My Poor Arthur

My Poor Arthur

A Biography of
Arthur Rimbaud

by

Elisabeth Hanson

HENRY HOLT AND COMPANY
New York

To

Frédéric de Heeckeren

Contents

	Preface	1
1	Cuif and Rimbaud	5
2	Schoolboy	22
3	Izambard	28
4	Runaway	40
5	Loose End	59
6	The Seer	77
7	Verlaine	97
8	Rimbe and Verlomphe	103
9	Exile and Return	123
10	Annus Mirabilis	132
11	End of a Poet	165
12	Winged Feet	185
13	Trader	209
14	Gunrunner	245
15	Fame and Fortune	252
16	Homecoming	264
	Epilogue	283
	Bibliography	297
	Index	301

List of Illustrations

THE FOLLOWING ILLUSTRATIONS FACE PAGE 100:

Arthur Rimbaud (*Henri Matarasso*)
The Rimbaud home 1869–75, Quai de la Madeleine, Charleville (*Musée Rimbaud*)
The Gindre House, Douai (*Faidherbe*)
The College of Charleville in 1873 (*Musée Rimbaud*)
Place Ducale, Charleville, in 1870 (*Musée Rimbaud*)
Baudelaire (*Nadar*)
Paul Demeny (*Nadar*)
Roche, the Rimbaud Farmhouse, in 1914 (*Herr*)
Roche in 1914 (*Herr*)
Verlaine just before the meeting with Rimbaud (*Henri Matarasso*)
Mathilde Verlaine (*Henri Matarasso*)
Rimbaud in Paris, 1872. Sketch by Verlaine (*Musée Rimbaud*)
Verlaine and Rimbaud in London, October, 1872. Drawing by Félix Régamey (*Floury*)
Germain Nouveau (*Kehren*)
Isabelle Rimbaud (*Henri Matarasso*)
Isabelle Rimbaud. Sketch by Berrichon

My Poor Arthur

Preface

In the sixty-eight years since the death of Arthur Rimbaud a vast literature has been built up round him. The hundreds of books and thousands of articles are concerned almost entirely (critical studies of his work excepted) with the question, why did this brilliant boy poet abandon literature before he was twenty-one?

As the many answers suggest, few people have been able to agree; Rimbaud has been variously explained as demon, angel, superman, saint, pervert, prophet, magician, mystic, and the precursor of fascism and communism. Nor is that by any means the end of the incarnations. If the reader wishes to explore the Rimbaud legends, and to ponder on the apparently limitless range of human credulity, he has only to dip into the thousand witty pages of M. Etiemble.

Disillusioning pages too; after he had finished his mighty work, M. Etiemble exclaimed in despair that even if he wished to write a life of Rimbaud he would never dare attempt it; he would be unable, he said, to set down a single sentence since he could no longer trust a single statement.

When my husband and I began work on Rimbaud some years ago we did not take this extreme view, perhaps because we had not delved so deeply as M. Etiemble into Rimbaudiana. But, more than a little daunted, we did limit our aim. Bearing in mind his excellent advice, to return to Rimbaud's own words, we decided simply to try to cut a path through the jungle and write a readable, factual biography.

This we did. Our first draft had only one serious fault—it did not make sense; the attempt had failed as it was bound to fail. We had come no nearer to the truth than the romancers

1

and for the same reason: the evidence, though indisputable, if accepted at face value was so contradictory as positively to encourage the conjectures, theorizings, wishful thinkings, ingenious interpretations of the past sixty-eight years.

Rimbaud, for instance, said that he could not endure the restrictions of his home; yet he chose deliberately to return home again and again. Mme Rimbaud did not hide either her dislike of spending money or her disapproval of her son's wanderings; yet almost every time he set out she provided his substantial railway fare. The young Rimbaud who says "I hate summer, which kills me" becomes within a year or two the man who declares that he cannot live without summer heat. These are only three of the inconsistencies in the "facts" which met us at every turn, not to speak of the supreme mystery, the renunciation of poetry.

By the time these inconsistencies became clear to us, I had been living with Rimbaud for five years, reading, re-reading, reflecting. Not without result: dominating themes recurred, hints in the letters, a trend of thought in the poems. These themes were echoed by my own experience, on which I now began to draw as I should have done in the first place had I not been so intimidated by the "enigmatic" Rimbaud—the experience of childhood, which I shall be excused from enlarging upon, and my present everyday experience. For this book has not been written in university rooms or in a public library but in my home in a French village street. To say that the Anglo-Saxon or even the Celt can ever fully understand the French would be an impertinence, but many years of living side by side with French peasants cannot but give a certain insight into national character.

In the light of this experience inconsistencies vanished. With my husband's consent the joint book was put aside, and I began work on my own. I offer in this final version what I believe to be an illumination of the life of Arthur Rimbaud.

One further point: I am a biographer, and literary criticism as such has no place in a biography. Analysis of a poem, as of a letter, has been included when it leads directly to knowledge of the writer. For a textual study of Rimbaud's work the reader cannot do better than consult the admirable editions of M. Bouillane de Lacoste.

I have been greatly helped during this long period. First by the wide knowledge of French literature and history of M. Roland de Margerie; by the generosity of M. Henri Matarasso who put at my disposal his famous Rimbaud collection; by M. St. Taute of the Musée Rimbaud where the greater part of the Matarasso collection now rests, together with much other material essential to the study of Rimbaud; and by Mme Renée Modot who first introduced me to the poet Rimbaud. I have many more kind people to thank whom I must list briefly: Mme Veuve Fricoteau of Roche; M. Ravioul of the Mairie of Dijon; Mlle M. Mestayer, Municipal Archivist of Douai; M. E. Herr-Faudemer of Attigny; MM. E. Pognon and Jean Adhémar of the Bibliothèque Nationale; Mme Marie Dornoy and M. François Chapon of the Bibliothèque Doucet; M. Jean Loize; M. René de Vrieze; Prince Pignatelli; the Keeper of the Colonial Museum, Rome; the Mayor of Reading; the Shipping Editor of Lloyd's; Miss Edith Marshall; Miss Jill Gallagher; and Miss B. Carpenter for her sterling work on several unreadable manuscripts and her patience when asked to do the whole thing over and over again. The debt to my husband is obvious.

My grateful thanks for permission to reproduce illustrations go to M. Henri Matarasso, M. St. Taute, the Bibliothèque Nationale, La Direction de l'Architecture.

—E. H.

CHAPTER ONE

Cuif and Rimbaud

1825–1865

O N March 10, 1825, a daughter was born to Nicolas Cuif at his farm at Roche in northeastern France. She was the second of three children and the only girl. Christened Marie Catherine Vitalie, she was known as Vitalie, a name which had been held by the eldest girl in the Cuif family for generations.

Vitalie grew up tall and strong like her father. In a severe way she was good-looking; she wore her dark brown hair drawn back into a knot on the neck, she held herself erect, her blue eyes looked out of a classical oval face with a forbidding directness which concealed a passionate nature. Her peasant origin declared itself in the strong hands and large wrists, her character and disposition in the thin nose, the mouth drawn into a hard, tight line and the sharp, commanding voice.

Some part of this stern manner and apparently inflexible nature was due to circumstance; her mother died when she was young and her brothers went to the bad. The first, Félix, decamped to Algeria to escape arrest for theft, the second, Auguste, was a weakling and drunkard. So instead of following the usual run of farmers' daughters, helping her mother to look after the house, Vitalie early found herself her father's mainstay; she ran the house and she worked on the farm like a man. She did both jobs well; within a few years she was dominating every corner of Roche.

The farm prospered. In the course of time Nicolas Cuif took an apartment in the nearest big town, Charleville, twenty-five miles to the north, so that his daughter could get some education. This education was spasmodic and not good but seemed likely to cover all her needs at a time when farmers' daughters commonly had little more education than the farm livestock. Her father's action was a significant one which would have been inconceivable to his forebears, peasant proprietors who stayed on their farm, saved every sou and brought up their children to do the same.

But Nicolas Cuif in his inconspicuous way was reflecting a remarkable upheaval in social history. From the 1830's, to date it no earlier, France, reacting against years of revolution, war and final defeat, had begun to turn bourgeois; the spread of railways, factories, shops, businesses, an industrial revolution in short, was creating a new and powerful class, a white-collared class with its own literature of romantic novels and sentimental poetry, its own painting of idealized portraiture and romanticized historical scenes, its own music in the flourishing operettas, its own moral code in which respectability was the presiding god, and its own ambitions in which the acquisition and display of money was used to force an entry into politics and the diminished and effete aristocracy.

This new class was drawn largely from the superior peasantry which began to leave its farms to the care of a foreman or poor relative, to set up house in the nearest town, and to send its sons into business, into the professions, the services, the church. It is well illustrated by the family with which Vitalie Cuif's second son was to be dramatically connected. In these years, across the country at Arras, Captain Verlaine met and married Stéphanie Dehée. Captain Verlaine was a ranker garrisoned at Arras. His father had been a small country solicitor, his grandfather a farmer, his great-grandfather a peasant. His wife's father was a sugar refiner near Arras, her grandfather had been a peasant proprietor. But the Verlaines' ancestry would have been impossible to deduce from their appearance, manners or way of life; to judge by their fearsome conventions, fine clothes, antimacassars, lace curtains, aspidistras, decorous teas, hands at whist, Sunday parades in the Bois, the Esplanade at Metz or wherever Captain Verlaine chanced to be stationed, they seemed, as they were, in another world from their parents, another aeon from their grandparents.

By the time Vitalie Cuif began to spend her winters in Charleville this class of which the Verlaines represented an important
section had been firmly set up all over northern France, was
everywhere beginning to direct opinion and taste and had already
taken over the government of the country, a more insidious
French Revolution reflected first by Louis Philippe and, when
Vitalie was twenty-six, by the self-constituted emperor, Louis
Napoleon.

Nicolas Cuif responded to this middle-class pressure, and the
winter months in Charleville, when the farm needed little attention, had their effect on his daughter; inevitably she got into her
her head ideas of social advancement. Not that Vitalie Cuif
would ever think of making a display of money; she remained
too much of a peasant; but gentility became one of her gods and
she began to look down on men whom in another age she would
have been glad to marry.

At this point, in the winter of 1852, when she was twenty-
seven, she met Captain Rimbaud.

2 ~~~~~

Frédéric Rimbaud's family is traceable to a Provençal ancestor
but had long since settled in and around the town of Dijon in
Burgundy. Frédéric was born in 1814 a few miles from Dijon in
the small town of Dole, famous as the birthplace of Pasteur. His
father was a tailor in Dijon, his mother came from Franche-
Comté. At the age of eighteen Frédéric joined the army as a
private soldier; nine years later, in 1841, he was made second
lieutenant in the light infantry, the Chasseurs d'Orléans. He
fought in the Algerian war from 1842 to 1844, was appointed to
the political service in 1845 and made chief of the Arab Bureau
at Sebdou in 1847. Three years afterwards, at the end of the
campaign against the Sultan of Morocco, he returned to France,
to the frontier garrison of Givet in the Ardennes. There he spent

two years. In 1852 he was promoted to be captain in the 47th infantry regiment stationed at Mézières facing Charleville across the River Meuse.

In those days Mézières and Charleville had little in common; Mézières, the ancient garrison town, looked down on its commercial and comparatively modern neighbor. Soldiers were of course seen in Charleville, the officers usually remained in Mézières. But the older town made a weekly gesture towards the upstart; every Thursday evening a military band played in the bandstand under the trees in Charleville's Place de la Gare. This event was something of a social occasion; the shopkeepers and businessmen of the town promenaded the Place with their wives and children whilst the band played; sometimes the young people would dance sedately round the bandstand under parental eyes.

Here one Thursday late in 1852 came Captain Rimbaud; his regiment's band was providing the music. And here came Vitalie. They met. They talked. He talked well. He was out of the ordinary run of rankers; a good administrator, humane and advanced, he was an educated man with a flair for languages and a hint of literary gifts. He talked well but looked even better. He had exceptional charm; he was handsome, impetuous, fair-haired, blue-eyed, with a high noble forehead and pleasure-loving lips which opened in a smile difficult to resist—the typical dashing soldier of romance but with brains.

There were disadvantages too; in spite of the open-hearted, friendly manner which made him such popular company, he was selfish, he was cold; if he felt strongly about anyone or anything but himself and his interests of the moment, it was about the army and the quiet and beautiful capital of Burgundy in which he was to spend his last years. But the attractive exterior carried away the passionate Vitalie for the first and last time of her life. They met again and again. He was the first man of the world to show an interest in her—she was too austere and too masculine to attract such men—and was skilled in the art of dealing with women as the plainspoken Ardennais were not. Her

rigidity melted, her conventionality loosened, her piety temporarily withdrew. She agreed to an engagement and early marriage.

No two people could have been less well suited but Vitalie
did not or would not acknowledge the obvious. If she needed
justification for what must have seemed a miraculous encounter,
she could find it in her suitor's rank; from the social point of view
the marriage promised her the longed-for betterment.

Captain Rimbaud's feelings are not so clear. Vitalie presented
such a contrast to the Burgundian and Arab women he had
known as to appear temporarily piquant; she had the aristocratic
bearing of so many pure-blooded peasant women. Perhaps he
flattered himself that he would have the pleasure of melting
the stiff and inexperienced countrywoman. He respected her
integrity of mind, her will to work, her strength of character, as
everyone did. More important to such a man, he discovered with
excitement the magnetism of the aroused Vitalie—the magnetism
which his children were to feel so strongly in their turn. That he
was ever in love with her is improbable. But he was not a man to
live easily on his pay; for him, money was to spend and his
tastes were expensive; Vitalie brought with her a large dowry
(300,000 francs her elder son said later) with a promise of
more to come on the death of her father. To a Frenchman of the
1850's, and especially a soldier who did not reckon to be often
at home, that could be attraction enough.

3

On the 8th of February, 1853, they were married in Charleville. It was a military wedding with Captain Rimbaud's superior
officers as witnesses.

Vitalie's pride and happiness did not last long. Such a marriage was unlikely to prove successful, but she made certain
that it was not. She could not help herself; character and circumstance made her difficult to live with. The short honeymoon
period over, she reverted instinctively to the exacting puritan

she was, despising tact and tenderness, her peasant thriftiness giving constant offense to a generous man careless of money.

Worse, fruit of twenty years of domination over an easy-going father, she had the instinct to rule. All must bend to her will. Nearly fifty years later she was to tell a story typical of herself at all ages: she had bought a new family grave and met workmen at the graveyard to arrange the exhumation of her father and dead children from the old grave; the workmen were accompanied by a foreman experienced in this kind of work but "I direct the operations, I tell the workmen what to do," says Madame Rimbaud triumphantly. "When the work began, it wasn't done as I wanted. I said what I thought and the fore-man said to me 'Well! you seem to know all about it; direct the workmen yourself and get the work done as you wish. . . .'"

She was then seventy-five. And at twenty-eight the passion to mold her happy-go-lucky husband in her image proved greater than her love for him. She was strong, determined, she would have her way, she gave him no rest; gaiety, flirtatiousness, ex-travagance, everything that had attracted her to him, became, in the home, grievous weaknesses which must be rooted out for the good of his soul. Convinced that the truth was in her, slave of her nature and beliefs, she struggled stiffly, implacably, to impose on him her somber version of the earthly pilgrimage.

Captain Rimbaud paid heavily for his 300,000 francs or for what part of it he could extract from a close-fisted wife. All charm left their ménage which soon began to resemble a series of revivalist meetings. By the time the first child, Frédéric, was born, at the end of 1853, scenes were frequent, and had Captain Rimbaud not been a soldier the marriage would no doubt have collapsed quickly. But he was often away on duty, and in the following year was moved to Lyons en route for the Crimea. His wife, already pregnant for the second time, could not follow him, and her second child was born on October 20 in her father's apartment at 12 rue Napoléon in Charleville. This was Jean Nicolas Arthur.

The Crimean war, in which Captain Rimbaud distinguished

himself for bravery, gave the marriage a fresh lease on life, expressed as always in those days by the birth of children; first, in 1857, a girl, named after her mother. This child died after a few months—another healing episode in relations beginning once more to deteriorate. A second girl, also named Vitalie, was born the following year.

Again war stepped in to restore a temporary harmony; Captain Rimbaud was sent off to the Italian campaign of 1859, where he earned another decoration. After his return another child, Isabelle, was born in 1860. Isabelle was the last. No more wars, no more deaths came to postpone the inevitable. Some time before 1862, when he retired from the army after thirty years' service, the Captain separated definitely from his wife; he set up house at Dijon where most of his relatives lived, and remained there for the rest of his life. At his death towards the end of 1878 he left his small fortune, just under three thousand francs, to his children.

4 ~~~~

Some forty-five years later Madame Rimbaud was to tell her last child: "Many soldiers are passing by just as I'm getting ready to write. This makes me feel a very great emotion, reminding me of your father with whom I should have been happy if I had not had certain children who caused me so much suffering."

The "certain" can be disregarded; as she was writing to one of her children, she could do no less than qualify the remark. In fact she believed to the end of her life that had she been childless and free to follow Captain Rimbaud from garrison to garrison she would never have lost him.

She was mistaken. Her husband may not have cared for the children—he made no effort to get in touch with them during his sixteen years of retirement in Dijon—but he fled primarily from their mother. His will would have made this clear, a will in which his wife is not mentioned, did not Madame Rimbaud's disposition render all other forms of proof unnecessary.

She was mistaken, but from her children's point of view the only fact of moment was that she believed them to have come between herself and her husband. And with this perpetual grievance at heart she found herself, in 1862, a passionate woman of thirty-seven facing a lifetime of dissatisfaction, with four children to support and educate. No consolation appeared in her possession of these children, for she was no more maternal than her husband was paternal; in everything but her one feminine surrender to Captain Rimbaud she was like a man, a hard and resolute man; to her the children were harrowing symbols of a bliss which, she persuaded herself, they had destroyed.

Nor was this the whole of her unhappiness. She had broken the code of her class. The bourgeois laws of conduct presupposed a formal unity between husband and wife; she had to face her world as a deserted wife, and, divorce not then being legalized, for all practical purposes a divorced one.

"I have been most wretched. I have suffered much, wept much. . . ." So she was to write in middle age, and she was saying no more than the bare truth. She suffered greatly. But she was a woman of character; she turned her thwarted feelings as much as she was able, not to the children but to the church, and to that other great consoler of the disappointed, money. Her love of land, which to the peasant is money incarnate, grew into a sort of worship which her religion not merely sanctioned but sanctified. "Fight without ceasing against what is called the injustice of fate . . . be strong and courageous in the face of every adversity; drive all bad thoughts from your heart . . . work hard and give your life an aim to follow . . . never despair of God's help . . . He alone can console and heal." This was her advice twenty years after the break-up of her marriage; it was her strength in the first months of the separation. And she could add after "I have suffered much, wept much" the proud "I have been able to turn all my afflictions to my advantage."

"To my advantage": revealing words; yet her religion preached duty as well as personal salvation; love she could not give her children, duty she performed with grim relish, the relish of one who, deeply hurt, turns the screw a little tighter. She was incapable of generosity but she did her duty punctiliously. And when she said "Give your life an aim to follow" she was thinking of her aim after the disappearance of her husband, to give the unwanted, guilty children the kind of education in life that he would or ought to have wished.

That is why, although her story was known in Charleville where nothing could be hidden, she decided to brave it out in splendid isolation. She could have retired to Roche. When she married, her father had given up the farm to his younger son as compensation for her large dowry. Two years after the marriage Félix returned and claimed his heritage and as Auguste had neglected the farm his father bought him out and installed Félix there. One year afterwards Félix died. By this time Auguste had become a byword in the district as drunkard, his wife had left him, and in his sister's view the farm would have been thrown away on him; she seized it before he could act and began to put it in order, fobbing him off with occasional sums of money. When her father died two years later, just after the birth of the second Vitalie, Auguste lost his only possible court of appeal and Roche remained firmly in his sister's hands.

But at Roche the children could not have given the only satisfaction left to her, the satisfaction of seeing them take the place in the world set aside for the family of a military officer. So she remained in Charleville.

5 ~~~~~

There, then, in the early 1860's was this unmotherly and still youthful woman applying herself to the ambitious task of educating four fatherless children into her husband's class and as far as possible from her brothers'. She had the field to herself; the younger boy's one memory of his father was a violent argument in the course of which each infuriated parent in turn dashed a heavy silver bowl to the floor. The effect of this on a child who could not have been more than six at the time is not

difficult to imagine but there are always exceptions; Arthur
said later that he was simply amused. Yet he may not have been
telling the truth; he was given to boasting. What Frédéric
thought of his father is not known. The girls were too young to
have remembered him.

All therefore was in favor of Madame Rimbaud's design;
and the walks, processions rather, to market in Place Ducale—
the great square in the center of Charleville—and to church a
few years after the final departure of Captain Rimbaud seemingly show virtue, if virtue it is, triumphant. In front trotted the
small girls, Vitalie and Isabelle, hand in hand; behind them
marched the boys side by side, white-gloved, hands clasping
blue umbrellas, clothed in black on Sundays and on market days
wearing conspicuous home-made trousers of heavy slate-blue
serge; round hats perched on the heads and heavily starched
white collars clasped the necks of all four. In the rear stalked
the mother in black from head to foot, a physical and spiritual
ramrod, contemptuous of the ironical comments which (if report
is true) the odd appearance of her children aroused.

At a glance all four children seemed of a piece; all appeared
demure, all had the oval face and blue eyes of the Cuifs. But
they were not alike and their mother's feelings towards them
differed; there are degrees in the disagreeableness of doing a
duty. The girls were obedient children from their earliest years;
the boys were less amenable.

Frédéric was not a bright boy; no amount of cuffs, smacks
and ear-tweakings could din book-knowledge into him. Nor
did he please his mother in disposition. He was lazy, amiable,
even sunny-natured outside the home, but inside it appeared
at his worst, forever trying to lie himself out of trouble. But
what his mother most detested and feared in him were his social
inclinations; he was absolutely without pride and took his pleasures, when he had the chance, in the humblest company; he
was the very reverse of respectable. To Madame Rimbaud he
was an irremovable thorn in the flesh, his idleness a scandalous
reflection on an ever-occupied household, his evasions criminal,

even his bonhomie an offense in a home where smiles were seldom seen and laughter subdued. For her he was a problem child without the problem; he was the living image of his Uncle Auguste and her duty towards him stood clear; he had to be put down and kept down.

Arthur presented problems of a more complicated nature: he was a beautiful child but his beauty was of a kind which gave his mother more pain than pleasure; Frédéric might be like his uncle but with God's help the Auguste in him could be crushed; but what could one do with a physical resemblance and a startling one at that? For Arthur appeared to her in emotional moments as nothing but a miniature edition of his father; he had Captain Rimbaud's startlingly clear blue eyes and wavy chestnut hair, his father's high forehead, slightly tip-tilted nose and more than a hint of his pleasure-loving lips. Most alarming, the likeness carried over into disposition; the boy had his father's volatile nature, his passion for travel, adventure, excitement. Alarming but fascinating too; this reproduction of the man she loved created a special bond between mother and son, a special antagonism too.

In fact, though they were to become more obvious later, Arthur bore signs of his mother also; not only the oval face but the big bones were hers, as was the setting of the blue eyes with their direct open stare, innocent or insolent as his mood dictated. Even more fundamental resemblances were to raise themselves later; but superficially at least the small boy was the spit of his father and was forever reminding her of him.

6

The Rimbaud home, though often somber, was not an unhappy one. The strong French family instinct was strikingly exemplified under the sway of Madame Rimbaud. In theory all the Rimbaud children ought to have been wretched; in fact, deprived of a father, all not only submitted to but loved and admired as well as feared their mother. Frédéric apart, she acted with scrupulous justice, and, though unable to show demonstrative affection, tried to be kind and successfully gave them security; the Rimbaud children were disciplined, their day mapped out for them, their future made clear, their actions supervised, they were never left idle. However much they may make motions of dissatisfaction, all children appreciate firm handling; this close attention was, if not love, a compliment of a kind that could almost be mistaken for love, and, in an age when strictness in the home went without saying, did not seem, as it can today, a sort of terrorism.

There were times, as the incident of the silver bowl indicates, when Madame Rimbaud's passionate nature burst its bonds. "Tyrannical rages," rising abruptly out of the blue, fell on her children. Not one escaped. For a short time she would be "unapproachable." The family trembled. But the rages, like summer storms, passed as rapidly as they appeared, and were "transformed into apologies." Stiff apologies, no doubt, but sincere, since nothing horrified her more than naked emotion; and the children did not think the less of her; the first fright over, any evidence of strong feeling was reassuring.

And they needed all the reassurance they could get; their interest was centered in the home and each other, with their mother as dea ex machina, and this close family attachment formed a kind of emotional phalanx against which other relationships were measured. The attachment was not paraded, and so co-operative were the children that even the dour Ardennais of Charleville would see them as preternaturally solemn.

Rue Bourbon, where Madame Rimbaud took an apartment soon after Captain Rimbaud's desertion, was a short street which began respectably and dwindled into near slums. It was an unwise choice for a woman with her ambitions. She perhaps overrated her powers of discipline, she may have been short of money after her husband left her or she may have wished to save whilst she put the farm at Roche in order. Whatever the cause, even the respectable end of the street bristled with difficulties for a woman with four small children and a strong sense of the proprieties. She took extraordinary precautions to preserve her two boys (alone old enough to worry about) from contamination. Other children ran freely about the street and into each other's apartments; hers were kept indoors, allowed no visitors and taken out under escort.

In vain. Frédéric responded to the appeal of like to like—or so his mother saw his truancies—and Arthur, like most small children, did not think in terms of class, only of playmates; they could not come to him so he slipped out to them, for his mother could not keep perpetual guard. At first the escapades were no more than childish curiosity in the form of life so far removed from his own: "His only familiars were children, stunted, bareheaded and with cheeks wet from running eyes, who hid thin fingers yellow and black with filth under old clothes stinking of diarrhea, and used to talk with the meekness of idiots!"

The companions were conversational only, for the seven-year-old Arthur ventured no further than the garden where he whispered through the fence. And when finally initiated into the rough and tumble of slum games he, being small for his age, had a struggle to keep his end up: "When the eight-year-old daughter of neighboring workpeople appeared, brown-eyed and wild, in her cotton frock, with a toss of her hair the little brute used to spring on his back in a corner where, finding himself beneath her, he bit her bottom (for she never wore knickers) and, pummeled by her fists and heels, carried back to his room the savor of her skin."

The escapades were discovered and presumably punished; presumably, because it is far from certain that, except on rare occasions, Madame Rimbaud recognized the necessity of punishing her second child. The boy speaks of his mother "taking fright" when she found him consorting with other children, a fright which he tried to soothe by "warm caresses." The caresses were returned and the look in her blue eyes told him that he was loved, or so he thought then. Her hand would naturally fall on the elder boy. Frédéric showed in the next years all the signs of the child in fear of scoldings, the child who is forever racking his brains in vain for the right answer. The state of apprehension in which he lived was made clear by a forehead perpetually wrinkled and by his nervous habit of rubbing these wrinkles with both fists, a habit which left ugly permanent red lines across his forehead. His younger brother's forehead remained "white and smooth."

After two years Madame Rimbaud decided to leave rue Bourbon. She was feeling more secure financially and was alarmed by Arthur's penchant, not easily hidden, for picking up bad langauge. So in 1862 she moved to a highly respectable quarter of the town, the Cours d'Orléans. She had been teaching the boys at home for some time past, and poor Frédéric came in for more punishment and scorn; his small brother showed him up unmercifully as a dunce. Arthur had no difficulty with these home lessons but this, though it spared him from his mother's anger, could not compensate for his "repugnance" to homework and discipline. He had early conceived an idea of abstract justice, and this justice seemed to play little part in the life of Arthur Rimbaud; he wanted to do this, he had to do that. For the most part he kept his dissatisfaction discreetly hidden. But even in these early days his face and an occasional remark gave him away. He had caught the habit, and the manner, from his mother; for from time to time Madame Rimbaud expressed in biblical terms a bitter awareness of the plight in which Providence had placed her. This reflection of his mother was also a method of getting her attention; and Madame Rimbaud, whose attitude towards this child was the sole unclear thing in her mind, bore with her youthful echo—not surprisingly since Arthur looked irresistibly the part of sulky angel—until he and his complaints became a kind of family joke. Besides, pout or murmur though he might, he mastered his lessons with contemptuous ease, and the main revolt was always out of sight: "Every day he pretended to sweat at obedience; very intelligent; yet some black habits, certain mannerisms seemed to suggest sharp hypocrisies in him. In the darkness of a passage with moldy hangings he would put out his tongue in passing, his two fists pressed into his groin, and would see spots in his closed eyes."

That was Arthur Rimbaud at eight, a boy running so far ahead of his mother that, her book knowledge exhausted, and anxious that both boys should learn Latin and Greek, she supplemented her home teaching by sending them to the Institution Rossat, a small preparatory school near the river.

She explained what she expected of them; she hoped that they would fit themselves to enter the Hôtel de Ville, the foundation stone of all respectable civil service careers in Charleville. To Frédéric, toiling hopelessly in the rear of his brother and cowering under one cuff after another, this must have appeared a dream indeed; nor did the prospect of a white collar and clean clothes for the rest of his life enchant him. From his brother this plan, and the double pressure of schoolwork and homework which was to ensure it, produced a precocious explosion: "Why, I ask myself, learn Greek or Latin? I can't think. No one has the slightest need of them . . . Why learn Latin? No one speaks this language." As for fitting himself for a good post: "I don't want a job; I shall be a *rentier*." It was true that one read Latin expressions from time to time in the newspapers, "but God knows I shan't be a journalist . . . And as for Greek, that dirty language isn't spoken by a single person in the world. Ah! saperlipote de saperlipopette! sapristi! I shall be a *rentier*. What's the point of wearing one's breeches on a bench, saperlipopetouille! To be a shoeblack you have to pass an examination; for the jobs you are offered are shoeblack, swineherd, or drover. Thank God *I* don't want any of them, saperlipouille. With that one is given a box on the ears for thanks . . . Ah! Saperpouillotte!" . . .

This reaction to cramming was confined to a notebook; publicly, butter would not melt in the mouth of this pretty boy. He resented the black and endless Sabbaths "when, his hair pomaded, he sat reading a Bible with cabbage green edges on the mahogany center table," but the resentment was obliged to accumulate until it broke out in dreams which "oppressed him

each night in the alcove" where he slept. He dreamed of open
rebellion: "He would not love God"; of escape, to the meadows
"luminously gleaming," to the crowds he watched enviously and
often from his station by the window. He did not love God, he
loved "the men he could see on a gloomy night, grimy-faced,
in their working clothes, in the busy street where the town-crier
and his three beats of the drum and the hawkers with their
funny announcements made the crowd laugh and roar."

These glimpses of a child reacting to discipline by daydreams
and defiant gestures in dark corners were by no means a proof
that he was not enjoying himself or that his public appearance
was a lie. In the strict but united home his mother still seemed to
offer in her severe way something of the love he expected, and
Charleville even without the excitements of slum children, the
Charleville he was to castigate in later years, presented many
opportunities for pleasure. Even today factoried outskirts, vulgar
street lighting, glaring shop fronts and motor car parks cannot
do more than dim the charm of this town built within a spacious
loop of the Meuse; a hundred years ago the tree-lined avenues
with their wide pavements, the noble colonnaded Place Ducale,
perhaps above all the river front with wooded hills rising across
the water to the Belgian frontier a few miles away—all this provided playground unlimited on a fine stage and with a romantic
background.

And Arthur was a romantic child. The river fascinated him
and when, a little more than two years later, in 1865, he was
sent with his brother to the College of Charleville he used to
wait for the opening of the school—Madame Rimbaud having
packed them off in very good time—in an old boat imagining
himself on the sea he had never seen.

The material for his dreams came from illustrated papers and
from books which he pored over in the one place free from
maternal correction: "In summer specially, vanquished, stupid,
he locked himself obstinately in the cool lavatory: there, calm
and drawing deep breaths through wide nostrils, he thought." In
a dozen solitary moments and places he "made up romances,

about the life of the great deserts where stolen freedom glitters, about forests, suns, shores, plains! . . . stared at pictures of laughing Spanish and Italian women." He glutted himself with the world's marvels as shown in a popular weekly educator taken by his mother, lingering specially over accounts and illustrations of the sea.

Arthur Rimbaud was neither the first nor the last small boy to wish himself away from reality into some dream of the past where he is great, respected, feared, adored; his ability to express these dreams is shared by many, as any kindergarten or junior school mistress could demonstrate. But there the likeness ends; at heart the child of his mother, the only dreams to interest him permanently were to be practical ones.

That is a long step from the small boy in his boat dreaming the minutes away. But a shadow of the future can be seen in the attitude of his companion; from what little is known of the relationship of the two brothers Frédéric provided an at times worried, for the most part uncomprehending, but always obedient henchman to his junior. There he was, eleven years old, rocking the boat at Arthur's bidding to simulate sea waters, doing this, doing that for Arthur as well as—who can doubt— taking punishments which passed over the head of that disarming young enthusiast.

CHAPTER TWO

Schoolboy

1865–1870

By the time Arthur Rimbaud begins what could without much exaggeration be called his sensational career at the College of Charleville he is coming into focus. Though big-boned he remains absurdly small for his age; in public he looks demure and behaves shyly. Any feeling he roused beyond instinctive pleasure at the sight of his cherubic face was, by the few who were on speaking terms with Madame Rimbaud, that he was hardly done by at home; more than one heart was moved by the pensive expression and sedate gait of the queerly dressed little boy. Difficult to imagine that the frank blue eyes were often ugly with resentment, that the thoughts behind the fine open brow were frequently caustic and twisted, that the full, slightly pouting lips spoke a language already childishly foul. Impossible to imagine that volcanic possibilities of enthusiasm and love smoldered beneath that pedantic façade. The general and obvious view of the ten-year-old who looked seven or eight was that, apart from his immediate appeal, he was an ordinary and rather spiritless child.

At first he behaved like one. His earliest school friend, Ernest Delahaye, says that some of the boys used to see him off the premises each evening with boos or catcalls, though he does not explain whether this was because of Arthur's homemade clothes, his mother's habit of waiting at the gates each evening to make sure that he and Frédéric came straight home, or her refusal to let them join in the games which she regarded as waste of time. In school, he had to endure the condescending "bit of a boy" or "little Rimbaud" from the masters and a contemptuous "little brute" from the boys.

Endure is a strong word but not too strong for this boy. For some years he had alternated between adoring his mother and putting out his tongue and clenching his fists against her in dark corners. A poor revenge against her restrictions, this, as he well knew, but sufficient until the day when he began to doubt whether his love was returned. Arthur was sharper than most unloved children and more demanding; once he had admitted a doubt his secret revolts became futile. Nothing would satisfy him but some dramatic stroke to force this unresponsive woman to acknowledge his importance in her life. The struggle opened between opponents curiously alike and in nothing so much as the pride, vast beyond reason, which dominated both.

His first year at the College inflated this pride into egoism, although apart from the jeers his reception seems to have been mild enough as the little savages go. He kept himself to himself, hugging his superiority until the moment when all should recognize it.

Consolation came quickly, though it might well have seemed a lifetime to Arthur. Within a year all was changing, within two or three years his nonentity was gone as though it had never been; he still wore the ridiculous trousers, he was still undersized, his mother still waited at the gates, but the attitude towards him in the school had become, some envy and dislike apart, respectful, admiring, almost incredulous; for "little Rimbaud" had become the prize pupil.

An account of his progress makes this clear. He joined the school after Easter in 1865. He and Frédéric were put into the seventh form. In October he moved into the sixth, leaving his elder brother behind. The following year he "jumped" the fifth and was put into the fourth. Two years later he was in the third and, in May, had sent Latin verses to the Prince Imperial to celebrate his *première communion*—verses which brought him the public thanks of the headmaster on the instructions of the Prince Imperial's tutor. The next year, 1869, three of his Latin compositions appeared in the *Moniteur de l'Enseignement Secondaire de l'Académie de Douai* which printed the educational feats of the academic area to which Charleville belonged.

At the Concours Académique of that year at Douai one of these compositions won the first prize; in his own form he won every first prize.

Arthur Rimbaud was, in short, a very clever boy. How clever it is impossible to say. The level of education at the College of Charleville in the '60's of the last century is difficult to gauge since the school was destroyed soon afterwards with all its papers. Rimbaud, for example, writes on a set theme a series of Latin verses for each of his form-mates—each version differing from the others—whilst the master demonstrates a geometrical theorem on the blackboard. Remarkable indeed, showing, it seems, an almost contemptuous attitude towards the composition of Latin verses. Or was it a contemptuous attitude towards the standard of Latin taught at the College? For not one of these exercises exists today. Arthur's lightning display of virtuosity presumably satisfied the master—though even this has to be assumed—but the value to be placed on this satisfaction remains uncertain. Six points about the schoolboy Rimbaud are indisputable: he had a gift for Latin, an excellent memory, unusual powers of assimilation and application, a flair for parody and a most facile pen.

What matters in his life, however, is that he was generally accepted as a genius in the school and by those Charlevillians who interested themselves in it. Admiration was the order of the years from 1867 to 1869. This admiration the boy accepted with outward modesty, but the universal praise and wonder justified every belief he had held in himself. Yet this demonstration of superiority for which he had worked was in practice nullified from the outset. He had convinced himself if he needed convincing, he had convinced the outside world, but he had not convinced his mother; he could not wring from her a single sign of admiration.

Madame Rimbaud's attitude, she being what she was, presents no surprise. Ironically enough, even had she loved him she would never, for fear of rousing the devil of pride, have dared to say the word which might have changed her son's life. She

must have been gratified by his triumphs, but they would cause
her publicly to lean over backwards. He was a hero at school?
He should be shown at home that God required humility and
implicit obedience, that in His eyes all men were sinners. Arthur,
perplexed and hurt, must have thought resentfully that he could
not have met greater severity if he had been another Frédéric.

A year after entering the College he and Frédéric took their
première communion. From this event dates their first photograph. At a glance the boys appear like enough as they face
the camera with the mesmerized expression customary in those
days of early photography. The illusion of likeness, however,
rests in this expression, in the clothes—clothes, by the way,
with which no fault can be found since they were those worn
by almost every French boy on this occasion—and in the oval
Rimbaud face. What chiefly strikes one are the eyes of Arthur,
eyes beautifully set, and the noble high forehead. He looks the
picture of virtue, a troubled virtue—the photograph is an excellent illustration of the front he wore in public.

After this he became notorious at school for a fanatical religiosity and the first of his many first prizes was taken in
catechism one year after his *première communion*. Delahaye tells
the story of the small twelve-year-old boy flying at older boys
who were amusing themselves after church one Sunday by
playing with water from the font. This outburst from the well-
behaved and reserved Rimbaud—he kicked, scratched, bit—
earned him the epithet of "dirty little hypocrite," an epithet
which he hugged to himself with a martyr's pride. There was
more in this pride than met Delahaye's eye and more in the
religious fervor than the *première communion* for it coincided
with Rimbaud's first suspicions that his mother's "blue look lied."
He cast about for a substitute. The substitute was not, apparently, hard to find, was in him, about him, everywhere: God.
God was always on his mother's lips, but not the God whom
Arthur began to worship rapturously in his thirteenth year. His
God was primarily loving. The boy returned this love with a
passion.

Yet before the "hypocrite" had become the wonder scholar, before even the year of the attack was out, Arthur's fervor had slackened. He discovered that the love of God can be cold comfort. He made another, more chilling discovery. This first attempt to find a substitute for his mother was also the first of a lifelong series of attempts to force feeling from her, in this case either sympathy or jealousy. And it was the first of a life-long series of defeats. Anything that smacked of emotionalism was anathema to Madame Rimbaud; her God was a practical conception who would not dream of interfering with a profitable career, and her son's impetuous championship, which might jeopardize his chances at school, forced nothing from her but anger. So Arthur is soon admitting that his mother has punished him for reading an "impious" book. Not that this indicated a deliberate apostasy; Madame Rimbaud's definition of impiety was so wide as almost to be all-embracing, and the boy's desire for knowledge was driving him to read everything that he could lay hands on, the poets for preference. He had also become a secret smoker—a habit caught no doubt from the children of rue Bourbon—which shows that his powers of evading detection were as strong as ever and that his mother's supposedly rigid control had its lax side. He was a tireless walker and, Delahaye says, would often go with him through the woods to the Belgian frontier to buy smuggled tobacco. The chief interest of the smoking is, who paid for the tobacco? Madame Rimbaud was careful to the point of meanness; her income was estimated to be not less than seven or eight thousand francs per year by the end of the decade, yet she lived like a poor woman. Nevertheless it is an open question whether Arthur purposely exaggerated when he said that she gave him no pocket money, or whether he simply allowed Delahaye to pay the two or three sous each time; in view of the future, either explanation could be true.

Delahaye was a cautious boy, a boy bound from birth for the Hôtel de Ville and the schoolmaster's desk. His one departure from reason was his infatuation with Arthur Rimbaud;

listening to his brilliant friend, he sensed a future with which he wished to associate himself. But he tried to sail on the windward side of the brilliance; when Arthur talked wildly or revealed a hint of the real future his assent was provisional merely.

The friendship was one-sided, as all Rimbaud's friendships were to be, and he remained in an imaginative and emotional world of his own. A disillusioned world, too. He had his little band of school devotees, he was a perpetual wonder to Frédéric and a hero to his sisters; only his mother remained unconquered. She had to be conquered, or supplanted. But by whom? How could the amiable, unexceptional Delahaye compare with that tower of strength, Madame Rimbaud?

In retrospect the school years can be seen as a misfortune. Arthur needed understanding, he experienced simultaneously the belief that his cleverness could conquer any world and the desolating suspicion that he could not have the one thing which would give point to the praise. This ironic situation distorted a character and disposition which in other circumstances might have developed very differently. Some suspected another Rimbaud beneath the smug and charming exterior but this Rimbaud remained hidden until January, 1870, when the master of his class was replaced by a young man from Douai. This young man, Georges Izambard, was the first to encourage Rimbaud the poet and the first to offer a serious challenge to the supremacy of Madame Rimbaud.

CHAPTER THREE

Izambard

1870

G EORGES IZAMBARD belonged to the world-wide type of kind, earnest, bespectacled young schoolmaster. He was just twenty-one and this was his first post. In the masters' common room he was told about the pupil who took all the prizes, the model boy of fifteen with the brain of a double first. He was curious but, after he had taught the prodigy for a lesson or two, rather disgusted. Rimbaud sat primly in the front row "tiny and timid, 'a dreamy Tom Thumb.'" Izambard found him "well-behaved, smooth-spoken, rather priggish with clean fingernails, spotless notebooks, exercises astonishingly correct, notes taken in class with scholarly precision"; found him in short "one of those exemplary and impeccable little monsters incarnating to the nth degree the examination fiend, the college 'swot.'"

Such was Izambard's first impression, the impression long since formed by the college and those townspeople who saw Rimbaud proceeding demurely to and from school—without escort after his mother moved in 1869 to a riverside apartment close by. But Izambard soon discovered another Rimbaud. The boy's impression of him had been more favorable than his of the boy. Rimbaud was starved and keeping a sharp eye for food, starved and desperate; his mother not only held him at arm's length in love, she presented a closed mind to his new enthusiasm, literature. Madame Rimbaud was interested only in the practical details of education; poetry was useless when not positively harmful; there could be no talk of it at home, books of poetry had to be hidden and no mention made of the poetry that he had begun to write secretly. Frédéric, lagging far behind his brother at school, disliked everything to do with books, the two little girls were growing up as genteel editions of their mother.

So to Rimbaud the arrival of this master, reputedly clever, said to be politically republican and a poet in his spare moments, was an irresistible temptation to unburden himself. One day Izambard found waiting for him at the college gate a Rimbaud who begged to be allowed to accompany him to his rooms in the Cours d'Orléans.

To walk unaffected day after day by the side of this Rimbaud, one would have to be either strong or hard. Izambard was neither; he was young, affectionate, even quixotic. He fell under the spell of the infectious enthusiasm lighting up the angelic face and spurting out by awkward fits and starts in the voice which was to cause such havoc. The "swot" became "a true intellectual, vibrating with lyrical passion, ingenuously proud of revealing himself as such, happy to have found at last someone to whom he could speak of poets and poetry . . . This boy who I had been told was 'good at his lessons' proved to possess a brain of the highest class." And when Rimbaud began to produce his "new-laid poems always lovingly copied for me in his beautiful script" and "with his modest air of the mere schoolboy" begged the master to read and criticize, another form of appeal made itself felt: to vanity. But Izambard was by nature anything but envious, and though he recognized these poems as imitations of the poets Rimbaud had been able to read—Hugo and the leaders of the Parnassian group, Leconte de Lisle and Théodore de Banville—he had the wit to see beyond the imitation to the original charm. For they had, most of them, a charm, the fresh charm of youth so difficult for youth to convey. He was impressed; he corrected, made suggestions, discussed at length, always with a reassuring "I am not 'teaching' you," encouraged the boy to continue his writing, lent him books and gave him lessons out of school; but again not as a master: "this child," he said, "treated from the first as a young comrade, little by little became a dear friend." The "little by little" is not to be taken

literally; neither is the "child"; the two boys were soon as in-
separable as Madame Rimbaud permitted.

Madame Rimbaud was told of the friendship and, as Arthur
was careful to write openly on the sitting-room table only what
his mother could safely overlook, with cautious approval saw
him sitting down evening after evening to this extra homework. Nevertheless she kept a weather eye open, and sure
enough less than four months had passed when she discovered
that her son had fallen into the embraces of a wolf in sheep's
clothing. His vigilance slipping for once, Arthur left a book
unhidden; Madame Rimbaud found, opened, read and, horror-
struck, sat down to write a note to Izambard. That done she
put on her outdoor clothes, walked out, the book in one strong
and bony hand, walked to the college where she left the letter
with the concierge and asked to see the headmaster.

The next morning Izambard, "stupefied," read: "I cannot
thank you sufficiently for all that you are doing for Arthur;
you are unsparing with advice, you give him lessons out of
class; we have no right to such attention. But there is one thing
I cannot approve, the reading of a book such as the one you
gave him a few days ago (*les misérables, V. hugot*). You ought
to know better than I that much care is needed in the choice of
books for children to read. Although I must think that Arthur
procured this without your knowledge, it would certainly be
dangerous to allow him to read any more such books." A moment later he was summoned to the headmaster's study. The
headmaster apologetically handed him the book left by Madame
Rimbaud; the complaint was absurd, he agreed, but Madame
Rimbaud had been much annoyed, had insisted that he repri-
mand the teacher, and parents had to be humored. He advised
Izambard to go to see her. Izambard went and was met by a
storm of protest: Hugo was the enemy of the Church and the
throne, he had been exiled and rightly for the depravity of his
works. "Do you think it right to teach such things to your
pupils?"

Izambard, producing the book, pointed out that it was not

Les Misérables but *Notre Dame de Paris,* and that it had been
lent to Arthur to help him to provide a background for a school
essay on Villon. Useless: Hugo's books, replied the angry
mother, were on the Index; that one, *Les Misérables* or *Notre
Dame,* call it what Izambard chose, was impious. "What right
have you to make Arthur share in your impieties?" she demanded.

There was nothing to be done but to retire with what dignity
a young man of twenty-one could summon; and with secret
thanks that Madame Rimbaud did not know that the essay on
Villon had been written two months earlier, but that the book
had remained with Arthur; did not know either that her son had,
carefully secreted, other books lent by Izambard of which she
could with more reason have complained. But there was much
that Madame Rimbaud did not know: that the Villon essay had
put thoughts into her son's head—might he not become another
Villon?—and had led him to read history which supported his
elder schoolmates' criticisms of the government of Louis Napoleon and enabled him to work off emotional dissatisfaction. He
was soon one of the hottest revolutionaries in the college.

Izambard's carefully correct attitude changed after the interview with Madame Rimbaud; he came away with a dislike of
her which he was never to lose, and a determination that Arthur,
who had been given a good box on the ears for his share in the
affair, should as far as possible be rescued from her.

The reaction was natural enough, many a heart was to be
touched by the thought of this eager spirit cramped by "brutal
tyranny"; and the "goody-goody" attitude at school, the reputation of college "swot" were, in Izambard's mind, at last explained: he went in constant fear at home. Even his lack of
manners—Izambard noticed that he seemed incapable of saying
"Thank you"—was put down to the way in which he had been
brought up. He was not to discover until much later that the
boy's meek and guileless manner represented "the modesty of an
inward arrogance." As his own experience of "the maternal lap"
had been unfortunate, he assumed that his view of her must

be shared by all, her children included. Arthur helped him to think so. From time to time, slightly shocked, Izambard conscientiously tut-tutted the outbursts against La Bouche d'Ombre, one of the boy's nicknames for his mother. He would have been more than shocked had he known what the son actually felt for the mother he blackguarded so freely, but emotional subtleties were beyond his ken; he mistook for dislike and fear the bitterness of a born poet at his enslavement to a born philistine; he understood the poet, the nature of the slavery not at all, and Rimbaud could not have enlightened him.

So from the 5th of May, the date of his interview with Madame Rimbaud, Izambard changed his tactics; to protect Arthur from further trouble at home he invited him to his rooms and told him to do all his forbidden reading there. This defiance of Madame Rimbaud made Izambard's conventional deprecation of her son's diatribes quite worthless, as the boy was quick to see. Nor was the refusal to talk politics of any greater value, for Arthur, spending every possible moment in the master's rooms, heard "bitter remarks on the Empire" by Izambard and his friends.

The chief of these friends was Léon Deverrière, professor of rhetoric at the Institution Rossat where Rimbaud had spent his first school years. Deverrière was a shaggy young man with a hint of plumpness and a delight in controversy; with all the ardor of the essentially peaceful man he burned to be away from his desk and at the barricades which, if he had his way, would long since have been set up in the streets of Paris. If Izambard had scruples about speaking politics before the boy, he had none.

Nor did scruples worry the other notable friend of Izambard at Charleville, Charles Bretagne. Père Bretagne, as he was known to his intimates, was a tax collector by profession but an eccentric by nature, "big-bellied and rabelaisian." Izambard regarded him with the reverence of the aspiring poet for a man who had actually spoken to Paul Verlaine. The tax collector's first circuit, in the Arras area, had included the sugar refinery of Verlaine's uncle Dehée at Fampoux, where the young Verlaine spent many holidays. Bretagne spoke freely of him, too freely perhaps since he had not met the published poet, but understandably to the ravishment of Izambard. Rimbaud, by this time "my friend and familiar," says Izambard, "often took part in these tumultuous collisions."

It is not difficult to imagine the horrific charm to these hot-spoken but essentially respectable young provincials of this not-so-old cynic, the type of "satanic" dandy still to be found in Paris cafés, beard clipped to a neat black point, precise voice uttering would-be abominations without a flicker of the cold eye. Usually such men are harmless, a general spitefulness the height of the machiavellian element, almost always they are musical and mildly talented. Bretagne was also "vaguely tinged with literature" and had a favorite quotation which "after contortions of the enormous lips and with the blare of a hunting horn" he would bring out time and again.

Et son haleine pue épouvantablement!

His breath had a dreadful smell!

he would roar, with a "What wonderful liberties the man takes!" and concluded the performance with "a tiny noiseless laugh like a tinkle of crystal."

The quotation was from Verlaine's first book *Poèmes Saturniens.* "It was the only line he knew" says Izambard. "We knew the others." Possibly. Possibly again the line by line knowledge of *Poèmes Saturniens* was in the future. Certainly Verlaine, apart from Bretagne's spicy and inaccurate recollections and the periodical shout of admiration about his technical license, was a poet dimly known in Charleville, even in the literary salon of Izambard. Certainly, too, the eagerly listening Rimbaud was the one person there who could be described as more than "vaguely tinged with literature"; the one person, also, who was to make practical use of the license all discussed.

2 ~~~~

Rimbaud's respect for Izambard rose still higher when he
discovered that his friend not only loved poetry, wrote poetry
and encouraged him to write poetry, but was on intimate terms
with a published poet. Izambard often spoke about the Douai
poet, Paul Demeny, and lent his pupil Demeny's *Les Glaneuses*.
The boy memorized the poems, praised them beyond all reason,
and expressed an ardent wish to meet the author.

Yet despite his raptures he was not the naïve child that
Izambard naïvely imagined, his smallness, baby face and ex-
citability misleading the master as everyone. For he himself
was already a published poet; a few days before Izambard
took up his post at the College his "Les Etrennes des Orphelins"
had been printed in *La Revue pour tous*. This triumph he did
not mention to his new friend. *La Revue pour tous* was a journal
of little importance and "Les Etrennes" an imitation of François
Coppée notable only for its loss of mother theme, ending with

Ayant trois mots gravés en or: "A NOTRE MERE!"

With three words engraved in gold: "TO OUR MOTHER!"

Yet even if the boy realized the insignificance of the poetry
and the journal it was printed in, his silence would have struck
the transparent Izambard as most peculiar. Not that he was
a fraud; impetuous and confiding by nature, he had learned to
be mistrustful. He appeared to Izambard as one dedicated to
poetry, which was true; anxious to be led, which was true up
to a point; and delightfully modest, which was not true at all.
And as one poem after another was diffidently shown, discussed
at enormous length, re-written, polished and re-polished during
those first six months of 1870, Izambard's affection and admiration went out to this strange and lonely boy who had so obvious
a gift.

So Rimbaud wrote his poems and showed them to his encouraging friend, he read and talked endlessly of the great

"moderns" the master had lent him. His enthusiasm, like his poems, was fascinating; Izambard could scarcely be blamed for thinking that he had won his entire confidence. Yet not only had Rimbaud failed to mention "Les Etrennes" but at some point in the first part of the year he was writing a poem and meditating a course of action about which he said nothing.

Banville, whose poems they discussed more than any others and with greater admiration, was, the exiled Hugo excepted, the most popular poet then writing. He was also one of the three men composing the Comité des Graces of the second *Parnasse Contemporain,* the anthology of the Parnassians. Izambard possessed a complete set of the first *Parnasse Contemporain* of 1866 which Rimbaud had read and re-read page by page. The second series, though announced the previous year, 1869, had not yet begun to appear and Rimbaud made up his mind to try to get his poems included. In May, without a word to Izambard, he sent three of them to Banville with this letter: "We are in the months of love; I am nearly seventeen. The age of hopes and chimeras, as they say—and here, a child touched by the Muse's finger—forgive me if this is a commonplace—I've begun to express my faith, my hopes and sensations, all of those poet's feelings. I call this springtime. And if I send you some of these lines by way of the good publisher Alphonse Lemerre it is because I love all poets, all good Parnassians—for the poet is a Parnassian—in love with ideal beauty; and it's because in you I admire, very naïvely, a descendant of Ronsard, brother of the masters of 1830, a true romantic, a true poet. That's why. It's stupid, isn't it, but never mind. . . . In two years, in one perhaps, I shall be in Paris. And then *anch'io,* gentlemen of the press, I shall be a Parnassian. I've got something in me, I don't know what, that wants to soar. I swear, dear master, always to worship the two goddesses, the Muse and Freedom. Don't purse your lips too much when you read these lines. . . . You would drive me mad with hope and joy, dear master, if you could manage to find a little place beside the Parnassians for the piece *Credo in unam.* . . . I would like to be in the last

series of the *Parnasse:* this would be the Credo of the poets!
. . . O mad Ambition!"

He added a postscript on the copy of "Credo in unam": "If
only these verses could find room in the *Parnasse Contemporain!*—Aren't they the faith of poets?—I'm not known but
what does that matter? poets are brothers. These verses believe,
they love, they hope: that is everything. Dear Master, help me;
raise me a little; I am young; give me your hand. . . ."

There were two ways of reading the letter, and Banville,
caught no doubt at an unfavorable moment, saw overdone
humility and imperfectly concealed arrogance and missed the
rapturous overflow of feeling of a repressed boy unable to
restrain himself in the excitement of writing to a revered poet.
Rimbaud did himself a disservice by advancing his age, natural
though it was. Banville replied and filed both letter and poems.
His reply has been lost but obviously said, what was the fact,
that the lists were closed. But it seems unlikely that he read the
poems. He was a kind man, renowned for the helping hand he
had held out to so many young poets, a fairly perceptive man
too, with a charming trait of over-enthusiasm for the work of
others. Had he read these poems he would probably have tried
to get them printed, for he had never handled work of greater
promise. All three were good; the poem on which Rimbaud had
written his postscript, the poem afterwards named "Soleil et
Chair," compared favorably with anything printed in the *Parnasse
Contemporain.* As with almost all his work of the first half of
1870 he had faithfully followed his masters; in this case, aping
the studious objectivity practiced by the Parnassians, he attempted, as they had so often done, an evocation of ancient
Greece, attempted and succeeded.

He was, after all, a boy who lived most of his life in the
imagination, who put his faith in the imagination to deliver
him from the reality of a prosaic home life lived against the
prosaic background of a commercial town. To recreate past
ages had been a favorite game with him for years; when he
walked sedately from school to home he walked, not the fa-

miliar streets but the deck of a ship, the cobbles of Rome, the
pavements of the Acropolis. "I dreamt that I was born at Reims
in the year 1503" he had written at the age of eight. And in
this spirit, almost without conscious use of the imagination, he
wrote "Credo in unam"; but he wrote it with a technical ability
beyond his years.

The authenticity of atmosphere which he conveys was not
wholly due to an exceptional imagination.

> *Je regrette les temps de l'antique jeunesse*
> I regret the age of antique youth

is one of the many striking lines, and the whole poem is a sigh
of longing for the unimpeded flow of mutual love which he
saw as the main distinction between ancient and modern worlds;
with all the passion of romantic, unsatisfied youth he opposed
his conception of ancient Athens to the modern Sparta personi-
fied by Madame Rimbaud.

3 ⤳

Not until July 18 did he show this poem to Izambard. Izambard remembered the day until the end of his life; it was the
middle of a memorable triad. On the first, July 17, three days
after the end of term, the *Concours Académique* award was announced of first prize to Arthur for his set of Latin verses on
Sancho Panza, the successful culmination of much out-of-school
work by the boy and his master.

The next day as they were walking along the leafy Sous les
Allées, as the townsfolk called the Cours d'Orléans, Rimbaud
suddenly handed the manuscript of "Credo in unam" to his companion. He had spoken about it a few days earlier "as an effort
in which he took some pride" but would not show it; because,
Izambard afterwards surmised, he hoped to hand it over with a
"Banville has accepted it for the Parnasse." It could be so only
if Banville delayed his negative reply to the May letter for two
months. However that may be, term over and Izambard soon

due to leave for his holidays, the poem was at last produced. Both stopped, Izambard to read, the boy "remaining close to me, silent, waiting for my first impressions."

Discussion of the poem continued in Izambard's rooms and with a slightly larger audience than usual, for his aunt, Caroline Gindre, had come over from Douai to join him for the last days of term. Izambard prefaced her coming by an outline of her virtues to Rimbaud and Deverrière. The outline included his own history, for, carried off to Douai by the sixteen-year-old Caroline following the sudden death of his mother six months after his birth in Paris, he had been adopted by the family to console them for the loss of the only Gindre boy in the Crimea. Caroline had grown into a blue stocking who was also an efficient household manager. She had been responsible for the successful beginning of Izambard's career; he had taken his *baccalauréat* at the age of fifteen and his teaching *licentiat* at the University of Paris three years later.

Whether she, Izambard, Deverrière or Bretagne realized what a remarkable poem the boy had written remains unrecorded because the very next day another piece of news swept everything else from their minds; on July 19 France declared war on Prussia. Ever since Prince Leopold of Hohenzollern accepted the throne of Spain seventeen days earlier the declaration had been expected, and to many people in France had been foreseen long before that as Louis Napoleon's final throw for a continuance of power. Foreseen, expected, but not always accepted; propaganda was necessary; and a few days before the declaration of war the little group which met in Izambard's rooms had read in the local newspaper "with a unanimous outcry of indignation": "War at this moment is imperiously decreed for us by the interests of France and by the needs of the dynasty . . . The government of Napoleon III owes it to the government of Napoleon IV to remove all stones from its path."

Rimbaud was far removed from the boy who had dedicated his Latin verses to the Prince Imperial; in March he had written "Le Forgeron," a Hugoesque deification of the old revolu-

tionaries, and he went off from one "outcry of indignation"—
for every day the newspaper shocked them with crude propaganda—in a mood of cynicism which he wrote into the savage
"Morts de Quatre-vingt-douze." When asked to sign a petition
to pupils to forfeit prizes as their war effort, he refused with a
brusque "Useless piece of nonsense."

However, war it was and on the surface a popular war, with
a Charleville blatantly expressing the chauvinism which had
spread over France. Rimbaud saw the bragging posters outside
the bookshops, heard the shouts of "*A Berlin*" from the conscripts
who began to march east through the town, heard in the streets
and market the latest recruiting songs from the *café-concerts*—
saw and heard with a sneer. With a sinking heart too, for within
a few days Izambard would be in Douai with Deverrière who
had been invited to spend part of his holiday there. His bitterness and desperation broke out one evening in Izambard's rooms
just before the three—Izambard, Deverrière and Caroline—were
due to leave: "What am I going to do when Monsieur Izambard
has gone?" he demanded of Deverrière, and answered himself
with "One day I shall escape, that's certain: I can't stand another
year of this life. I want to earn my living. I can write, so to begin
with I'll be a journalist in Paris."

"You think that's easy?" asked Deverrière, whose ambitions
stretched in the same direction.

"I don't care," cried the boy. "I may collapse on the road,
I may die of hunger on the paving stones, but I'll go."

"You'll do nothing of the kind," said Izambard. "I tell you,
you must stay here, finish your studies and pass your *baccalauréat*. Be patient for another year; all the prizes you'll win
will make your mother more indulgent."

"You don't know her!" was the bitter answer, how bitter no
one understood.

A day or two later, on July 24, Rimbaud saw his friends off
from Charleville station.

CHAPTER FOUR

Runaway

1870

IZAMBARD had not left Rimbaud without consolation; he persuaded his landlord to let him have the key of his room on demand. Whenever he could slip away or wheedle permission to go out, which was not seldom, the boy shut himself in the little library and read. Yet this pleasure was limited— he read fast and Izambard's books were few—and could not always compensate for what he felt to be a total desertion; for Bretagne, the one member of the Izambard clan still in the town, manifested no inclination to make an intimate of an excitable and apparently priggish child who talked like the Bible. So the child relieved his feelings in poetry; the savage irony of "Morts de Quatre-vingt-douze" descended into the coarseness of "Vénus Anadyomène." He had borrowed the idea from Coppée but the attempt to shock was all his own.

> *Et tout ce corps remue et tend sa large croupe*
> *Belle hideusement d'un ulcère à l'anus*

> And this whole body stirs and offers its broad rump
> Hideously beautiful with an ulcer at the anus

he ends with youthful satisfaction. If his mother believed that the "bad words" learned in rue Bourbon had been a passing phase, she was mistaken.

On August 6, the college prize day, his vanity was soothed by the customary pre-eminence; he won more than half the class awards in addition to the academical area honors. But by that time he was hugging a greater pleasure, the acceptance of a second poem by a Paris journal. This was *La Charge* and the poem, in another world from "Vénus Anadyomène," the charming "Première Soirée."

The publication of this poem on August 13 was a high-water mark. From that moment all went wrong. The war which had been launched to such a chorus of acclamation was already declaring itself a major disaster. For a week or two all had gone well and when, on August 2, Saarbrucken fell, there was a general expectation of victorious French armies driving on to Berlin under the nominal lead of the great Napoleon's nephew. Then one reverse followed another and an uneasy certainty spread over the country that Louis Napoleon was not a second military genius and that the much vaunted French army was wretchedly equipped as well as badly led and had no chance of making a fight of it. By the middle of the month one French army had been shut up in Metz, another in Strasbourg; by the end of the month a third army, under MacMahon and Louis Napoleon, had retreated as far as Sedan, fourteen miles up the Meuse from Charleville, where it was cut off and surrounded.

Before this final ignominy, which settled the fate of the Empire, Rimbaud had left Charleville, but he stayed long enough to see gleefully his townsfolk realizing that they and not the faraway people of Prussia were to be in the thick of the battlefield. He may have heard the gunfire from Sedan; certainly he watched with a grimace conscripts still streaming through the town mechanically shouting "A Berlin," shopkeepers, businessmen and clerks climbing into volunteer uniforms, soldiers hurriedly strengthening the defenses. He relieved his spleen in the sarcastic "A la Musique" of one of the Thursday concerts in the Place de la Gare, where his mother and father had met, and there too he drew his clever caricature "Three bourgeois of Charleville."

But neither poems nor caricatures could relieve his feelings for long. He was bored, angry, frustrated. He had nothing to do. No one noticed him; the great Charleville prizewinner had dwindled into an anonymous little boy who walked about scowling; his mother, silent and preoccupied, could not be drawn into a show of interest even by his complaints. He panted to be away. What a town! When it wasn't buried snout-deep in the

making of money it was being hysterical about war; patroniz-
ingly permitting poets to practice their childish game in days
of peace; in war, brushing them aside as frivolous excrescences.

When, some time before the month was out, Frédéric, grown
into a big boy, fell hopefully in with one of the squads march-
ing to the railway station, managed to squeeze himself into a
truck and was forthwith adopted by the men as mascot and
carried off to Metz whilst Madame Rimbaud helplessly raged,
Arthur then had to grapple with jealousy as well as the rest;
the despised and amiable clod of a brother had at least acted.
Behind his mother's anger was there not some tinge of pride
too? His fury boiled over into a letter to Izambard marked
"Very urgent": "You're lucky not to be in Charleville any longer.
Of all small provincial towns my native one takes the cake for
idiocy. I've no more illusions about this. Because it's next door
to Mézières—a place no one's ever heard of—because one sees
two or three hundred *poilus* ambling along the streets, this
blessed population gesticulates, pompously playing the bravo—
very differently from those besieged in Metz and Strasbourg!
They are frightful, these retired grocers who go back into uniform! Stunningly chic, these lawyers, glaziers, tax collectors,
carpenters and all the paunchy who make the motions of patriotism at the gates of Mézières. My country rises! I'd rather
see it sitting. Don't stir a foot! that's my principle.

"I'm without a country, sick, angry, stupid, upset; I long for
sunbaths, enormous walks, rest, travel, adventures, in short for
bohemianism; I long specially for newspapers and books . . .
But nothing! Not a thing! The post doesn't deliver anything
more to the bookshops; Paris makes nice sport of us: not a single
new book! This is death! For papers I'm reduced to the honorable *Courrier des Ardennes,* proprietor, manager, chief and only
editor A. Pouillard! This paper expresses the aspirations, wishes
and opinions of the population, so you can guess what it's like!
it makes one's gorge rise. I'm an exile in my own country!!!

"Luckily I have your room. You remember that you gave me
permission to use it. I've swept through half your books! I've

taken the *Diable à Paris!* Tell me, has there ever been anything more idiotic than Granville's drawings? I have *Costal d'Indien,* I have *Robe de Nessus*—two interesting novels. Beyond that, what can I tell you? I have read all your books, all; three days ago I descended to *Epreuves* then to *Glaneuses*—yes! I have re-read that book! And that's the lot! Nothing left; your library, my last plank, is exhausted. I have just come across *Don Quichotte;* yesterday I spent two hours on end studying the Doré woodcuts: now I have nothing more! I enclose some verses; read them in the morning, in the sun, as I made them: you are no longer my teacher, I hope!"

At this point the letter is damaged; Rimbaud used simply to fold the sheet of paper and seal it with a wafer, which when opened frequently took some of the paper with it. He is praising a poetess he has "discovered," Louisa Siefert, and quotes one of her poems to whet Izambard's appetite, a poem which he claims, his critical sense deserting him, "is as beautiful as the lamentations of Sophocles' Antigone."

He ends with another and very different recommendation. He had got hold of Paul Verlaine's *Fêtes Galantes,* which he says is "most unusual, very funny and truly adorable. Great license occasionally: for instance.

> *et la tigresse épou/vantable d'Hyrcanie*
>
> and the frightful Hyrcanian tigress

is a line in this book. I advise you to buy *La Bonne Chanson,* a small book of poetry by the same author, just published by Lemerre; I haven't read it; nothing reaches here; but many newspapers speak favorably of it. Goodbye, send me a letter of 25 pages—poste restante and very quickly!"

He added a P.S. "Soon, some revelations about the life I'm going to lead after the holidays."

This letter was dated August 25. There is no sign that Izambard regarded it as anything but blowing off steam; if he needed reassurance that nothing much was wrong with the boy he would find it in the poem enclosed, which was either the verses published in *La Charge* or *"Ce Qui Retient Nina."* Both poems are lighthearted, breathing high spirits and happiness, every line contradicting the prevailing tone of the letter. And it was true enough that Rimbaud remained the child in many things; he could shelve all his miseries the moment he strolled in the country; the poem reflected him as accurately as the letter.

Izambard, then, thought nothing of the postscript, and the letter itself he dismissed with sentimental reflections on the extravagances of youth; he was preoccupied—these were anxious days for Frenchmen in the line of the advancing Prussians—and did not reply immediately. This perhaps decided the boy; he was not to be invited to Douai, that was clear. Then why not Paris? All the poets were there. The triumphant escape of Frédéric rankled; then he heard that the railway to Paris might be cut at any moment. That was enough: four days after he had written to Izambard, on August 29, whilst MacMahon was fatalistically crossing the Meuse nearby, he suddenly ran away. He had been walking with his mother and sisters in the meadows outside the town. The girls sat down with books whilst their mother paced up and down, a parasol protecting her from the sun. Arthur asked if he might fetch his book from their apartment not far away. His mother raising no objection, he walked straight to the railway station, bought a ticket to Charleroi with all the money he possessed and boarded the first train.

In his poem "Mémoire" he was to re-live this prelude to his first escapade, stating symbolically the problem that was to dog him all his life:

Mon canot, toujours fixe; et sa chaîne tirée
Au fond de cet oeil d'eau sans bords—à quelle boue?

My boat, ever stationary; and its chain pulled
To the bottom of this brimless eye of water—to what mud?

2

Not until he reached Paris that evening was he asked to show his ticket. When he was found to have no ticket beyond

Charleroi and no money he was taken to the prefecture for examination. These were the days of defeat and near panic, with every other man suspected of being a "red," as the extreme revolutionaries were called; a spy scare was at its height; the train had come from the threatened areas; only with these facts in mind is it possible to understand how a small boy could have been arrested and put into prison. He was unwilling, or unable through sudden fear, to explain why he had come to Paris. In his pockets were found poems, not all of the happiest kind for a government official to read; humor was at a low ebb at that moment, the usual respect for the arts practically submerged.

The examination, followed by a prison cell, verminous and crowded, sobered the boy but did not immediately cow him; five days later, cheered perhaps by an issue of the regulation tobacco, he celebrated Louis Napoleon's surrender at Sedan with a defiant recopying of his "Morts de Quatre-vingt-douze." But that was a final flicker of spirit. The great events of the next day, the famous Quatre Septembre, when the republic was proclaimed in the Place de l'Hôtel de Ville, fell flat with him; he was not, as he later confessed wryly, "very much in the mood" for rejoicing. Even his longing to meet the literary men of Paris had foundered in the wave of homesickness. And when, that same evening or the next morning, the governor, belatedly puzzled by this unusual prisoner, interrogated him again, he spoke freely and begged to be allowed to go home.

As a result on September 6 Izambard received a covering letter from the governor enclosing this from Rimbaud:

"I have done what you advised me not to do; I went to Paris, leaving the maternal home! I did this on August 29.

"As I stepped out of the train I was arrested for owing the railway thirteen francs and not having a sou to pay it with, was taken to the prefecture and today I am waiting for my trial at Mazas! Oh! I TRUST IN YOU as in my mother; you have always been like a brother to me; I ask at once for the help you always used to offer me. I have written to my mother, to the imperial prosecutor, to the police commissioner at Charle-

ville; if you haven't heard further from me by Wednesday, before the train leaves Douai for Paris, *take that train and come
here to claim me, by letter or by appearing before the public
prosecutor and begging him to let me go, by answering for me,
by paying my debt! Do everything you can,* and when you get
this letter, write, yes, *I command you, write to my poor mother*
(Quai de la Madeleine, 5, Charleville) *to comfort her; write to
me* also; do everything. I love you as my brother, I will love
you as my father. I shake your hand; your poor A.R." He added,
"If you can come to free me, take me back to Douai."

"I TRUST IN YOU as in my mother." Here, under stress of
youthful panic, is plain speaking. And the "write to my poor
mother to comfort her" provides a view, not so much of Madame
Rimbaud as of the son who had to imagine that she was wretched
without him.

Izambard, having been asked by the governor to remove
the boy, at once wrote to Paris enclosing money to pay both
the debt and the fare north, explained, guaranteed, and begged
that the runaway be put into a train for Charleville or, if that
was not possible, for Douai. Charleville was not possible, the
Prussians having already cut the line, and a day or two later a
"dishevelled, crestfallen but happy" Rimbaud was received into
the snug Gindre home at 29 rue de l'Abbaye des Prés at Douai,
received "exactly like the prodigal son and without any ser-
monizing." The first thing was to let Madame Rimbaud know
where Arthur was. Both wrote to her, the son penitently, Izambard advising her to treat him leniently since he had already
been punished severely for his escapade. That duty done they
sat back to enjoy themselves; direct communication between
Douai and Charleville was broken and letters had to take the
long route via Belgium; a reply from Madame Rimbaud could
not be expected for a week or more. The boy, cleaned and re-
clothed, was given a pleasant bedroom containing the books of
the dead Gindre brother and was treated as an equal by all—the
all including Deverrière who was showing no inclination to leave
such good company.

What struck everybody about the new arrival was his self-possession. Izambard was amused by the rebound into jaunty much-travelled man of the world; the sharp-tongued Caroline soon became riled by it. It was a talkative household, and the discussions, on politics, literature, art, came to a climax at the evening meal; all had something to say; and Caroline, who was serving-maid as well as other things, often paused by the table with a pile of used plates, eager to hear the end of an argument or to throw in her own word. One evening Rimbaud, talking briskly, was the last to finish. Then, having wiped his plate clean with a piece of bread, French fashion, he was ready for the next course; and seeing Caroline standing and making no move to fetch it, he ostentatiously bent across the table in the midst of the discussion and put his used plate in front of her. This broad hint ("cheeky but unthinking" Izambard kindly says) struck dumb everyone but Caroline. "Rimbaud," she said, "when I serve Georges and you and my sisters I do it kindly and whole-heartedly, like a mother. It is quite all right if you don't want to help, but to take it for granted as your action implied is not good. I'm sure your mother would never tolerate such a thing."

This last conventional remark was more effective than the speaker could have hoped. Rimbaud colored and was silent. A dozen times he could push forward a plate, himself, a theory, anything; he had only to unloose that ravishing, innocent, en-thusiastic smile of his and the deed was done; but when his bluff was called, as then, his small stock of self-confidence col-lapsed; he became the uncertain little boy, mute under his mother's reproaches. He did not revive again until alone with Izambard. They walked happily about the town and into the country beyond it, with Deverrière sometimes making a hearty third, discussing books and politics. Rimbaud, on top of the world again, joyously quoted Montaigne on the poet into every rare silence. They visited Douai's poet Paul Demeny whom the impressionable boy cultivated with a fervor. No more was *Les Glaneuses* the tedious book to be read when one was at one's last gasp, but the work of a friendly published poet. Demeny

took the over-earnest view of his position so often forced on
the second-rate and Rimbaud burned to show him what he
could do. He wrote "Les Effarés." Demeny was impressed; the
poem about poor children watching the baker at work and
hungrily sniffing new bread through the bakehouse grating is
one of Rimbaud's most effective paintings in verse.

Not less happily he and Izambard tried their hands at amateur
soldiering. The republic declared, the war became all at once,
for Izambard as for most Frenchmen, a war of national defense;
Louis Napoleon gone, he no longer wished to shelter behind
the shortsightedness which had saved him from service in the
Garde Mobile, the special militia formed as soon as war began, but, eager to help, volunteered for the infantry. As neither
rifles nor uniforms were available he was assigned for the moment to the Garde Nationale, the home guard, of Douai.
Rimbaud went along with him to the headquarters; at first "for
the walk" but as the walk progressed announcing without ceremony "that he would put down his name when I did." Izambard
pointed out that this was impossible without Madame Rimbaud's consent. Rimbaud declined to believe that such an
"enormity" was possible; and when, at the barracks, his offer
was peremptorily declined, he walked back with his friend
cursing his "pestilential luck" and the "flabbiness of officialdom."

When Izambard left for his rifle and bayonet drill the next
day Rimbaud insisted on accompanying him and watched the
exercise enviously, an envy unimpaired by the fact that most
of the men were armed with broomsticks. At the end of the
display he begged his friend to ask the sergeant-instructor if he
could take part in future as "garde nationale volontaire." His
request was granted, an extra broomstick was obtained for him
from the "arms depot" and he joined the drill every day.

Having had his way, he quickly aspired higher, to the possession of a real rifle. He was not alone. He heard the grumbling
after a parade before the mayor in which the men had been
told that no arms were available, heard several men ask Izam-

bard to write out a protest for them to sign. In the Gindre house again, before Izambard had had time to put pen to paper, the boy had written out on three large sheets of paper a protest which he laid proudly before his friend.

The protest, as Izambard says, was written in the best journalese; Rimbaud, ever the imitator, had learned his lesson well; for Izambard had also turned journalist whilst waiting to be called up. Douai being without information except by the town crier since the surrender at Sedan, a printer began a small news sheet. Izambard, anxious to propagate "a very discreet political note conforming to the new spirit," suggested collaborating with an article or two and a leader and was soon installed for part of each day in the little office of *Le Libéral du Nord* as he christened the paper. Here came Deverrière and Rimbaud, the latter "blooming in printer's ink and letting himself go"—in more ways than one.

The launching of the little newspaper led quickly to a public meeting of Douai's left wing republicans. Rimbaud was there; so, too, was the co-director of a factory, one of the big men of the town. The next day Izambard took a day off, handing over the preparation of *Le Libéral du Nord* to a friend, the editor of a Douai republican newspaper which had been suppressed a few months earlier. He introduced Rimbaud to this man and left them in the office together. Later, when a copy of the day's issue arrived at the Gindre house, Rimbaud hung about watching Izambard tear off the wrapper; watched "with a detached air so much overdone" that Izambard was intrigued. He opened the paper and began to glance through it. On the third page, under Local News, he found a report of the meeting, a report in which everyone who had spoken, including the big businessman, was described as "le citoyen."

Rimbaud, "as red with modesty as a young virgin after her first kiss," waited for compliments on his first essay in printed journalism.

"So this is how you abuse my trust!" Izambard said, laughing.

"Bah! your friends will be pleased."

"I'm not so sure. One or two perhaps. But the others, Monsieur . . . ?" Izambard named the businessman.

"Well? Have I spared him compliments?"

"Will they be the kind he likes? He's a serious man, by no means a bourgeois but with a reputation in the town for steadiness, in short he's a personage, and you've dealt him the blow of 'citoyen' as if he called himself Marat . . ."

"Not at all; it's a title one gives to everyone under the republic; in '92 and '48 it was just the same."

Izambard, more amused than worried, dropped the subject and set off for the town, alone for once, to try to make the peace.

3

This was Rimbaud's last fling at Douai. The date of *Le Libéral du Nord* which carried his report was September 25; four days earlier a letter had arrived from Madame Rimbaud for her son; a letter, says Izambard, "so violent, so denunciatory, so brutal towards him, me, my family and everyone who sheltered him *instead of turning him out* that Rimbaud, losing his self-control, clenched his fists, cursed and swore that he would not return home at any price." This outburst shocked everybody; he was reproved; and after an injured "You're like all the rest," his mouth distorted into "an enormous sulk," he calmed down and promised to do what they thought best. Privately, he wrote out his agitation in "Les Poètes de Sept Ans" which included the reproach to his mother that her "blue look" was a lie. Izambard, whose dislike of Madame Rimbaud had turned to detestation, read the poem without reproof and encouraged Rimbaud to give it to Demeny. He replied to Madame Rimbaud, telling her that if he turned her son out of the house he would only come to further harm. He offered to pay the fare home but refused to give Rimbaud the money because he felt sure that in the boy's present state of mind he would get off the train at the first stop and disappear again. He suggested that Deverrière might cut his holiday short and accompany Rimbaud to Charleville.

Before she received this letter Madame Rimbaud wrote again: "I am very much disturbed and don't understand Arthur's prolonged absence. He must have known from my letter of the 17th that he was not to stay a day longer at Douai; on the other hand the police are making inquiries as to where he has gone, and I much fear that before you receive this the little silly may have got himself arrested a second time; but if so he need not trouble to come back, for I swear that never in my life will I receive him again. How can one understand the stupidity of this child who is ordinarily so quiet and sensible; how could such madness have entered his mind; did someone prompt him to do it? But I must not believe that; one is unjust when one is wretched. Will you please be kind enough to lend ten francs to the unhappy boy and turn him out so that he comes home quickly. I've just come from the post office where they have again refused to issue a money order as the line is not open as far as Douai. What can I do? I am greatly troubled. May God not punish the folly of the unfortunate boy as he deserves."

The violence of the first letter, caused by the shock of sudden relief, had given way to an uneasy attempt to shift responsibility. The "did someone prompt him?" was as uncalled-for as the "how can one understand the stupidity?" was disingenuous; but Madame Rimbaud was uncertain what confidences her son had indulged in to this household he seemed so reluctant to leave. On the night of her son's disappearance she had walked distractedly through Charleville calling at all the bars, cafés, bistros and at the station. She was frightened, thinking that Arthur had followed Frédéric's example and her fear was aggravated by guilt. She knew that Arthur was not irresponsible by nature; if he had run away to join the army it was not for the same reason as Frédéric. Consciously or unconsciously, she knew the reason. But Arthur discovered, every feeling gave way to anger, an anger whipped up by pride; for the runaway to linger in the Gindre house was an insult not to be borne calmly.

The morning after this second letter arrived, September 27, Deverrière, Rimbaud and Izambard set out by train for Charleville. Izambard joined the others because although, having volunteered for the army, he could not return to the college he was worried about his books and furniture; the Prussians were advancing on Mézières and he decided to pack and store everything while there was still time.

The train had to travel by the way of Belgium, and the deviation reminded him of an invitation he had received that morning from an old schoolfellow then living in Brussels; he would, he told Deverrière, spend a day or two with this friend, Paul Durand, on his way back from Charleville. Rimbaud, sitting in a corner of the compartment, did not speak a word. Izambard, looking at him with pity, imagined romantically that his thoughts were far away, perhaps with some future poem.

At Charleville master and boy walked to the Quai de la Madeleine, Izambard at least uneasily. With some cause, since this second visit of his to Madame Rimbaud proved even more unpleasant than the first. "Very vinegarish as usual," he says, "mother Rimbaud gave her small prodigal son a colossal thrashing and admonished me in terms so harsh that at first I stood there as if thunderstruck."

It was an unhappier moment than Izambard realized. Madame Rimbaud treated them both like naughty children and her son did not forget the sight of Izambard struck dumb and looking foolish in front of her. She did the punishing and, as far as her son was concerned, received the respect.

Izambard neither saw nor heard of the boy for the next week; he had forbidden Arthur to visit him without Madame Rimbaud's consent, and after packing his goods he made a tour of the battlefields round Sedan. When he returned he found a note from Madame Rimbaud who had been looking for him all over the town: would he call on her? With an effort he did so. Arthur, she said, had run away the previous night: would he try to find him? Izambard then remembered certain remarks which suggested that Arthur might have visited a classmate who lived at Fumay a few miles north of Charleville. His route back to Douai passed through Fumay; he offered to call there. Madame Rimbaud asked, if her son was found and refused to return home, that Izambard put him into the hands of the police with a request that they bring him back.

The next day, October 9, Izambard left Charleville for Fumay, called at the house of his pupil, Léon Billouart, and found without much surprise that Arthur had spent the night there and had left the next morning en route for another classmate, Arthur Binard, who lived a few miles further north, at Vireux.

At Vireux he heard a similar story, but this time Rimbaud had announced his intention of going to the home of a third college boy, Des Essarts, at Charleroi, the first big town over the Belgian frontier. There he hoped, on the somewhat feeble strength of his Douai experience, to be taken on as sub-editor by Des Essarts' father who published a small newspaper.

The tireless Izambard went on to Charleroi where he interviewed M. des Essarts. Yes, said the publisher, a young man had called and had at first made such a favorable impression that he was invited to dine with the family. Unhappily for Rimbaud's hopes his head was easily turned by drink, even a little of it. The wine or beer at dinner made him incautious; when the conversation moved on to politics, he, wishing to show himself au fait with the latest developments, launched into what quickly rose to a revolutionary tirade. It became a question which most shocked the sensibilities of his listeners, his preferences or his language, the "weathercock" politician degenerating into "dirty cad" as the evening advanced.

At this point Izambard ran into an impasse: "I declined his offers of assistance," explained M. des Essarts, "and he did not honor me with details of his future movements." So Izambard decided to forget Rimbaud for a moment and to make a surprise

visit to his friend in Brussels. Arriving at the door he was greeted
by Durand with a "Here you are! We've been waiting for you.
Your room is ready."

Izambard looked his bewilderment. "You were expecting me?"

"Yes, your pupil 'little Rimbaud' has been here to warn us
that you would soon be on your way."

Izambard thought back suddenly to the small silent figure in
the corner of the railway carriage a few days earlier.

"Yes, and how gentle, how nice he is. By the look of him the
poor child had done a lot of walking; he was dusty, muddy and
his collar was dirty and tie twisted. Naturally I rigged him out
with my best things."

Was he still there? asked Izambard, hoping that his search
was ended. But Rimbaud, he was told, had stayed only two
days, declaring that he must "look round Belgium to improve
his education" and assuring the kindly Durand and his mother
that "he knew how to look after himself." He had not left empty;
Durand, being given to understand that his funds were low—
indeed one look at him was enough—gave him money and told
him to keep the clothes he wore.

At this Izambard "shouted with laughter" and settled down
to enjoy a week with his friend. He simply saw Rimbaud's odys-
sey as "colossal cheek." On his return to rue de l'Abbaye des Prés
he was greeted by a Rimbaud whose tour of Belgium had ended
in Brussels' railway station where he straightway bought a ticket
to Douai with Durand's money, walked to the Gindre house and
presented himself to the astonished aunts with a perky "Here
I am. I've come back." He "strutted about the house and town
in a stiff butterfly-wing collar from which flowed a bronze silk
tie across his chest with dazzling effect; a true *dandy:* Paul
Durand had chosen well." So Izambard thought with fond amusement as he listened to the recital of the boy's adventures: the
chocolate given him by Billouart at Fumay; the unsuccessful
attempt to find a sergeant recommended to him by the same
schoolfellow, and the meal he hoped for, at Givet, the frontier
garrison town where his father had been stationed twenty years

earlier; his stolen sleep on the sergeant's empty bed in the Givet barracks; the state of his feet by the time he reached Charleroi; and his hunger: "I dined on sniffs of the smells wafting through ventilators of roast meats and chickens being enjoyed at the bourgeois tables of Charleroi."

He showed Izambard with pride the poems composed on his journey, "Au Cabaret-vert," "La Maline," "Roman," "Le Buffet," "Ma Bohème," this last with its Rimbaudian

Mes étoiles au ciel avaient un doux frou-frou

My stars in the sky made a gentle rustling

and

je tirais les élastiques
De mes souliers blessés, un pied près de mon cœur!

I was tugging at the elastic bands
Of my wounded shoes, with one foot near my heart!

Making himself at home as soon as he entered the house, he spent most of his time copying out these poems, copying with a dedicated air and a fussiness that made Izambard laugh secretly. He insisted on using foolscap paper and whenever he made the slightest error, began again on a fresh sheet. Several times a day he would cry out "I have no more paper" which was understood correctly to mean that he wanted a few sous so that he could walk up the street and buy more. The aunts watched this display of riotous living with dismay; they had hard work to make ends meet with their nephew temporarily out of work. At last, unable to bear the sight in silence, Caroline cried, "Why can't you write on the back?" To which Rimbaud replied, with a scandalized air, "No one ever writes on the back; printers don't like it."

"Very wise, very fine, very powerful and perfectly intelligible," said Izambard, not without humor, of these poems. He added, "they had the effrontery to be charming" and this was more to the point. This second excursion from home was to be one of the happiest periods of Rimbaud's life, and the happiness is reflected in the poems; they are a delight to read as he, in the mood in which he wrote them, was a delight to meet. They are more than a delight, they are a delightful novelty. They deal time and again with incidents then regarded as unpoetic—the tying of a bootlace, the prick of stubble on the ankles—just as the Impressionists were to reveal the poetry of supposedly unpainterly "common" life and scenes. But the Charleville boy did not know the work of the painters still struggling for recognition in Paris; he was an original poet and could cheerfully write, with homely realism:

> *Ça sentira l'étable, pleine*
> *De fumiers chauds,*
> *Pleine d'un lent rhythme d'haleine*
> *Et de grands dos*
>
> *Blanchissant sous quelque lumière;*
> *Et, tout là-bas,*
> *Une vache fientera, fière,*
> *A chaque pas . . .*

> It will smell of the stable, full
> Of warm manure,
> Full of slow rhythmic breathing
> And of large backs
>
> Turning white beneath a vague light;
> And, over yonder,
> A cow, proud, will drop her dung
> At every step . . .

Most of these early poems convey the very essence of their young author as he appeared to his Douai friends—eager, keen-eyed, in love with life. They tend to be underrated by the critic with his eyes on later events, but Izambard is not the only reader to consider them as some of the most delightful ever written, presenting a Rimbaud whom all can find sympathetic.

At times more than sympathetic. These youthful poems have another peculiarity, their frequent references to love, as if in his fresh and charming world of artless incident a free and generous love moved in the very air. The incidents are snatches of experience, the love wholly imaginative. One poem ended

"Car elle aime d'amour son fils de dix-sept ans,"

For she is in love with her seventeen-year-old son,

but Rimbaud was still a year away from this self-revelation; he was celebrating his sixteenth birthday happily in the Gindre house. Nor did his mood change when Izambard made clear as soon as he reached home that his uninvited guest could not stay there. "You understand what a quandary you put us in," he said. "We don't want to turn you out but we have no right to keep you." The boy, said Izambard, an Izambard sorely conscience-stricken by his thankless role, remained "the living image of the *fait accompli* and kept his air of smiling serenity." Kept it even when, Madame Rimbaud having been written to once again, she replied as expected, that he was to leave at once and, to save money, was to be delivered to the commissioner of police and returned to Charleville by the police.

The next day, the last day of the month, Izambard handed Rimbaud into the police station. On their way he tried to encourage him, speaking of the bright future, of the high dignity of the art he had chosen to follow. He talked "from the heart" and said afterwards, "I had the impression that he understood me, that he was heavy-hearted but inwardly moved."

But he adds: "Perhaps I was mistaken. He was so impenetrable."

Izambard had some reason for his doubts; he could not feel quite sure of the boy because the mainspring of so many actions and responses was out of sight. How account, for instance, for the "smiling serenity" so different from the scowls of the first journey home? Izambard could not guess that his happy guest had looked in vain for strength of purpose in his host, for romance, for high seriousness, that he had been measured against Madame Rimbaud and found wanting. To Izambard the mere idea would have seemed an insult or an excuse for his easygoing laugh; and this accurately fixes the value and forecasts the end of his relationship with Arthur Rimbaud.

For the boy was no longer being torn from a serious alternative to his mother but leaving an intellectual and emotional diversion which he hoped would be repeated. He had had his fun, was ready to return and willing to pay for it. He left pleasant memories behind him, even to the farewell poem of thanks which he fastened to the doorknob on his way out. It was a good ending. For ending it was; he was never to see Izambard, the Gindre aunts, the Douai house again.

CHAPTER FIVE

Loose End

1870–1871

H IS reception on his return home from this second escapade was not what he expected. No thrashing, but words so wounding that Douai regained a temporary place as an absolute paradise and Izambard as a friend without blemish. In this mood he wrote to Izambard the day following his return a letter "for you only":

> I reached Charleville the day after I left you. My mother took me in and here I am . . . with absolutely nothing to do. My mother won't send me back to school until January.
>
> Oh well, I have kept my promise.
>
> I die, I rot in the midst of platitudes, ill nature, drabness. What can you expect? I persist in adoring most awfully real freedom, and . . . heaps of things that are "deplorable," aren't they?
>
> I meant to clear off again this very day; I could have done it, I have new clothes, I could have sold my watch, and, *vive la liberté!* But I stayed! and I shall long to get away many more times yet. Off we go, hat on head, coat on back, hands in pockets and away!—but I shall stay, I shall stay. I haven't promised that I would, but I'll do it to deserve your affection: you told me so. I shall deserve it.
>
> I can't express the gratitude I feel any more than I could the other day . . . I'll prove it to you. If it were a question of doing something for you I would die doing it—I give you my word. I still have lots of things to say . . .
>
> The "heartless"
A. Rimbaud

He had as postscript: "War; no siege of Mézières. When? No one speaks about it . . . Some sniping now and then. Abominable itching disease of idiocy—such is the mind of the population. One hears some good stories about it! This is disintegration."

The change from the intellectual freedom of the Douai house-hold to the rigid morality of Madame Rimbaud was hard to bear yet not so hard as her accusations of heartlessness. Be-wildered by the cruelty of this ironic situation, a situation quite beyond a boy of sixteen, he worked off feelings he had been taught to suppress by extravagant political discussions with Deverrière.

A few days later, having passed on Izambard's reply to Rim-baud, Deverrière was summoned to the Rimbaud apartment.

"You are M. Deverrière living at 95 Sous les Allées? You are looking after the affairs of M. Izambard? You gave my son a letter coming from Douai?"

"Yes, Madame."

"I can't accept the unreasonable requests of M. Izambard and I shall wait until I can settle the matter with him personally. In the meantime I propose to give you 15 francs 65 centimes. Are you prepared to take it?"

"Yes, Madame."

"You will give me a receipt."

"Yes, Madame."

He wrote out a receipt for Izambard's loan to Rimbaud when he left Douai, and Madame Rimbaud put the money on the table. "I thought," said Deverrière disgustedly, "of weighing it, of testing it—for who knows?" And from that moment he kept Izambard's letters for Rimbaud to collect at his lodgings, and tried to help him to free himself from the clutches of the "brutal tyranny"; he had forsaken school-mastering for journalism and hoped to get work for him on the left-wing newspaper *Le Progrès des Ardennes* which had just been launched by a Mézières photographer, Jacoby. The plan did not get far; Deverrière wrote an article for the first number and read it in print "twelve days later, out of date and wretchedly cut and corrected. Jacoby has reduced it to the level of his own bourgeois and thieves' argot prose. He is an ass." His indignation suggested that he might soon part from the paper, and Rimbaud's hopes of striking further republican blows dwindled.

For the rest there was "absolutely nothing to do." A youthful exaggeration, for though the College had been taken over as a hospital, he read, wrote poems, walked with Delahaye, talked with Delahaye and Deverrière. At home he used idle moments to attack Frédéric who had returned soon after him, having escaped from Metz and made his way through the enemy lines. This was action and romance too, but whatever Arthur really felt he chose to jeer at his brother's patriotism. Frédéric was not to be roused; his invariable reply was a calm "You disgust me" in between puffs of his pipe.

Disgusting no doubt to the simple-minded Frédéric, these cheap jibes and witticisms of the armchair critic. Yet of the two Arthur had the better right to complain; the war which had made a man of his brother, made him strike cynical attitudes. By the time he returned to Charleville for the second time all the enthusiasm which had shot him into the Douai home guard had evaporated. That had been in September, a few days after the declaration of the republic; now he was in November. Far from heralding the millennium, the fall of Louis Napoleon seemed to have accomplished nothing; there was no "Citoyening" in the streets, no sense of universal brotherhood; the spirit of '92 had not returned. He saw the old muddle, selfishness and waste, heard and read the old ignorantly defiant boasts, witnessed day after day all the sights he had castigated in his holiday letter to Izambard; the bourgeois enjoying their losing battle. Even from besieged Paris came rumors of mismanagement, treachery, unrest in the Garde Mobile, monarchist plots and, in response, the first abortive proclamation of the Commune in the Place de l'Hôtel de Ville. Nothing had changed except the position of the advancing Prussians.

His lofty hopes disintegrating before his eyes, the youthful idealist reacted by sneers, at Frédéric, at the frailty of human institutions, the preparations for the defense of Mézières. He used to walk across the Meuse bridge into Mézières every morning to see Delahaye and stroll with him in the public gardens or the grounds of an old château outside the town which had

been made into a small public park. There they found themselves a nook where they could smoke and talk. Rimbaud took
the lead as befitted an adventurer and practising poet, reading
poetry, talking poetry and politics. Politics would intrude; and
when their parks were laid waste by the Mézières garrison and
Delahaye moaned to see the beloved trees fall, Rimbaud's reply
was a threatening: "Some destruction is necessary. Some old
trees which have stood for hundreds of years must be cut down.
The axe must be applied to the roots of the society in which we
live. The wealthy will be razed to the ground and the arrogant
laid low."

This pontifical denunciation—and there was much more of
it, all taken straight from his readings in revolutionary writers—
by a youth of sixteen struck Delahaye with amazement but then
to him Rimbaud was a very god, beautiful and of a superlative
genius. How he looked, how he talked! Delahaye would perhaps
not follow him to the death; but to hear Rimbaud declaim his
poetry, to hear him demolish governments and classes and build
a new world, this was a safe excitement he was never to forget.
To what end, these defenses, this war? Rimbaud asked himself
and the few companions he mooched about with, Deverrière,
Delahaye and their school friends Louis Pierquin and Ernest
Millot chiefly; to make life secure once more for M. and Mme
Bourgeois and their quiverful? Where was the selfless enthusiasm
for the cause? Not in Charleville. Not, at least, outside the office
of *Le Progrès des Ardennes.*

A new hero arose in his mind, the would-be Marat the second,
Eugène Vermersch, editor of the satirical Paris journal *Le Han-
neton* and already notorious as a fanatical communard. The
wish to see France victorious had left Rimbaud since a victorious
France promised, by the look of Charleville, a perpetuation of
the social regime he loathed. A defeated France, on the other
hand, could lead to the rise and triumph of the communards who
were working through the discontented Garde Mobile in Paris
and whose main mouthpiece was Vermersch. Then the glories of
'92 would be repeated, and not only men but literature be free

once more. For behind the revolutionary thought and talk moved
realities: the outlet for emotional dissatisfaction which was as
old as the schoolboy; and the hopes of a brilliant literary future
which were as old as the poet. "I've got something in me, I don't
know what, that wants to soar," he had written to Banville; and
"poets are brothers." A revolution to him was not simply a political event, but an opportunity for him to "soar" inspired by
the company of brother poets in a world in which all men would
be brothers. He saw a Paris free in spirit, where men wrote,
talked, painted as they felt. His poems of this time express his
disappointment that this freedom was so long in coming.

He soon had an opportunity of seeing, in his part of the world,
France in the dust. By December 20 Mézières had been cut off,
and ten days later was bombarded, half the town being destroyed
before the flag was hauled down. The casualties included the
printing office of *Le Progrès,* a favorite haunt of Rimbaud still
not hopeless of picking up a job which would please his mother
and console himself. He had not succeeded in becoming employee or contributor. His poems were dismissed unkindly by
Jacoby, who took his new role seriously, with a "the present times
don't lend themselves to rustic pipings." And when, taking the
hint, he submitted a critical article on Bismarck, Jacoby showed
interest but cautiously demanded "please lift your mask a little,"
the article having been written under a pseudonym. This was on
December 29; the next day came the enemy bombardment and
the disappearance of the paper until the following spring.

Madame Rimbaud locked her family in the apartment until
the bombardment slackened. This was her only satisfaction. All
the rest, as far as the boys were concerned, was one moral defeat
after another. Frédèric, too big to punish, had gained self-confidence from his months in the army and displayed a carefree
determination to live his own life. Arthur had twice run away,
had lived happily with a family of which the only member
known to her was an infidel apparently anxious to lead the boy
to destruction; and when she questioned him she could get no
better explanation than that he wanted to lead a free life, that he

loathed Charleville and all the people in it. "Deplorable" sentiments, as she said; but what to do about it? She could not put him back to school, into the army or the civil service; the school was closed, he was too young for the army, the civil service was disorganized and not accepting recruits and in any case he had still to take his *baccalauréat*. She never knew when he would go off again and, short of locking him up all day, could not prevent it; she could only make it difficult by withholding money.

For his part, Arthur resented the way in which his mother was standing between him and the fame which would bring her to his heels. He imagined cloudily—as he had said in Izambard's rooms months earlier—that to be a journalist in Paris, another Vermersch, was at that moment the most romantic and most practical task even for a poet. Yet even if he managed to screw a loan from his friends, communication between Paris and Charleville was still cut, enemy troops were everywhere, and in the capital the reactionaries, as he now styled the republican government, remained in control.

So his attention was drawn temporarily from Madame Rimbaud and from the ever-detested bourgeois, now making the best of a bad job by selling at absurdly high prices to the invaders, to a new bête noire, the Prussians, who marched the streets with insolent correctness, sat stiff and resplendent at the cafés in the Place Ducale and stared with haughty frigidity at the degenerate Frenchmen they had conquered. He, with Delahaye making faint motions to copy him, slouched past the Prussians on the pavements with a look of disgust on his face, as if he passed an open drain; and once at least, sitting at his favorite "Café de l'Univers" listening to one Prussian boasting to another, he laughed openly in contemptuous disbelief, to his companion's alarm. When Delahaye said gloomily that the Germans had proved themselves unmistakably superior, he replied prophetically: "No, they are our inferiors . . . The asses! They'll march home behind their blaring trumpets and beating drums to eat their sausages and believe it's all finished. But wait a bit. They are now militarized from top to toe and will swallow all the rot about glory that their treacherous masters choose to feed them with while they rule them with a rod of iron . . . All for nothing. For in the end they'll simply be crushed by some coalition."

This perceptive remark is an excellent example of the young Rimbaud's intelligence. It has perhaps been expressed by others of the thousands of young people who have experienced German occupation, but, Rimbaud having said it, the world was to hear and wonder. The Germans did more than wonder; when they occupied Charleville for the second time forty-five years later they made a point of destroying the bust which had been placed by Rimbaud's belatedly admiring townsfolk in the Place de la Gare. The bust cried aloud for destruction, but the Germans, needless to say, destroyed it for the wrong reason.

Except for a rare panic dread of confinement Rimbaud was virtually fearless and, not content with facial contortions and audible remarks, defied enemy instructions that no one was to leave the town without a pass. He knew every footpath and track for miles around, and often slipped out to see Delahaye whose parents, losing their house in the bombardment, had moved into the country. But in general the coming of the Prussians and of a hard winter drove him to heavier reading. And, the books which Deverrière was able to lend him and the books he "borrowed" from the stalls outside bookshops proving insufficient for his enormous appetite, he launched a prolonged assault on the public library.

Assault is the mot juste, for he met at the entrance an all but immovable object in the person of the librarian. This man, known as Père Hubert, was of a slothfulness and conservatism excessive even in his calling; Pierquin claims to have been chased out of the library because he asked for the *Fables* of La Fontaine, which is going rather far even for the seventies. The arrival of Rimbaud, baby-faced, undersized and demanding in a voice not yet broken the most inaccessible and, in the librarian's view, improper books, was treated as a joke. The joke died quickly when Père Hubert discovered that this angel in trousers was serious, was not to be turned from his purpose and, if thwarted, was capable of an unangelic coarseness. Rimbaud intended to use the library and although every obstacle that the outraged librarian could summon was put before him, he persisted in prising from forgotten shelves several books buried in dust.

His arrival came to be dreaded, not only by the librarian but by all the old men sleeping peacefully through the newspapers in the reading room. They were awakened rudely day after day by the exchanges between the brat demanding his rights as a citizen and the librarian fighting to the last ditch to avoid demeaning himself by service. Their sympathy was so patently for Père Hubert that Rimbaud tore them to pieces in "Les Assis," one of his cleverest and most original poems, sparking with hatred.

The books forced from the near-apoplectic Père Hubert are referred to vaguely by Verlaine years later as "a great many Oriental tales and libretti of Favert interspersed with scientific books, very old and very rare." The list given by Delahaye of his reading at this period included Daudet, Flaubert, Proudhon, Leconte de Lisle, Banville and Gautier. The library contained a book on the occult, Lévi's *History of Magic,* which may have had some slight influence on him. More to the point—a historic moment—is Delahaye's story of Rimbaud visiting him with a Baudelaire translation of Poe. The discovery of Baudelaire was decisive. The great poet had been dead more than three years but to all but a handful of the avant-garde he remained either unknown or a bogey figure incarnating the morbid. Rimbaud read all the Baudelaire he could lay hands on and saw instantly that he was a revolutionary poet of the greatest importance, a remarkable instance of critical understanding in a boy of his age. He read with joy Baudelaire's denunciations of the bourgeoise, denunciations as violent as even he could wish, was ravished by his metrical experiments, and in "Les Déserts de l'Amour" at once began to try his hand at the prose poem, encouraged by the master's "Who . . . has not dreamed of the miracle of a poetic prose, musical without rhythm or rhyme, supple and sudden enough to conform to the lyrical swayings of the soul?" He could not know and was never to know that there was a deeper correspondence between them, that Baudelaire's life too had been governed absolutely by devotion to a mother who was embarrassed by it. He and Baudelaire, he felt, were blood brothers, speaking with the same voice, expressing similar aims. He began to worship Baudelaire as his god.

2

The absorption in Baudelaire, books, poetical experiments was given strong impetus by the political events which quickly rose to a crisis in the new year. From Paris came one dramatic rumor after another. At the end of November the failure of the great sortie at Champigny led to the first appearance of the communard's red posters demanding the impeachment of the government. The second and last big attempt to break the siege, the sortie of Buzenval, failed with heavy loss of life halfway through January. A few days later an angry crowd led by mutinous Gardes Mobiles rescued the communard leaders from the prison into which they had been thrown after the unsuccessful October proclamation of the Commune. The next day, January 22, the Commune was again proclaimed in the Place de l'Hôtel de Ville. This second revolt was put down after a struggle but the position in Paris had become so critical after months of siege —practically no food, far too much drink, mass unemployment and the Garde Mobile and regular troops at each other's throats —that the government asked the Prussians for an armistice.

The armistice was signed on January 27, the government resigned and elections were held. The results of the elections shocked Rimbaud who had been excitedly following the news as it came through to Charleville; instead of the swing to the left that he, encouraged by Deverrière, had expected, most of the country outside Paris voted right with a leaning to royalist and Thiers became chief executive of the new government. The indignation of the little left-wing group in Charleville was a feeble reflection of communard reaction in Paris, where ugly scenes occurred day after day. The Garde Mobile, which had been allowed to keep its arms, presented such a threat to government that Thiers moved to Versailles. Disorder in Paris increased after Bismarck joined Thiers on February 19 to discuss the terms of peace; details began to leak out—surrender of Alsace-Lorraine, payment of a large indemnity, a symbolic occupation of Paris by the enemy—and the Garde Mobile prepared to resist.

These events did not merely inflame the boy's revolutionary fervor, they pointed the way to literary triumphs in a Paris cleansed of reaction. And at this point, when the successful establishment of the Commune seemed to be a matter of days, trouble arose at home; on February 15 the College reopened in a temporary building; Delahaye, like the rest of the boys, went back; Rimbaud refused.

After ten days of reproaches from a mother who saw, horrified, his years of education being thrown away, another reopening— the railway between Charleville and Paris—broke the stalemate. Rimbaud did not hesitate; on the first day of the re-establishment of communications, February 25, he sold his watch and took the train for Paris.

On his arrival he went straight to the only man whose address he knew, the caricaturist André Gill, a regular contributor to *La Charge*. Gill was not in but the boy pushed open the door made famous by its white rabbit and, seeing a bed and feeling tired, laid himself on it and slept as he had slept in the sergeant's bed at Givet. But this time he was interrupted; Gill, returning late from the cafés, shook him awake and asked what he was doing there. Rimbaud complained sleepily that his pleasant dreams had been broken into; to which Gill replied with a laugh "I have pleasant dreams too, but in my own bed."

Gill was kind. He questioned the "urchin" who explained that he wanted to make a name by his pen. To this romantic announcement Gill replied that he had chosen a poor time to launch himself into the literary life of Paris; people were too much preoccupied by attempts to scratch a living after the long-

drawn privations of the siege to bother themselves about poets
or poetry. He advised him to return home, gave him all the
spare money he had, some ten francs, and saw the "lugubrious
little monster" out of the door.

Rimbaud did not take Gill's advice; he was in Paris, he had
a windfall of ten francs in his pocket, he was immensely curious
and hopeful too, whatever Gill might say. Gill did not know
that he was talking to a reincarnated Baudelaire whose head
buzzed with dreams of greatness. Leave Paris, indeed, the
moment he had reached it!

He had, besides, another plan, to get in touch with Vermersch
and take a paid part in the demands for the heads of priests,
nobles and bourgeois which that worthy was making with considerable journalistic skill in his revival of Marat's *Père Duchesne*.

Even when he failed to find Vermersch's address at the
Artistique Bookshop (Demeny's publishers), Paris remained,
and some at least of the ten francs. He "saw" Paris; how and
with what result he told Demeny: "I saw some novelties in
Lemerre's shop: two poems by Leconte de Lisle, 'Le Sacre de
Paris,' 'Le Soir d'une bataille'; of F. Coppée, 'Lettre d'un Mo-
bile breton'; Mendès, *Colère d'un franc-tireur;* A. Theuriet, *L'In-
vasion;* A. Lacaussade, *Vae Victoribus;* some poems of Félix
Franck and Emile Bergerat; a *Siège de Paris,* a big book, by
Claretie . . .

"Every bookshop has its *Siège,* its *Journal de Siège*—Sarcey's
Siège has gone into its fourteenth edition. I have seen such
streams of boring photographs and drawings of the siege—
you would never credit it. I was struck by the engravings of
A. Marie, "les Venguers," "les Faucheurs de la Mort"; above all
the comic drawings of Draner and Faustin. As for the theaters,
abomination of desolation. The things of the day were *le Mot
d'Ordre* and the admirable work of Vallès and Vermersch in the
Cri du Peuple.

"Such was literature from February 25 to March 10."

"Such was literature"; and so eager was he to make himself
au courant with the latest artistic developments in this city of

the arts that he did not even bother to mention to Demeny or to Delahaye that he had been in the thick of dramatic political events. Yet three days after his arrival the anniversary of the Second Republic was celebrated by an enormous meeting in the Place de la Bastille when the crowd called for the establishment of the Commune; three days later, on March 1, the Prussians marched in amidst a disdainful silence, stayed two days ignored by the entire population, and marched out, again in absolute silence; and on the morning of March 10 Paris was placarded by red posters "Unite to save the Republic"—a preliminary to the setting up of the Commune eight days later.

Yet on this day, March 10, Rimbaud left the city and walked back to Charleville. His indifference to what would normally have delighted him was caused by the shock of a capital in which literary men were demeaning themselves by writing popular accounts of the siege, artists turning out cheap war sketches by the dozen, and the theater pandering to the masses with vulgar rubbish. So this was Paris! Even his enthusiasm waned after a few days of lighthearted inspection; he had no wish to conquer a pigsty. His mortification carried over into the letter to Demeny in the shape of a pathetic would-be sophistication.

He suffered shocks of another kind. His money running out, he made early morning raids on dustbins for food and slept on one of the coal barges moored in the river. Paris was filled with down-and-outs, the demoralized dregs of the siege; Gardes Mobiles roamed drunkenly everywhere, the mean streets swarmed with youngsters running wild. At night the quays were thick with sleepers, all the boats were jammed with men and boys seeking a free night's shelter. Rimbaud was not alone on his barge.

The puritanical idealist was lightly hidden beneath the adventurous boy; shocked and disgusted, he suddenly made for home, all interests and ambitions shrunk to regaining the security there. Having no money he had to walk the whole way. This week's walk, with its enforced crossing of enemy lines, was adventurous enough but he gilded the lily by declaring that he

passed himself off as a franc-tireur and demanded food and
lodging at village *mairies*. The truth was—and his reluctance
to stick to sober facts can be understood—that a small boy
with such an immediate appeal was in no danger of going without food or a bed, no women and very few men being able to
refuse him; still less was he in danger of being mistaken for a
franc-tireur who could be shot at sight. The real hardship was
the walk, 150 miles of it in all weathers.

3 ~~~~

The announcement of the Commune, which coincided with his
arrival in Charleville, brought out all his mother in him—that
side of Madame Rimbaud which freely expressed mordant disapproval of a sinful world. Annoyance at missing the triumph
he had longed to see mingled with hurt pride and shocked feelings at the scurvy reception Paris had given him.

He, Demeny and Izambard corresponded desultorily and he
sent poems to both. The poems followed his mood and Demeny
did not care for them. Rimbaud replied sarcastically to his comments: "As for what I asked you, am I a fool! Knowing nothing
that one ought to know, determined to do nothing that one
ought to do, I am damned, always and forever. Hurrah today,
hurrah tomorrow!"

He had not abandoned hope of journalism; one of his old
schoolfriends told Izambard that "he has great ideas about becoming sub-editor of a newspaper, or so Billouart tells me." The
newspaper was *Le Progrès* which had just reappeared. He was
given work of a kind by Jacoby, only to have to report ruefully
to Demeny in this same letter of mid-April: "Since the 12th I
have been sorting letters for *Le Progrès des Ardennes;* today,
it's true, the paper is suspended. But I've appeased la Bouche
d'Ombre for a while."

He continued: "For the rest, for today, I advise you earnestly
to ponder on these lines, as wise as they are romantic, from
'Ecclesiastes.' 'That man has seven layers of folly in his soul who,

having hung his clothes in the sun, complains when the rain comes.'" He did not live up to the text (which was not, in fact, taken from "Ecclesiastes" or from "Ecclésiastique") for he began as soon as he had lost his job to complain as never before. The suspension of Le Progrès indicated precisely where his home town stood politically; in Paris the Commune, in Charleville the old bourgeois stagnation. The comfortable citizens had learned nothing and he set himself to teach them by example. No longer was he content to write scathing poems and letters, smoke and indulge in anti-social diatribes secretly whilst behaving publicly with the quiet discretion of the town's prize pupil. He walked the streets dirty, unkempt, long-haired (it reached to his shoulders, Delahaye says) and with a perpetual sneer on his face. A clay pipe hung from his lips, "vulgar side" up. Accompanied by an uneasy Delahaye he would sit at the Café de la Promenade or the Univers, a scornful eye on the respectable promenaders. Some old school companions would stroll in, amongst them those who had once booed him away from school. They had blossomed into the town dandies and would cry, twirling the inevitable malacca cane, "Rimbaud! Hullo! And what are you up to?" Rimbaud, inviting them to his table, would launch casually and with a plentiful use of gutter slang into a recital of horrors; in Paris he had done this, in Charleville that, theft, assault, rape, everything or anything that came into his head. He employed a wealth of detail "so ferociously circumstantial that it was enough to bring fire from heaven down on the café windows. The young men would look at each other in consternation, too much astonished to grasp his meaning fully . . . they gave little goatlike laughs and, trying to keep themselves in countenance, could find nothing better to do than to tap their chins with the ivory head of their canes, and ended by taking themselves off with an amiable and dignified air. Rimbaud, seeing them retreat, chuckled, amused a little by their disgust but"—and it is Delahaye who tells the story—"specially in seeing me distressed by such imprudent jokes."

The dandies provided sport but his real aim was his friends.

Delahaye, Pierquin, Millot kept him company in the cafés,
Deverrière talked politics, literature and philosophy in the
same breath and Bretagne, hypocritically smoothing his beard
with a soft hand, would "constantly give him the wisest and
most prudent advice about leading a practical life whilst listening affably and with a joyful curiosity to his audacious flights
of imagination." All professed much the same revolutionary
sentiments as himself but he suspected the sincerity of his old
schoolmates and amused himself by pushing them to what he
saw as logical conclusions and watching their efforts to conceal
uneasiness, a game he had learned from Bretagne. Pierquin describes a typical Rimbaud tirade, over drinks one evening at the
Café Dutherne, against those "spoil-sports" the mediocre, who
ought to be wiped off the face of the earth by slow torture to
make room for the truly gifted. "All that rubbish must be swept
away, whatever the cost!" he declared to the half-amused, half-
apprehensive Pierquin. "I wouldn't hesitate to murder them and
I'd take the greatest pleasure in watching their death agonies."

The practical protests were few; the worst he could think of
was to scrawl "M . . . à Dieu" in white chalk on walls, benches
and church doors.

His poems too reflected the disturbed adolescent in their pre-
occupation with sex and violence, but no adolescent had ever
written with such power, such original use of language. Their
strength, however, is also their weakness; they are often too
clever, with the cleverness of the boy who cannot resist a parade
of adult knowledge. "Paris se Repeuple" recreates bitterly the
effect of the "cité douloureuse" on the poet. "Les Premières
Communions," composed when Isabelle was initiated, cynically
exposes the confusion of sexual and spiritual longings. Both
types of poem—he wrote about a dozen during this period—
sprang, as far as their obscenity, violence and cynicism go, from
the two weeks in Paris. The scurrilous and very youthful attacks
on girls had a second source, his personal failure to attract
one. All his friends and companions at the Charleville cafés told
the usual tales of their conquests of local girls. He had to outdo

them in this branch of life as in all the rest, and his egoism forced him into more tall stories. These stories were swallowed wholesale by Delahaye and Pierquin—such was the boy's compelling manner and their own naïvety—and solemnly repeated.

Yet neither Delahaye nor Pierquin nor any other of his companions ever actually saw him with a girl, they simply repeated what he chose to tell them. The scurrilous poems, which make nonsense of the tall stories, lead to a single conclusion: Rimbaud, unable to interest girls or afraid to try, invented them. As he makes clear when he says to Demeny, just married, "Oh yes, you are happy. I tell you that—and also that he who doesn't find his *Sœur de Charité* either as woman or idea, is one of the wretched." And when he says of himself at concert time in the Place de la Gare, the recognized Charleville center for decorous meetings between the sexes, "je ne dis pas un mot: je regarde toujours," he is telling the truth; he looked longingly at "les alertes fillettes" but did nothing, fearful of rebuff or comment on his littleness.

The face-saving brag is common amongst schoolboys and youths, and he had better excuse than most; for a sixteen-year-old who wanted to be the man of men he was unfortunately equipped physically. At the beginning of the year he measured just five feet, some inches less than most girls in their early teens, and still possessed the innocent rosy face of a choirboy. Young girls are not interested in little boys, however clever or beautiful, and poor Rimbaud was given no chance to demonstrate his superiority to the husky Charleville clods who, brainless, insensitive, plain, carried all before them.

Nor could his sisters help him. The apartment of the Rimbaud family might just as well have been placed on the moors of Haworth for all the people they met; the family was as self-contained as the Brontës and the children as emotionally thrown back on one another. Isabelle's access of religiosity reduced her hero-worship of Arthur who reacted by spitefully underlining the reverse side of this religiosity. He evidently got his facts from reading medical textbooks and observing his mother rather than from listening to his sisters, but Isabelle and Vitalie were obvious targets for an attack on the whole feminine sex. They had not only abandoned him for God, they offered no consolation in the form of girl friends; they had none.

His attempted revenge, against his self-sufficient sisters, his successful friends, his timid self, can be read in the poems. They were on a par with the secret scowls and clenched fists of earlier years and as ineffective.

4

The citizens of Charleville who passed this unsavory boy in the streets, read his scribbled defiances to God or heard him boasting in the cafés, may have felt disgusted, but that any took him seriously is unlikely. The anecdote of the man who stopped him in the street one day, handed him a coin and said "Better get your hair cut, Sonny" is from the life.

To behave badly is no answer to disappointment or disillusion, as every child discovers, and Rimbaud's behavior, as if he believed himself hopelessly sullied, was uncharacteristic as well as futile. The neat and clean-fingered little boy who, at ten, had written approvingly that his mother kept her house "in perfect order" was a true portrait; Rimbaud remained one of those who prefer to restrict revolution to the mind although the mind often forced him to act against the grain.

No lasting satisfaction there, then. Nor could he scratch even the semblance of notice from his mother. He could not believe that she would tolerate his continued refusal to return to school and the mock he was making of her careful cult of respectability. He found in a quarry outside the town a kind of grotto formed by the explosion of a mine; he would spend his days there, he told Delahaye fiercely, and his nights in the quarryman's hut, if his mother would not let him go his own way; all he asked of his friend was to bring bread on his way to school each morning. But this dramatic resolve was never put to the test. To his chagrin as well as to his relief, his impersonation of the Paris gamin in the streets and cafés of Charleville stirred so little interest outside some old college boys that his mother never even heard of it. She had accepted the escape to Paris with nothing more dramatic than a lecture, and for the rest she showed an unexpected and infuriating forbearance: she threatened him, berated him for laziness, tried to clean him up, urged him in and out of season to go back to school or get a steady job, but she did not turn him out of the house and she fed him as usual; his growing pains, she said (he had just begun to put on inches), had unsettled him and his peccadilloes must be humored, under protest, for a time.

On the surface he had won his fight; she had given way. Yet he was far from pleased. Her leniency disconcerted him; he demanded notice even if only by abuse, and he chose to be insulted by the reason she gave for her ungracious indifference. He showed his displeasure by renewed complaints of her, complaints always made beyond her hearing.

But he did not give up hope. He had a plan. Whilst he slouched the streets of a provincial town, playing the idle and dissolute youth, he was meditating a daring ascent to universal greatness; and when Delahaye and his school friends saw him ostentatiously pass the windows of their classroom, reversed clay pipe puffing hard, he was actually on his way to the library next door, the fumes of rank tobacco lingering about him, the scourge of Père Hubert and "Les Assis." The poems he had been writing since the return from Paris, though brilliantly done, led nowhere, as he well knew, and under the spell of Baudelaire he was already experimenting in a verse form and an approach to poetry which he believed to be new. He first tried this out in a letter to Izambard.

CHAPTER SIX

The Seer

1871

THE letter had a background. Soon after Rimbaud left Douai for the second time, Izambard was called up to the infantry and, with Demeny who had volunteered at the same time, was posted to Abbeville, where he saw the rest of the war out. Peace made, he was demobilized and returned home at the beginning of May. There, whilst waiting to be appointed to a new school post (his post at Charleville having been filled) he received a tempting offer from his brother in St. Petersburg: a Russian Duke was willing to engage him as tutor to his children. Izambard was intrigued but cautious, fearing that after the expense of the journey he might find himself "a disguised domestic," a form of "gilded slavery" that his pride would not endure.

Unable to decide, he asked the advice of Rimbaud and Deverrière. Rimbaud was emphatically in favor of St. Petersburg and "champing at the bit himself, pawed the ground with impatience at the idea that I could even hesitate."

The advice was no sooner sought than Izambard made up his mind. The Lycée at Douai offered him a post until he had officially been placed elsewhere, and he accepted. He wrote at once to tell Rimbaud.

This letter annihilated what was left of Rimbaud's hero worship. When Izambard brought him home from Douai in September, his idol, standing speechless before Madame Rimbaud, had rocked on his pedestal. Now he rejected the chance of a lifetime, a journey into the unknown, a heaven-sent opportunity of broadening his mind, for which Rimbaud would have given his right hand. And why? For an insubstantial fear, a reluctance to expose himself to uncertainties. The boy felt despair—was he to

be allowed to respect no one but the enemy in the poet's camp?
—and the heavily ironical reply did not disguise it: "So you are
a professor once more. One owes it to society, you tell me; you
are a part of the teaching profession; you're sticking to the good
old rut. I follow the principle too; cynically I allow myself *to be
kept;* I dig up the old idiots from school; I give them, in word
and act, everything stupid, foul and bad that I can think up;
they pay me in glasses of beer and pints of wine. *Stat mater
dolorosa, dum pendet filius.* I owe it to society, right enough—
and I am right. You're right too, for today. At bottom you only
see subjective poetry as your rule; your obstinacy in going back
to the academic feeding-trough—excuse me!—proves it. But
you'll end up as one of the self-satisfied who has done nothing,
never having wanted to do anything. Not to mention that your
subjective poetry will always be horribly insipid. One day, I
hope—lots of others hope the same thing—I shall see objective
poetry in your principles, I shall see it more sincerely than you
will make it! I shall be a worker: it is this thought which holds
me back when mad rage urges me to the battle of Paris where
so many workers are dying while I write to you! But to work
now—never, never; I'm on strike.

"At the moment I'm debauching myself as much as I can. Why?
I want to be a poet and I'm working to turn myself into a *seer.*
You won't understand and I scarcely know how to explain it to
you. It's a question of reaching the unknown by the derangement
of *all the senses.* The sufferings are enormous, but one must be
strong, one must be a born poet, and I know that I am a poet.
This is not my fault at all. It's wrong to say, 'I think.' One ought
to say, 'I am thought' . . .

"*I* is another person. So much the worse for the wood which
finds itself a violin, and to the devil with the unthinking who
quibble about something they know nothing of!

"You aren't *teaching* me. I give you this. Is it satire, as you
would say? Is it poetry? It's fantasy anyway. But I beg you,
don't underline it with pencil or with too much thought.

Le Cœur Supplicié

Mon triste cœur bave à la poupe,
Mon cœur couvert de caporal:
Ils y lancent des jets de soupe,
Mon triste cœur bave à la poupe
Sous les quolibets de la troupe
Qui pousse un rire général,
Mon triste cœur bave à la poupe,
Mon cœur couvert de caporal!

Ithyphalliques et pioupiesques,
Leurs quolibets l'ont dépravé!
Au gouvernail on voit des fresques
Ithyphalliques et pioupiesques.
O flots abracadabrantesques,
Prenez mon cœur, qu'il soit lavé!
Ithyphalliques et pioupiesques,
Leurs quolibets l'ont dépravé!

Quand ils auront tari leurs chiques,
Comment agir, ô cœur volé?
Ce seront des hoquets bachiques
Quand ils auront tari leurs chiques:
J'aurai des sursauts stomachiques,
Moi, si mon cœur est ravalé:
Quand ils auront tari leurs chiques
Comment agir, ô cœur volé?

My sad heart oozes at the stern,
My tobacco-covered heart;
They cast streams of soup at it,
My sad heart oozes at the stern
Beneath the jeering of the soldiers
Who all burst into laughter,
My sad heart oozes at the stern,
My tobacco-covered heart!

Ithyphallic and soldierish,
Their jeers have depraved it!
At the rudder one sees frescoes
Ithyphallic and soldierish.
O abracadabrating waves,
Take my heart, let it be washed!
Ithyphallic and soldierish,
Their jeers have depraved it!

When they have shut their traps,
How are we to behave, o stolen heart?
There will be Bacchic hiccups
When they have shut their traps:
I'll have stomachic cramps,
I will, if my heart is disparaged:
When they have shut their traps
How are we to behave, o stolen heart?

"This doesn't mean nothing. REPLY TO ME by way o M. Deverrière, for A. R. Hearty greetings."

This was a test letter, and Izambard failed to pass the test. He knew from Demeny, if not from Rimbaud himself, how the boy had roamed the streets and quays of Paris. He knew from Demeny, who had been there, of the appalling state of Paris between armistice and commune. He had Rimbaud's plain warning "this doesn't mean nothing." He had the feeling so obvious in the poem. He even had direct clues in some of the lines. But pedantry and hurt vanity prevailed over the understanding of a friend; irritated by the jibes, he could not or would not respond to the appeal. He refused to take the poem seriously, or the effect on Rimbaud of the experience it described; he could see only extravagant diction which "startled" him. He decided to give the boy a lesson. So, after protesting against the "detestable buffoonery" of the Latin quotation, he continued: "I don't want to say that you are mad, I'll leave that to the angels. But if you really think this is the last word I should like to show you that everyone can be ridiculous if they choose."

Then followed a clever parody of the poem with a "You see, it's very easy; you take the most incoherent thoughts, the most unusual words, you put them together somehow or other and from this interbreeding is born prematurely a delightful little foetus that you put into a jar carefully labeled. But take care, with your theory of the *seer*, that you don't end in a bottle yourself, a museum monstrosity."

Rimbaud found the skit "most amusing," as it was, and said so, but this was mere face-saving; Izambard had shown himself in his true colors and Rimbaud was not prepared to sail under them. He turned to Demeny. On May 15 he sent him a long letter, beginning with studied flippancy:

"I've decided to give you an hour of the latest literature. I'll begin right away with an up-to-date psalm."

He then wrote out his "Chant de Guerre Parisien," a savage attack on Thiers and the government troops who were just beginning their drive from Versailles on Paris.

"And now," he continued, "comes a dissertation on the future of poetry. All ancient poetry leads up to Greek poetry, the life harmonious. From Greece up to the romantic movement— middle ages—there are the literati, the versifiers. From Ennius to Theoroldus, from Theroldus to Casimir Delavigne everything is rhyming prose, a game, the glory and decline of innumerable idiotic generations. Racine is pure, strong, great. If his rhymes had been blown out, his hemistiches mixed up, the Divine Dolt would be as little known today as the original author of *Origines*. After Racine the game grows moldy. It has lasted two thousand years! . . .

"Romanticism had never been correctly estimated. Who was there to criticize it? The Critics!! The Romantics? who prove so well that the song so seldom conveys the complete idea, that's to say the thought sung and understood by the singer.

"For *I* is another person. If brass wakes up as a bugle, it isn't its fault. That is clear to me: I am present at the birth of my thought: I watch it, listen to it: I make a bow-stroke: the symphony stirs in the depths or bounds on stage.

"If the old fools had not given only the false meaning to the I, we should not have to sweep away these millions of skeletons which, from time immemorial, have accumulated the products of their one-eyed intelligence, proclaiming themselves authors!

"In Greece, as I said, lines and lyres rhythmed Action. Afterwards, music and rhymes became games, relaxations. The study of this past charms the curious; some take pleasure in reviving these antiquities. That's all right for them. Universal intelligence has always thrown off its ideas naturally; men picked up scraps of these fruits of the brain: they acted by them, wrote books about them. So it went on, man not using his own experience, neither fully awake nor dreaming great dreams. Civil servants, scribblers! Author, creator, poet—this man has never existed!"

After this résumé of his reflections on his readings in the poets, he tried to explain more fully than in his cryptic and sensational outline to Izambard what had been passing in his mind whilst he was "debauching" himself in Charleville. "The first task of the man who wants to be a poet is to know himself completely; he seeks his soul, he examines it, puts it to the test, understands it. When he knows it he must cultivate it! This seems simple; every brain fulfils a natural development; so many *egoists* proclaim themselves authors; many others attribute their intellectual progress to themselves! But the real requirement is to make the soul monstrous: after the fashion of the comprachios, the masked men, for instance! Imagine a man planting and cultivating warts on his face.

"I say that it is necessary to be a *seer*, to make oneself a *seer*.

"The poet makes himself a *seer* by a long, vast and reasoned *derangement* of *all the senses*—every form of love, of suffering, of madness. He searches himself, he works out all the poisons in himself so as to keep only their quintessences. He will need all his faith and superhuman strength during this ineffable torture and will become above all the great diseased, the great criminal, the great accursed—and the supreme Savant! For he reaches the *unknown!* since he has cultivated his soul, already richer than any other! He reaches the unknown and even if, maddened, he ends by losing all understanding of his visions, he has seen them! If he dies after his leap into these unheard-of, unnamable things, more workers in the horrible will come; they'll begin at the horizons where the other has collapsed!"

At this point Rimbaud broke up the letter with a "To be continued in six minutes" and a "Here I interpose a second psalm outside the text; lend a sympathetic ear and everyone will be delighted. Bow in hand, I begin."

He wrote out "Mes Petites Amoureuses," an unpleasant but clever poem, every stanza, sometimes every line containing at least one word never before used in French poetry. He ended his parenthesis with a "There you are. And mind you, if I weren't afraid it would cost you sixty centimes or more at the door—I, *pauvre effaré* [a reference to his poem of hungry children watching a baker] haven't seen so much as a copper coin for seven months—I should also send you my 'Amants de Paris,' one hundred hexameters and my 'Mort de Paris,' two hundred hexameters!"

He went back to his argument with "I pick up again.

"So the poet is truly a stealer of fire.

"He is responsible for humanity, even for *animals;* he will have to make his inventions felt, smelled, heard; if what he brings back from *down there* has form he gives form; if it is formless he gives it formlessness. A language must be found; in any case, all speech being idea, the hour of a universal language will come! One would have to be an academician—more dead than a fossil—to finish off a dictionary, no matter what the language. Weak-minded people who began to *think* about the first letter of the alphabet would quickly go raving mad!

"This language will be of the soul for the soul, combining everything, perfumes, sounds, colors, one thought grasping another and pulling. The poet would express the amount of the unknown awakening in the universal soul of his time; he would give more than the formula of his thought, than the annotation of *his march towards Progress!*—the abnormal becoming normal, absorbed by everyone, he would be truly *a multiplier of progress!*

"This future will be materialist, as you see. Always full of

Number and *Harmony,* these poems will be made to last. At bottom it would be rather like Greek poetry.

"Eternal art would have its duties since poets are citizens. Poetry will no longer rhythm action; it *will be in advance of it.*

"These poets will be! When the endless serfdom of woman is smashed, when she lives for herself and by herself, man— hitherto abominable—having freed her, she too will be a poet! Woman will find the unknown! Will her world of ideas differ from ours? She will find strange things, unfathomable, repulsive, delicious; we shall take them and understand them.

"Whilst waiting, let us ask the *poet* for the *new*—ideas and forms. All the sharp practitioners would soon believe they'd satisfied this demand—but it is not what they think!"

By this time Rimbaud had said what he had to say about the poets of the past. He continued with a devastating résumé of 19th-century French poetry. "The first romantics," he went on, "were *seers* without really knowing it; the cult of their souls began by accident; abandoned locomotives, still hot and keeping to the rails for a time. Lamartine is sometimes a seer but strangled by old form. Hugo, *too stubborn,* shows much insight in his last volumes; *Les Misérables* is a true *poem.* I have *Les Châtiments* at hand; *Stella* shows approximately the limit of Hugo's *vision.* Too much Belmontet and Lamennais, too many Jehovahs and columns, old outmoded enormities.

"Musset is fourteen times execrable to us, suffering generations rapt in visions—whom his angelic laziness has insulted. Oh! the sickly tales and proverbs! Oh the "Nuits!" oh "Rolla," oh "Namouna," oh "la Coupe!" it's all so French, that's to say hateful to the last degree; French, not Parisian! Still the work of that evil genius who inspired Rabelais, Voltaire, Jean la Fontaine with commentary by Monsieur Taine! Springlike, Musset's wit! Charming, his love! There you are, solid poetry, enamel painting! *French* poetry will be enjoyed for a long time—in France. Every grocer's boy can reel off a Rollaesque apostrophe, every candidate for church carries the five hundred rhymes about with him in the secrecy of a notebook. At fifteen these flights of passion make boys ruttish; at sixteen they are already contenting themselves by reciting them *feelingly;* at eighteen, even at seventeen every schoolboy who can manage it behaves like Rolla and writes a Rolla! Some may still be dying of it. Musset achieved nothing; there were visions behind the gauze curtains; he closed his eyes. French, spineless, dragged from bar to school desk, the beautiful corpse is dead and from now on we won't even take the trouble to wake it with our execrations!

"The second romantics, Théophile Gautier, Leconte de Lisle, Théodore de Banville, are really *seers.* But as to examine the invisible and to hear the unheard is quite another thing from recapturing the spirit of dead things, Baudelaire is the first seer, king of poets, *a very God.* Yet he lived in too artistic a circle; and his much vaunted form is paltry. The discoveries of the unknown call for new forms."

He then reviewed the contemporary scene under the headings: "the harmless . . . the Mussets . . . the dead and the fools . . . the schoolboys . . . the bohemians . . . the fantasists . . . the talented." Only three poets escape from this wholesale slaughter, the man to whom he was writing, and finally "the new school called Parnassian has two seers, Albert Mérat and Paul Verlaine, a true poet. And there you are. So I work to turn myself into a seer."

By this time he had become oblivious of his audience, continued with "Let us end with a pious chant," wrote out "Accroupissements," a scabrous account of a kneeling monk, and ended with an exhortation. "You will be abominable if you don't reply: quickly, because perhaps in a week I shall be in Paris."

2

Demeny did not reply. He was angry, thought Rimbaud, unable to believe that anyone could read his wonderful idea of the poet of the future without an immediate response, and overestimating the shock of poems so different from Demeny's idea of poetry. Demeny was, in fact, amused by the boy's presumption and, having talked the matter over with Izambard, decided to let him cool his heels for a while. Much of the letter recalled the charm of Rimbaud in spate, talking extravagantly and with a wild assurance made acceptable by his eager, absurdly young face. He would move mountains, he would do this and that; and under pressure from that persuasive voice, those startlingly blue eyes, the critical sense was liable to sag. But Rimbaud was not walking back and forth in Demeny's study at Douai, he was writing a long, confused, egoistical letter; derivative, too; for if Demeny knew his Baudelaire and his Bible the origins of the letter were no mystery to him. Baudelaire, describing the effect of hashish, had written of the ecstatic sense that "all things have been created for me, for me, for me! . . . I have become God!" The Bible was filled with descriptions of the efforts of the mystics to get in touch with the Infinite, to become one with God. The idea of flagellation as a form of spiritual discipline was as old as the first witch doctor. The need for a universal language, for a new poetry, was a thought freely canvassed in poetic circles. But if the poems enclosed by Rimbaud represented his idea of the poetry of the future, Demeny felt that he would be better in his old tracks, a charming and invigorating companion and the writer of poems altogether delightful.

If Demeny had been able to take his young friend's program seriously, he could have put his finger on the weakness of the conception. Rimbaud might anticipate the Dostoievsky hero to the top of his bent, but to no purpose since he missed the first essential. The example offered at home was not of a kind to encourage humility; his mother could read her Bible, talk like the Bible, punctiliously attend Mass, bend knees, bow head, preach pious resolutions and practice good conduct, no matter, she remained a goddess in her own right, mistress of all she surveyed; she talked freely of God but left the impression that He had been made in her image; her word was law, her appearance, tall, erect, head held high, was majestic, and her outbursts of

anger, blue eyes blazing, sharp voice pronouncing sentence, fell
on the wrongdoer like the wrath of God Himself.

Indeed, feeling as he did, Arthur Rimbaud could not afford
humility. More important than his wish to make himself the
poet seer was the reason impelling the wish. Here too he followed Baudelaire, though without Baudelaire's self-knowledge.
Unsatisfied children ring all the changes of exhibitionism. Rimbaud's ambition was not simply a sign of a head turned by early
successes or a consciousness of great powers. He aimed high because his target stood high. Madame Rimbaud was no ordinary
mother to be won by ordinary achievements.

So the young Rimbaud—never younger than then—was confident, excited and impatient. Not only did he see himself on
the track of greatness, but he was living at a time of momentous
events—the Versaillais under MacMahon at the gates of Paris,
the Commune fighting for its life—and living them in an unbearably quiet provincial town.

"Perhaps in a week I shall be in Paris," he told Demeny. But
he is unlikely to have gone, anxious though he was to fight for
the Commune. Having begged for a reply to his letter, he would
not give up hope for two or three days. He had no money,
would have had to walk to Paris, and could not have arrived
before MacMahon's troops had finally routed the communards.

3

The next that is heard from him is another letter, sent from
Charleville on June 10, to Demeny who had not replied to the
letter of four weeks earlier. In spite of this snub, Demeny,
for want of anyone better, held his place in Rimbaud's hopes
as successor to the disappointing Izambard. He was now given
a fresh copy of "Les Poètes de Sept Ans" followed by "Les
Pauvres à l'Eglise," a Baudelairean picture but drawn with a
cynicism of a kind Baudelaire was incapable of, with a "Here is
—don't be annoyed—a subject for queer sketches; the antithesis of the everlasting sweet vignettes in which cupids frolic

or hearts soar with gaudy flames, green flowers, wet birds,
promontories of Leucadia etc. . . ."

Then, with another "Here is—don't be annoyed——," he wrote
out under the title "Le Cœur du Pitre" a variation of "Le Cœur
Supplicié" he had sent to Izambard a month earlier.

"That's what I've done," he announced; and followed with:
"I have three favors to ask you. Burn, *I wish it* and I believe
that you will respect my wish as you would respect the request
of a dying man, burn *all the poems that I was a fool enough* to
give you during my stay at Douai; have the kindness to send
me if possible and if you please a copy of your *Glaneuses* which
I want to re-read and which it is impossible for me to buy, my
mother not having favored me with a single brass farthing for
the last six months—shame!; finally, please reply, whatever it
may be, to this letter and to the one before it."

He sent this to Paris, hearing from Deverrière that Demeny
was there, but the postal system having been disorganized by
the civil war, he did not receive a reply for two months or more.
Long before that time was out he had begun to bombard another Charleville newspaper with poems. This paper, *Le Nord-
Est*, rose on the ashes of the unfortunate *Le Progrès*, carrying
on the revolutionary note slightly muffled, with Deverrière as
chief sub-editor and another acquaintance of Rimbaud, Henri
Perrin, as editor. Perrin had taken Izambard's place at the
College when it re-opened at the beginning of the year but like
Deverrière he preferred journalism. He soon formed one of the
little group—Bretagne, Deverrière, Delahaye, Millot and Pierquin were the others—who used to listen to the boy boasting
and swearing and anti-Charlevilling at the "Univers" under the
arcade of the Place Ducale and to pay him in *"bocks"* (glasses
of beer) and *"filles"* (pints of wine) for amusing them. But
though Perrin laughed at the extravagances he drew the line
at printing them; he consistently refused Rimbaud's poems and
eventually told his concierge not to accept further packets "from
the long-haired youth."

Rimbaud's failure to earn a sou from his pen led to his last letter to Izambard. Relations between them had virtually ended; each heard of the other through Deverrière—Rimbaud knew that Izambard had been posted to the College of Cherbourg— but neither made a move to get back to the old footing. Then, in July, Rimbaud fell into trouble, and a Rimbaud in trouble was not sensitive to fine distinctions about friendship: Izambard was kind and would surely help. Even so he could not resist a jab in the very first paragraph: "The Russians are far away, you won't be thinking any more of them." But he envied Izambard the sea, which he thought of longingly in the dusty summer streets of Charleville: "You bathe, you have been on a ship . . . I'm jealous of you, I who stifle here. For I'm ineffably fed up and truly I can't get a thing on to paper."

Then he got down to business. "An enormous debt—to a bookshop—has come home to roost, and I haven't a sou. I must sell some books. You'll remember that in September, having tried to soften a hard-hearted mother, you took away with you at my suggestion many books, five or six, which on your advice I had brought to your rooms the previous month."

He gave details of the books he had presented to Izambard, then: "If you knew the position my mother could and would put me in with my debt of 35 francs 25 centimes you wouldn't hesitate to turn over these gifts to me! You would send the parcel to M. Deverrière 95, Sous les Allées, who expects and waits for it. I would pay you back the cost of carriage and would be extra chockfull of gratitude to you!"

Another thought then occurred to him, starved of books as he was; why should not others be added to the parcel? So: "If you happen to catch sight of any books that are out of place in a teacher's library, don't stand on ceremony. But quickly, I beg you, I'm hard pressed!"

Rimbaud did not appeal in vain. The books had never left Charleville; they were still boxed up with Izambard's books in the cellar of his Charleville landlord. "Rimbaud ought to have known this," remarks Izambard, referring to the postscript of the begging letter in which the boy adds: "I see in a letter from you to M. Deverrière that you are worried about your boxes of books. He will send them to you as soon as he has received your instructions."

He should have known this, said Izambard. He should indeed and unquestionably did; the "35 francs 25 centimes" is a little too obvious. But he was frightened—this was another of the crises during which he suddenly relapsed into his age or below it—and Izambard took the kindly view. "His judgment was obscured by the meteoric 'enormous' . . . for him, poor thing, it was a fortune."

And not for him only; teachers' salaries were pitiful in those days, Izambard had just had to move house and "we were only in the middle of the month!" But he "scraped the money together" and sent it via Deverrière.

That was the last he heard of Rimbaud; no acknowledgment, no thanks. "I was neither surprised nor offended," said Izambard. "Our epistolary relations weren't regulated by the code of the publicans or pharisees; we weren't throttled by journalism. Besides, Rimbaud didn't know how to say thank you."

But whatever Izambard may have thought or felt, the matter no longer rested in his hands. Rimbaud's old friend and hero had declared himself as a man who was "sticking to the good old rut." Rimbaud had said this; he forgot nothing; he turned elsewhere; he wrote again to Banville.

Banville had already lost first place in his admiration; Baudelaire and Verlaine had supplanted him. But Baudelaire was dead, Verlaine not yet a power in the literary world. In the middle of August Rimbaud sent Banville a poem which he perhaps reckoned as the first example of the poetry of the future or at least as his first serious essay in the new form. The letter enclosing the poem said:

"Sir and dear Master.

"Do you remember receiving from the provinces, in June, 1870, one hundred or one hundred and fifty mythological hexameters entitled 'Credo in unam'? You were good enough to reply!

"The same imbecile now sends you the lines below signed Alcide Bava. Excuse me.

"I am eighteen. I shall always love the poems of Banville.
"Last year I was only seventeen!
"Have I improved?"

Neither the tone of the letter, nor the choice of nom de plume
(Bava, dribble, Alcide one of the names of Hercules) nor the
treatment of the subject of the poem could have appealed to
Banville. He might have laughed at the flight of fancy as he
read, but wryly, for "Ce qu'on dit au Poète à propos de fleurs"
made a mock of everything he thought and wrote about flowers;
and he had written quite a lot. As a technician, however,
he must have been intrigued by the bold imagery and the
remarkable mélange of words then considered unpoetic, and
as a poet famed for his verbal juggling he ought to have appreciated Rimbaud's ingenuity.

Distaste won the day; he did not reply, and Rimbaud began
to grow desperate. Matters between himself and his mother
were approaching a crisis. Frédéric had taken to selling newspapers in the streets of Charleville, and, finding the work congenial, could not be persuaded that he was disgracing the family name. Madame Rimbaud, turning sourly from this black
sheep to the brilliant and promising Arthur, could find no comfort there; she, the most upright of women, her own happiness
sacrificed to maternal duty, could produce as sons only a newspaper seller and a young idler who walked about the town
longhaired and unwashed day after day. Arthur's stories of work
in the library, of his literary hopes, were dismissed as excuses,
and she demanded that he get an honest job. That he had brains,
she knew well enough; let him use them profitably, she insisted.
He continued his passive resistance; he, who proposed to dare
heaven and hell and boasted that he cared nothing for the good
opinion of men, was as always reduced to a sulky child by his
mother. He resented his dependence, resented her philistinism,
but not whole-heartedly; feeling, respect, and the puritan in himself divided him.

Two weeks after the letter to Banville, he at last heard from
Demeny who, quite apart from his other engagements, had not
seen the necessity of replying by return of post to letters which

he now made clear in friendly fashion he regarded as amusing extravagances. Rimbaud, in difficulties, swallowed his pride and appealed once more, and more specifically, for help: "You make me say my prayer all over again. Very well. This is the whole trouble. I'll try to speak calmly but I'm a bit rusty in the art of calmness. Anyway, here it is.

"Case for the accused. For more than a year I have abandoned the ordinary life for the life you know about. Imprisoned without respite in this unspeakable province of Ardennes, associating with none, rapt in infamous, idiotic, stubborn, mysterious work, responding only by silence to coarse and illnatured questions and reproaches, carrying myself with dignity in my extra-legal position, I have ended by provoking atrocious resolutions from a mother as inflexible as seventy-three helmeted administrations.

"She wants to force me to perpetual hard labor in Charleville (Ardennes)! Get a job by such and such a day, she said, or out you go. I refused such an existence without explanation; that would be degrading. Up till now I've been able to dodge the issue. She has reached the point of wishing ceaselessly for my rash departure, my flight! Penniless, inexperienced, I should end up in a reformatory, and from then on I shan't be heard of again!—that's the disgusting handkerchief with which my mouth is gagged. It's all very simple.

"I ask for nothing but information. I want to work in freedom, but in Paris which I love. Look here, I have my two feet, nothing more; I shall arrive in the great city without a sou to my name. But you told me that whoever wants to work for fifteen sous a day should go there, do this, live so. I have begged you to tell me the kinds of jobs which take up the least time, for thought demands large slices of one's day. Besides, these material humbugs can become loved for themselves and swallow the poet. If I'm to live in Paris, a real *saving* is absolutely essential! Don't you find this sincere? It seems so strange to me that I should have to protest to you that I am serious!

"I have had the above idea, the only one that seems reasonable to me. I put it to you in other terms; I am willing to do what

I can, I speak as clearly as an unfortunate man is able! Why scold a child, not well up in the principles of zoology, who longs for a bird with five wings? One could make him believe in birds with six tails or three beaks! One should lend him a family *Buffon:* that would sharpen his wits.

"However, not knowing what you will say in reply to this I cut short the explanations and continue to have faith in your experience, in your kindness which I certainly blessed when I received your letter, and I urge you to interest yourself a little in my plans—if you will.

"Would you be too much bored to have some samples of my work?"

"It seems so strange to me that I should have to protest to you that I am serious." There was nothing strange about it to Demeny, and this last letter convinced him that he would be unconscientious to encourage the youthful enthusiast to try his luck in Paris. He had himself, as Rimbaud knew, been trying to get a foothold there and could not believe that a boy would succeed where a published poet had failed. Besides, though he had heard no good of Madame Rimbaud, he began to wonder after reading her son's letter whether there was not something to be said on the other side.

For the rest, Rimbaud's hysteria about Charleville, though understandable to a man who also intended to fly the provinces, struck Demeny as too much like an overdone echo of Baudelaire. He was nearer the truth than he knew, for Rimbaud was enthusiastic rather than profound; with his extraordinary poetic instinct he appreciated the great poet in Baudelaire, but he was too young, too inexperienced and too narrow to understand the great man.

Rimbaud's impatience with the humdrum was single-minded enough up to a point; it offended all the poet in him. It was far from offending the Cuif, and, sensing his weakness, he redoubled his abuse. But abuse could not give him a wholeness he did not possess. Superficially he was on common ground with Baudelaire in hating the bourgeois: each was a poet, each loved his mother, each detested the mother's cult of respectability. Fundamentally their hatred was rooted in causes entirely dissimilar: Baudelaire's was inborn, ineradicable, the disdain of an aristocrat; Rimbaud blackguarded the bourgeois to inartistic lengths because he feared the bourgeois in himself.

The fear drove him to grandiose plans to elevate himself out of reach of the common man. But how derange the senses in Charleville which did not offer one decent vice for him to endure resolutely? His most familiar experience in that sink of parochialism brought no aftermath but humiliation. This was the experience of his experiments rebounding harmlessly from an unimpressed Madame Rimbaud. So Paris it must be; a Paris where he could not be reduced to a speechless little Cuif but where he would arouse fear, amazement, awe.

When Demeny again delayed a reply he looked about for another helper. Madame Rimbaud's threats and prophecies, though no more than calculated efforts to frighten him into a job, were taken in deadly earnest. Impossible for him to accept calmly or at all the emotional implication of a mother who tried to drive her son away. The financial aspect of her heartlessness, if not so hurtful, was serious enough. The two weeks in Paris, or to be precise, the last part of them, had taught him a lesson; he had no intention of launching himself into the blue; he wanted a job to go to or a safe base from the security of which he could produce a poetry that would stagger the world. The job seemed impossible so he concentrated on the base. Within a week or two, in September, he was writing to Paul Verlaine.

Months earlier he had named Verlaine as one of the two Parnassian seers and "a true poet." More than a year earlier he had revelled in *Fêtes Galantes,* Verlaine's second book. In Bretagne he had as friend a man who knew Verlaine, a man who was often quoting Verlaine. Everything pointed to an approach to Verlaine rather than to Demeny. That it was not made earlier suggests that Rimbaud was insufficiently intimate with Bretagne to discuss his hopes for the future.

But when both Banville and Demeny were unresponsive he must have spoken to Bretagne who offered to write a postscript to a letter to Verlaine. Overjoyed, Rimbaud hastened to collect specimen poems—Delahaye says that he asked him to copy the poems in small copper plate to make them appear as much like the printed page as possible—and sent five of the most recent to Verlaine with a letter and Bretagne's postscript. The letter avowed his admiration for Verlaine's work and appealed to Verlaine to help him to practice poetry in Paris if his specimen poems seemed to warrant it. The letter was sent via Verlaine's publisher, Lemerre.

Rimbaud waited: no answer. Had he but known, Verlaine was also in the north, visiting his mother's family near Arras. Rimbaud wrote again enclosing three more poems. This letter has been destroyed but some lines have been quoted from memory by Verlaine and his wife: "I've formed the plan of writing a great poem and I can't work at Charleville. I'm prevented from coming to Paris, being without resources. My mother is a widow and extremely devout. She only gives me ten sous every Sunday to pay for my seat in church."

Later that month Verlaine returned to Paris, read both letters and the poems and was impressed. "You are prodigiously gifted," he replied in a letter—also lost—in which he balanced the compliment with a criticism; he did not care for Rimbaud's verbal experiments, particularly the vulgarisms: "Your lycanthropy makes me feel as if I'd caught a whiff from a sewer." He told Rimbaud that he would show the poems to friends before deciding what to do.

This letter, which must have caused a flutter in Rimbaud's little circle at Charleville, was quickly followed by another even more exciting. Verlaine had shown the poems to Léon Valade, Philip Burty and Charles Cros; all three poets agreed with him that they were exceptional; and Verlaine, hesitating no more, sent Rimbaud a typical: "Come, dear great soul, we summon you, we wait for you."

According to Mathilde Verlaine, her husband sent Rimbaud

the fare to Paris; according to Delahaye, Deverrière gave it to him. The two accounts are not necessarily contradictory; Rimbaud may well have accepted both fares as well as collecting a third from his mother. Madame Rimbaud certainly sent her son off in a new suit; backed by Verlaine's letters he had talked her round; he would become famous, would make money.

Towards the end of September, armed with a poem he had just completed, "Le Bateau Ivre," he left for Paris and Verlaine.

CHAPTER SEVEN

Verlaine

1844–1871

D ESPITE the school triumphs and the hopes of poetic immortality, despite all the brave and boastful words, the Rimbaud, still a month short of his seventeenth birthday, who traveled to Paris that autumn was in essence the small boy, a melancholy example of the child who, unsure of parental affection, remains unsure of himself in almost every direction. For a moment he saw himself as the despised people of Charleville saw him, and as his mother described him in angry moments, a rude, crude, useless creature without manners, conversation or savoir faire. How was he to act, talk, behave in Paris? he asked Delahaye at their last meeting. And whatever answer he gave —he would certainly give one, bravado being the keynote of his relationship with this admirer—the problem remained and he knew it.

Had he known the man he was going to meet, he would have felt reassured, for Verlaine was above all kind. Indeed Verlaine was in every respect Rimbaud's opposite and his life had been as different from Rimbaud's as any life could well be. Ten years older, he was an only child brought up in comfortable homes and indulged in everything. To most children this excess of love would have been almost as harmful as the scarcity of it in the Rimbaud house but the young Verlaine's affectionate and happy disposition seemed to have absorbed it painlessly; it encouraged a natural indolence but at school even this could not wholly disguise a lively intelligence; and after several pleasant years —pleasant because he was popular—he passed his baccalauréat without difficulty.

By the age of sixteen he was reading voraciously and roaming the bookstalls of the quays; there he discovered excitedly and learned by heart the "moderns" old and new—Banville, Leconte de Lisle, Gautier, Glatigny and Mendès—as Rimbaud did ten years later. Like Rimbaud again, he was an instantaneous admirer of Baudelaire.

He became a member of the literary group at school, planning and beginning plays and poems. He rarely finished them, for his poetic fervor never rose above the status of pleasant hobby. He was destined by his parents for the civil service and it never once occurred to him that a poet and a civil servant might be incompatibles; and when he began work at the Hôtel de Ville he discovered other poets sheltering there under the same happy delusion. He had one overmastering wish, to be at peace with all and to have a "good time," which included the writing of verses, plays, whatever it might be, when he felt inclined; and this he succeeded in doing without difficulty up to his early twenties, a year or so after the death of his father.

By that time he had become a confirmed young man-about-town, the lightly intellectual part of the town, and met all the progressive poets, painters and musicians at the cafés and the soirées held practically every day of the week at one or other of the leaders' houses. For the young Verlaine to meet men and women on such congenial ground, with plenty to eat and drink, some flirting, much fooling and a noisy exchange of ideas, was to find himself willy-nilly pushed into print; he was such good company, had such a good sense of humor and faithfully echoed the prevailing enthusiasm with such engaging exaggeration that his companions felt unable to leave him out of their literary plans.

Thus rather to his surprise some of his poems were included in the first *Parnasse Contemporain* which Rimbaud studied so earnestly. The fact that by nature and talent Verlaine was directly opposed to the Parnassian conception of poetry escaped him in the pleasure of contribution. He had not hitherto considered his gifts as in any sense out of the way, but membership, however accidental, of the Parnasse put ideas into his head; when his cousin Elisa, who had been brought up with him and helped to spoil him, offered to pay for the publication of a book of poems he accepted eagerly.

Hence *Poèmes Saturniens* of 1866, praised by Bretagne and read by Rimbaud. They were for the most part diligent imitations of the Parnassian masters and still more of the lone wolf Baudelaire, but this was overlooked by both readers in Charleville.

But Verlaine's hail-fellow-well-met air led to other, less comfortable discoveries; he not only loved poetry, he loved alcohol consumed in congenial surroundings and the right company; which, with this gregarious young man, embraced his rustic relatives in the north as enthusiastically as the café crowd in Paris.

For a while this other love kept its place but it was biding its time. The sudden death of Elisa in February, 1867, exposed the failings of a pampered upbringing. The unexpected loss struck the warm-hearted Verlaine with a terror unimaginable by the stronger, harder or better brought up. No cotton-wool antidote to death appeared automatically; he was left naked, hurt, in pain. But he had never known pain, would not endure it, fled it. A single remedy offered itself and he grasped at it; one had only to drink enough and the pain, any pain, was worsted. Within a few months he was in the grip of absinthe. The dandified young poet-civil servant declined into a down-at-heel, violent-tempered drunkard in disgrace at his office, avoided at the cafés and the bane of his mother at home.

But he could not live out the part of rake; at heart he was a gentle soul and when told of his behavior under absinthe he was horrified and tried to pull himself together. He tried again and again with no more than moderate success, hard put to it to resist the blandishments of the wilder spirits. He did, however, manage to write the poems which were published early in 1869 as *Fêtes Galantes*. Rimbaud admired its technical brilliance and *Fêtes Galantes* earned Verlaine a place in the boy's scheme of things as a modern seer. In one sense Rimbaud was not mistaken; the little book was a *tour de force,* mocking the age of

Watteau with exquisite cleverness. This would naturally appeal to a Rimbaud obsessed by the clever, despising the past and with a mordant streak clamoring for expression. His "Ce qu'on dit au Poète à propos de fleurs" was his idea of a *Fête Galante* and points the difference between himself and Verlaine; the satire is savage and the technical mastery is marred by the use of words whose only purpose is to be different.

Whether Rimbaud perceived the gulf between them is doubtful; he could be obtuse for a clever boy. Certainly *Fêtes Galantes* gave him a false idea of the author; Verlaine was uninterested in the objective, the brilliant; the circumstances of that time—the struggle against absinthe—were responsible for the book being as it was; the true Verlaine does not appear in it.

And had Rimbaud read *La Bonne Chanson*, Verlaine's next book, instead of merely reading about it, he would also have been deceived, for this too was atypical Verlaine in the opposite direction to *Fêtes Galantes*. A few months after the publication of *Fêtes Galantes* Verlaine, casting about helplessly for a woman to save him from absinthe, was introduced to the sixteen-year-old Mathilde de Mauté, half-sister of one of his wilder friends, the musician Charles de Sivry. Mathilde was pretty, promised a good figure and read poetry. That was enough to convince Verlaine that she was the wife for him. He was too busy admiring her appearance in a grey dress to notice her vanity, stupidity and ineradicable philistinism. The poet-lover became infatuated on the spot and proposed two days later.

The engagement was long and *La Bonne Chanson* the record of it and of the transformed Verlaine, sober, impeccably frock-coated and buttonholed once more, who called every evening at Mathilde's home to exchange formalities with her parents and to slip into her hand one of the poems which eventually made up the book. These sentimental love songs, though technically skilful, present a Verlaine as unreal as his devotion to a girl he did not know and, since he was forbidden to meet her unchaperoned, could not know. If the stern young Rimbaud with

Arthur Rimbaud

The Rimbaud home 1869–75,
Quai de la Madeleine, Charleville

(*Musée Rimbaud*)

The Gindre House, Douai

(*Faidherbe*)

The College of Charleville in 1873

Place Ducale, Charleville, in 1870

Baudelaire

Paul Demeny

Germain Nouveau

(Herr)

Roche, the Rimbaud Farmhouse, in 1914

Roche in 1914

(Herr)

Mathilde Verlaine

(Henri Matarasso)

Verlaine just before the meeting
with Rimbaud

(Henri Matarasso)

Rimbaud in Paris, 1872. Sketch
by Verlaine

Verlaine and Rimbaud
in London, October, 1872.
Drawing by Félix Régamey

Isabelle Rimbaud

(Henri Matarasso)

Isabelle Rimbaud. Sketch by Berrichon

his passion for naked sincerity and all the antibourgeois virtues could have read them he would certainly have disapproved.

Verlaine and Mathilde were married in the late summer of 1870 after the war had begun and it was not long before absinthe raised its head again. His wife, Verlaine discovered, was not the model of intelligence and sympathy he had imagined. To sustain himself under the shock he turned to his familiar and only comforter; there were scenes, blows, flights to the parents, reconciliations, more scenes.

The round was broken abruptly by political events acted out under the very eyes of the warring couple: the end of the siege of Paris, the civil struggle, the declaration of the Commune at the Hôtel de Ville on March 18, 1871. Verlaine, who in sheer good fellowship had been announcing himself for some years past as a red-hot revolutionary, counting among his friends some of the Communard leaders, suddenly found his bluff called. He remained at the Hôtel de Ville as press censor of the Commune, uneasily defying the order of Thiers to all civil servants to follow the legitimate government to Versailles.

The collapse of the Commune two months later and the widespread witch hunt which followed left Verlaine high and dry; he was afraid to present himself at the Hôtel de Ville, yet if he did not he would lose his job. He decided to lose the job and to earn his living as poet. As only Hugo, Banville and Leconte de Lisle were managing to make ends meet, this aim was on the optimistic side, but Verlaine was an optimist. Meanwhile until the royalties began to roll in—or, putting first things first, until he managed to steel himself to the labor of writing—he retired with Mathilde to the house of his parents-in-law at 14 rue Nicolet in the respectable part of Montmartre, calling on his mother for pocket money.

The move was not a success. Monsieur Mauté, a snobbish and upright retired solicitor, had never cared for his son-in-law; after the domestic scenes and the job under the Commune, he detested him. The house would scarcely stand two masters of any kind; two as disparate as Verlaine and Monsieur Mauté was an impossibility; and in the early summer Verlaine took Mathilde off on a round of visits to his relatives in the area of Arras. He was there, enjoying his ease with his pregnant wife, whilst Rimbaud some hundred miles to the east was writing to him in Paris.

Towards the end of September Verlaine, set up by northern air and food, came back to rue Nicolet. Monsieur Mauté being absent on a prolonged shooting holiday, Verlaine was his own master and, side-stepping reality as always, dreamed of beginning a new life, writing pleasant salable poems, he and his wife reunited by a child who would smoothe out all discrepancies. And it was in this fatuous if likable mood that he read and answered the letter of the boy who was dedicated to the destruction of fatuity. "Come, dear great soul" he wrote, cheerfully doing the honors in the merciful absence of his father-in-law; and on the appointed evening went off with the poet-inventor friend of the family, Charles Cros, to the Gare de l'Est to meet the provincial genius.

CHAPTER EIGHT

Rimbe and Verlomphe
1871

EXPECTING a full-grown man Verlaine did not recognize Rimbaud and waited for the next train. Rimbaud, arriving first at rue Nicolet, was left to the mercies of Mathilde and her mother. The women had been told by Verlaine, thinking of the technical virtuosity of the poems, that the guest would be in his twenties or thirties; they were astonished by the youthful reality. Astonishment quickly changed to dismay: "He was," Mathilde wrote years later, "a big, solid, red-faced peasant boy. He looked like an overgrown schoolboy, for his short trousers revealed blue cotton socks knitted by his mother. His hair was unkempt, he wore a cord tie, and his general appearance was slovenly. His eyes were blue and rather fine but had a sly expression which in our good nature we mistook for shyness. He came without luggage, not a single valise, neither linen nor clothes other than those he wore."

Rimbaud was not big at that time nor was he solidly built; he had, however, the large feet, hands and bones of his mother which indicated to a perceptive person that he would grow tall and strong. As for the expression in his eyes, Mathilde read wrongly.

From her, spoilt, thoughtless, snobbish and only a year or two older than himself, he could expect neither justice nor charity; she did not disguise her surprise, she looked and spoke with condescension. But Madame Mauté held out hopes of better things; unlike her daughter, she was both well-born and well-bred and had a genuine gift as a musician; a pupil of Chopin, she had become an excellent pianist and teacher; at that moment she was giving free lessons to the young Debussy for which he was grateful to the end of his life. So Rimbaud might have done very

103

much worse than meet this kind, generous and gifted woman who was fond of Verlaine and wishful to please him and who had a general benevolence towards artists. This benevolence, however, did not extend as far as uncleanliness, incivility or any of the peculiarities unknown previously to her which her guest was displaying with a certain relish.

For Rimbaud was at his most difficult. Mistrustful as he was, he could not have behaved pleasingly in any strange and socially superior milieu; the unexpected absence of Verlaine and the atmosphere of the Mauté house made sure of a savage reaction. His lofty spirit had not expected to find his chosen god living in Paris in a glorified example of the thing he had been castigating daily in Charleville. Yet so it was; an undeniably bourgeois milieu, the very silks and bows and smugness of which made him bristle and, even more outrageous, made him ill at ease. The attitude of his hostesses, which he understood and exaggerated, completed his discomfiture. For this humiliation, this frightful anti-climax he had longed and waited, he, the "seer"! The look in those blue eyes was neither slyness nor shyness, it was sullen fury.

By the time Cros and Verlaine arrived, having given him up, the evening was irretrievably wrecked. Thinking perhaps that food would loosen her guest's tongue, Madame Mauté sat them down to dinner, but Rimbaud went to some lengths to emphasize his proletarian origins and to shock his fastidious hosts; he ate noisily, bolted his food and, finishing first, lit his pipe from which, leaning his elbows on the table, he puffed smoke over the other plates. During dinner Cros tried to draw the boy out, questioning him about his reading, method of writing and opinions of other poets. To Verlaine, who was no pedant, watching the inquisition with forked eyebrows raised and faunish eyes glinting, Cros was "a little too much like a cross-examiner, analyzing without pity, going as far as to demand how such an idea had occurred to him, why he had used this word instead of that, asking in effect for an account of the genesis of his poems."

Cros, usually a kind and rather frivolous young man, had

evidently been affected by the general atmosphere. The class-room manner did not suit him and failed absolutely to rouse a spark from the resentful Rimbaud who sat there replying "rather wearily" in monosyllables. Soon afterwards he muttered that he was tired and was shown to his bedroom.

Looking back over that evening Verlaine could remember only one remark by Rimbaud and that not pleasant: at table the dog came round begging for scraps and Rimbaud said "Les chiens, ce sont des libéraux." Nevertheless Verlaine's impression was favorable. He understood the sulky monosyllables to be the defense of a youth out of his depth. This analysis was correct only in part, but Verlaine could not be expected to guess that he was entertaining a seer. He knew, however, that he had dis-covered a prodigy; the poetry he had admired became still more remarkable from the hands of the youngster he now knew its author to be. Even the use of gutter, patois, and scientific words which marred the poems became explicable when he saw the writer; they were simply expressing a youthful intoxication with words. And if he read "Le Bateau Ivre" before going to bed he must have been ready to believe almost any claim by the boy; he was a clear case of budding genius.

The next morning was to open his eyes still further, was in fact to settle his destiny. During the disastrous evening he had pitied the provincial visitor. To him, quick to love, slow to dis-like, Rimbaud's behavior and appearance "the round, ruddy face of a child on a bony body with all the clumsiness of the growing adolescent" and even more his voice "heavily accentuated in Ardennais, almost a patois, with the abrupt highs and lows of the breaking voice" were a little difficult to take seriously; they aroused compassion and interest.

What Rimbaud had thought of Verlaine during the evening is not known; he certainly deplored his choice of wife, home and clothes (the elegant civil service dress of the period) but something—the elder man's charm, his sympathetic silence or his poetry—persuaded him to exempt Verlaine from the other-wise complete condemnation of 14 rue Nicolet.

They went off in the morning for a round of the poets' cafés
so that Verlaine could introduce the boy wonder to his friends
and had not been out of the house ten minutes before Verlaine
was following the star that Frédéric, Delahaye, Demeny and
Izambard had followed before him. Rimbaud in the open air of
Paris, walking by the side of a well-known poet and about, as
he thought, to come into his own, was another being from the
country bumpkin of the Mauté salon. He bubbled over with
confidences, blue eyes gleaming, face radiant, voice cracking
adorably in his enthusiasm. Verlaine, making the first conventional though sincere references to his guest's poetry, found
himself cut off in midstream with an impatient wave of the hand.
"That stuff!" Rimbaud was no longer interested in *démodé*
literature. "He spoke to me of what he would do in the future,
and what he told me was prophetic. He began by Free Verse
. . . then by a prose, clear, vivid, breathtaking and calm too
when necessary." Verlaine listened, stupefied, to the unfolding
of daring plans for scaling the heights where the imagination of
man had never yet stood; he even had a vision of himself reborn,
a Verlaine no longer playing at poetry, a great originator. And
to come down to earth for a moment, the boy was extremely
good-looking and talked, if not well, with a crude fervor not to
be heard in sophisticated Paris; his very naïveties invited love;
he was the find of all time, a prodigy who was also more than
personable. He was, in fact (though this thought was slower in
coming), what Verlaine had dreamed Mathilde must be when
he first saw her and heard her "Oh, I love poetry too, Monsieur."
He proceeded down the hill to the cafés in a dream.

At the cafés yet another Rimbaud appeared—a Rimbaud who
completed the conquest. In the course of the next day or two,
perhaps even of that first day (for the Paris of the poets was a
small world) he had met all Verlaine's friends and companions.
These almost without exception formed a sort of left-wing section of the Parnassians. They even had a collective name. Just
before the war Coppée, one of the most popular of the younger
Parnassians and a special favorite of Verlaine's, had had a one-

act play accepted. All his young poet friends were at the first performance and applauded so boisterously that a theater critic wrote sarcastically the next day "that was a jolly meeting of the *vilains bonshommes.*" As the slightest of excuses provoked the group spirit a regular dinner of the *Vilains Bonshommes* was instituted right away. For the most part this meant no more than that the young men consciously defied the sneers of Leconte de Lisle and some elder Parnassians at Coppée's "success"—success not being a permissible word in the strict Parnassian vocabulary. But as the French are incapable of keeping politics out of art, seriousness out of fun or purpose out of pleasure, these high-spirited dinners, with all the ramifications of private parties and café discussions which spread from them, became a focal point of what the young men liked to think of as the new literature, demonstrated by readings and criticisms of their latest work.

By the time of Rimbaud's arrival this *avant-garde* had become a group within a group. During the siege of Paris the *Vilains Bonshommes* dinners were suspended, but a section of the young men began to meet spasmodically in the apartment which the Mautés had taken temporarily (to avoid the shelling) in Boulevard Saint-Germain. The leading spirit of these gatherings was Cros, the favorite of Madame Mauté. Cros was a restless, attractive young man who tried his hand at everything; he was at once poet, musician and inventor and displayed considerable talent in each direction. He was also a first-rate mimic and no respecter of reputations; and under his influence the literary tone became as hostile to recognized authority as the political tone—for one and all were fervent republicans.

Two "regulars" were the inseparables Léon Valade and Albert Mérat, who had worked with Verlaine at the Hôtel de Ville. As poets, the sharp Mérat and the shy Valade were unremarkable; as men they looked like a thousand others, black-bearded, black hair worn long and drooping over the forehead. Another habitué, Villiers de l'Isle Adam, was a "character"; a maker of stories after Hoffman and Poe, mystical, morbid, melancholy, his true forte was dramatic monologue. Not less strange in his stuttering withdrawn way was the yellow-bearded giant Ernest Cabaner who dreamed through the months of siege and the succeeding assault of Thiers' Versaillais under the impression that both were by the Prussians, and, incorrigibly bohemian, gently endured a life which many would consider unendurable. This tasteful composer who set his friend's lyrics to music and composed oratorios when he could was obliged to play the piano nightly in a cheap Left Bank café.

Beside Cabaner's inevitable tattered cloak of bright orange the trim dandyism of Etienne Carjat stood out radiantly. This slim and elegant young man, monocled, top-hatted, frock coat curving correctly in the latest hourglass fashion, wrote poetry like the rest of his world but was actually a photographer of genius. His faultless attire and old-style courtesy had not been permitted to vary by a hairsbreadth throughout the war and the sieges. The youngest of the band, Louis Forain, two years older than Rimbaud, was a protégé of Cros who purported in erratic bursts to be training him in the art of the poet, but even then Forain could not keep his hands from the pencil which was to make his name. This small, quiet boy concealed a wild spirit of mischief.

Of the rest, who included the André Gill already known to Rimbaud, Jean Richepin perhaps made the most noise. Like so many of the intellectuals of that time his versatility concealed a distressing emptiness; he could win a wager that he would talk in rhyme throughout a meal, he could turn out verses and playlets with an ease that earned him much admiration, he had a flair for the editing of journals, but as he had nothing to say his triumphs left him where he began. But he was an entertaining if slightly malicious companion and could tell an improbable anecdote against the mighty with great aplomb. "He is a skunk and a butcher of letters who writes like a badly bred pedant and thinks like an animal," said Verlaine not without truth; but this judgment was still to come; at the moment Richepin was accepted as a brilliant young man. Armand Silvestre made nonsense rhymes with dexterity but earned his place as a superb teller of dirty stories; he had also known Baudelaire which gave him a luster. The golden-haired Apollo, Catulle Mendès, was there too from time to time; he more than any man had been responsible for the eventual appearance of the first *Parnasse Contemporain* but, edged out from control, consoled himself in the rowdier cafés and brothels; a competent poet, he was destined like so many others to find his niche in journalism. The hairy young Raoul Ponchon wrote with a certain wit borderline poems which were eventually to land him in jail; but unlike Richepin who somewhat resembled him in talent and high spirits he was a goodhearted fellow. Emile Blémont, the last who need be noticed, had been taken up by Banville, published, praised some years earlier. He looked like the businessman he turned out to be, editing and publishing one journal after another with sense and efficiency, but at this time he remained the poet and, in amiable fashion, the revolutionary all present took for granted. Like his patron he was a nice man and good friend; a little out of place when the company grew wild, but always obliging.

This little collection of poets, musicians, caricaturists, photographers, inventors, playwrights, journalists to which Verlaine introduced Rimbaud had in good French fashion a private name, the Zutists. The purpose of the group, Cros explained characteristically some years later when the name became well known in Paris, was "nothing for use, everything for pleasure." Its one collective activity was also characteristic; the *Album Zutique,* a leisurely and occasional compilation, consisted of parodies, sometimes illustrated, of the living poets, great and not so great, including themselves. Before he met Rimbaud, for instance, Verlaine had written neat parodies of Banville, Heredia and Coppée.

The fun, shading occasionally into savagery, represents the group well enough, but there were some serious attempts at new poetic forms. They had, ironically enough, seceded in the indefinite manner of the time from the *Vilains Boshommes* (that is to say, they usually sat together at one end of the table) because of Coppée. Their objection to Coppée was not so much his continued success in the theater, though this caused some heart-burning, as his relapse into the respectable; he went on with his work in the War Office, which did not please the revolutionaries in politics, and his latest poetry—he was fast being accepted as the cockney poet of Paris, simple, sentimental, fluent—did not please the revolutionaries in literature.

Rimbaud had long since thrown off his fleeting "Coppée period." For that matter he had thrown off most succeeding influences too, as his "seer" letter to Demeny made clear; his scathing judgments of contemporaries had included the Zutists when he bothered to mention them; only Verlaine and Mérat had escaped criticism.

Nevertheless when he saw these men face to face in their new meeting place, the Hôtel des Etrangers in Rue Racine, where Cabaner had a room, Rimbaud became for a time the literary-minded boy from the provinces; for courage he needed not only Verlaine's support but what they soon pressed on him, drink. Though he conscientiously drank with what devil-may-care air he could muster, Rimbaud neither liked alcohol nor had a head for it. But it loosened his tongue and restored illusions of grandeur. He repeated his performance of the Charleville cafés, and Verlaine's friends were startled to hear foul language, declarations of forthcoming grandeur, savage criticism of French literature and promises of unheard-of orgies coming from the mouth of this baby-faced boy with the frank blue eyes, the tousled hair in childish disarray, the pathetic-comic big-boned hands waving far out of their too short sleeves, the breaking voice. Yet if his poems were to be believed—and several there had read them—he was the literary find of the century. And if he were to be believed, he was an archfiend too. He was in any case excellent entertainment.

He arrived on the eve of a *Vilains Bonshommes* dinner where he repeated the sensation. Mathilde heard of the boy's momentary triumph from her husband and from Cros, and a letter from Valade to Blémont gives an eyewitness account. Valade was that rare thing, a silent and diffident intellectual, and the brusque assurance of Rimbaud may have impressed him—he had already read the poems—rather more than it impressed some of his friends. But they too were struck, even if they treated the apparition more jocularly, as he shows. "You missed much," he says, "by not being at the recent dinner of Les Affreux Bonshommes. A most terrifying poet, not yet eighteen"—Rimbaud was in fact not quite seventeen—"was put on show by Paul Verlaine his inventor and John the Baptist. Big hands, big feet, the absolutely babyish face of a thirteen-year-old, deep blue eyes! His temperament is more turbulent than timid. Such is this boy whose imagination encompasses great power and unheard-of corruption and who fascinated and alarmed all our friends. D'Hervilly said 'Behold Jesus in the midst of the doctors!' Maître countered with a 'Satan more likely!' "

Valade explained that Rimbaud had come to Paris "with the firm intention of never returning home," urged Blémont to read the Rimbaud poems and judge for himself, and predicted that, Fate permitting, he believed all were "witnessing the birth of a genius." And this, he concluded, was not a first emotional reaction but a "considered opinion after three weeks of reflection."

Rimbaud, in short, caused a certain stir, and Verlaine displayed him triumphantly at all the recognized rendezvous of the poets. Carjat photographed him, Forain sketched him, he was taken to Banville's, Lemerre's, Gautier's, Nina de Villard's and to Hugo's where, Verlaine's friend Edmond Lepelletier declared, he was forthwith proclaimed "A child Shakespeare!" a remark which the child greeted with an aside, in part unprintable, on "the old dotard."

The object of Hugo's remark has been questioned. Years later Verlaine's last publisher Léon Vanier told Pierquin that "it seems to have been Glatigny who was in question. But as there is nothing to prove it let Rimbaud have the benefit." But if Hugo did not say it he ought to have said it; exclamations of that kind were his specialty; and if he applied the phrase to Albert Glatigny his judgment is even more suspect than usual. Rimbaud's reported aside rings true.

Sensations never last long in Paris; all this adulation, wonderment, speculation about Rimbaud occupied a few weeks only; but his effect on Verlaine was immediate and for life. Mathilde says that Rimbaud and her husband stayed out from morning to night on the first day and almost all the days that followed it. Rimbaud she scarcely saw again; he attended one family dinner with the rattle brother-in-law Charles de Sivry, a failure this dinner too; he was occasionally to be found stretched on the path in front of the house smoking his pipe; for the rest he was absent and so too was Verlaine.

Rimbaud broke into Verlaine's life when he was wavering between domestic ease enlivened by the occasional composition of undemanding poetry or books for operettas, and a return to the joys and pains of absinthe. The imminence of Mathilde's child swayed him to the domestic life but he was too intelligent not to divine that this was death to his poetic gift and to suspect that, child or no child, he would eventually break loose. But break into what? And it was this thought which restrained him when the longing for absinthe took hold of him, for he knew that absinthe, taken as he had taken it in the past, would kill him and his muse as effectively as domesticity. So, lazy and inclined by upbringing towards the bourgeois virtues, above all fearful of lacking a center for his affections, he was trying to make up his mind to live the life symbolized by Mathilde, her child and rue Nicolet. But not wholeheartedly. He was not wholly bourgeois and was, despite himself, a poet with aspirations. And if Verlaine was not wholehearted any wind would blow him from his course.

Then out of the blue came Rimbaud; not a wind but a gale which tore the flimsy sails to shreds. "Devilishly seductive" Verlaine was to describe him; the impulsive man did not look further than the face or the voice of the person who attracted him; his intelligence smothered by emotion, he neither saw nor thought nor cared where the intimacy would lead. His "Rimbe" (his letters were to be spattered with "n'est-ce pas, Rimbe?" Verlaine having a penchant for abbreviations) quickly became a necessity to "Verlomphe," Rimbaud neatly marrying the man to his chief distraction.

Yet when Verlaine said "devilishly seductive" he did not speak of personal charm only. He heard of his young friend's determination to be a seer, he heard, too, of his own role; he, with Rimbaud's aid, was to be restored to his "primitive state as a son of the Sun." Ominous words to a peace-loving man, words which Verlaine did his best to misunderstand; so successfully, that he often managed to extract a sensual appeal from what Rimbaud intended as a spiritual experience. "Derange all the senses," cried Rimbaud with puritan fervor; "suffer all things for the greatness to come." But Verlaine was no puritan; he mistook the fervor—deliberately, perhaps—for an invitation to license and his sufferings after a derangement of the senses were not at all the sufferings that the serious boy had in mind.

However the Rabelaisian Verlaine had a brain, had a gift, had ambition, and it was through these that Rimbaud eventually proved an irresistible attraction. Unlike Mathilde he attacked Verlaine on both sides; he was not simply a person to be loved, he was an artistic conscience. When he told his friend with all the fire of youthful charm and confidence that he would make him into a second seer, the great poet that he should and must be, Verlaine could not always laugh it away with his engagingly modest laugh. He, a son of the Sun! Absurd, yes; yet there niggled in him somewhere a sense of guilt. He was a poet, he had a power, he had played with that power. This, in such a mood, he could not deny. He could at least try his hand by the side of this fantastic boy.

And what could he reply to Rimbaud's daily blistering comments on the ménage at rue Nicolet, on the delights of domesticity, on his impeccable appearance? Mathilde was soon complaining not only that Verlaine was seen no more until bedtime, but that "he suddenly showed a liking for dressing most carelessly; he began to wear his dreadful mufflers again and soft hats; he sometimes went a whole week without changing his underclothes or cleaning his boots." Nor was this distressing sign of bohemianism the only or the worst effect of Rimbaud's arrival. Rimbaud was in search of new methods of deranging the senses; in Paris absinthe was to be had at every bar, hashish could be obtained without difficulty; Verlaine had the money to buy them. The hashish seems to have disappointed, though it produced the mild hallucinations, resembling the abrupt change of colored slides in the magic lantern of the day, which were to present *Illuminations* with its title and many of its sections. But the absinthe was effective at once, and Verlaine began to return home at night as he had returned from his garde nationale duties a year earlier, drunk and quarrelsome.

The reconciliations of the mornings after did not lessen Mathilde's antipathy to Rimbaud. She tried to discredit him in her husband's eyes but she was young and had little skill in the art. Rimbaud, she complained, had removed a crucifix from his bedroom; Verlaine laughingly made him return it. Rimbaud had broken some knickknacks; Verlaine shrugged his shoulders; they were hideous and better gone. Rimbaud left lice crawling on his pillow; he kept them in his hair, Verlaine explained solemnly, so that he could throw them at priests he met in the street. And when Verlaine reported a conversation he had had with the boy— "How did you get hold of my books in Charleville when you had no money?" "I took them from stalls outside bookshops, read them and returned them, but after a time, afraid of being caught, I took them, read them and then sold them"— Mathilde, losing no opportunity, commented, "That shows how unscrupulous your friend is." At this—they were talking before going to sleep—Verlaine without a word lifted her out of the bed and put her on the floor.

Nevertheless Verlaine did not feel so easy about his friend's behavior at rue Nicolet as he made out to Mathilde. There was, he discovered with perpetual surprise, a fly in every ointment. Rimbaud, prodigiously gifted though he was, invigorating companion, physically appealing, even he could show an ugly and indeed inexplicable side. What was the meaning of the senseless jokes he went in for, jokes rarely funny and almost always

cruel? Possibly, had he known the level of humor at the college
of Charleville or what so often passed for it in the town, Verlaine
might have understood. And again, possibly not; had he heard
Rimbaud in his worst vein at the Charleville cafés, no excuse
for the deliberate urge to hurt could have comforted him. Perhaps even at that early stage, when the jokes were directed
against strictly bourgeois targets, some uneasy premonition of
the future ruffled his mind. In any case a natural kindness resented "eccentricities of this kind, blemished I'm afraid with a
kind of sly malice and mischievous humor." He came to the
conclusion, from which he did not waver, that they were due to
"a partial and passing aberration which is suffered most often by
the most exceptional natures."

But he was uneasy, and about the middle of October Mathilde
managed to get rid of the boy; her father, who would certainly
not endure him in the house, was returning from his prolonged
shooting trip, she was expecting her child at the end of the month
and Verlaine agreed without argument that Rimbaud must go.
He beat about for a new home for him. Banville offered him the
attic of his house in rue de Buci, Madame Banville furnished it
and Verlaine, Cros and one or two others clubbed together to
give him weekly pocket money.

2

This marked the peak of Rimbaud's attempt on Paris. Already,
the first fine rapture over, he perceived that he could establish
himself there only by compromise; if he took part in the mutual
back-scratching he would "arrive." His answers, ranging through
the next months, were contemptuous negatives. There followed
a series of "aberrations" which effectively put him beyond the
pale. He began with Banville, the best loved poet and man of
the day. To Rimbaud, become horribly clear-sighted after the
carousals which made him bilious and bad-tempered, Banville
was a trickster, a juggler with words, a traitor to his gifts, a non-
serious man. He could imagine no more heinous crime, and no

kindness, no affability of Banville could wipe it out of his mind. On the evening of his arrival at Banville's house he was seen naked at the window of his attic, having just thrown his shirt into the courtyard below. Whether the alarmed neighbors called for the police is not certain, but the hubbub was sufficient to send Banville hurrying upstairs. His clothes were "full of fleas," Rimbaud explained, and unfit for the room in which he found himself. This gesture, not so much against luxury as the manner in which it had been earned, may have passed over Banville's head; if not, he ignored the sarcastic form of moral judgment favored by the boy, took him downstairs, fitted him out with clothes and invited him to dinner. The meal proved almost as difficult as the first night dinner at rue Nicolet; Rimbaud was looking for condescension and found it, and the evening ended with him gripping a knife threateningly when the conversation took a turn he could not approve—a gesture he was to repeat. He had drunk too much, of course, or could not hold his drink, which is not quite the same thing. Mallarmé, who tells the story, did not care for Rimbaud but is a reliable witness.

From that moment Banville's attic had to be exchanged as soon as possible for another home. Cros, who bore no malice, offered the boy a bed in his apartment. This arrangement also collapsed quickly; Rimbaud tore up and used as toilet paper sheets from a series of albums highly prized by Cros. Cros reproached him; they quarreled; and Rimbaud moved once more to Cabaner. Cabaner was a difficult man to dislike or to differ from, and Rimbaud lasted there until December. It was at Cabaner's that Delahaye discovered him. Delahaye, curious to know how his friend was faring in Paris, found him passing the winter in an old overcoat far too big for him and a large soft hat squashed on his head. He was lying on a couch just coming out of a hashish trance and rather pettish; he had seen only black and white moons chasing each other, he complained.

By this time he was being looked at askance for more than one reason; rumors were circulating, not only of his behavior at Banville's and with Cros but of the nature of his friendship with Verlaine. The man who first gave this friendship a sinister twist was Edmond Lepelletier. Lepelletier was a political journalist who paraded advanced republican views but in his private life remained extremely correct. With a horror not far short of Mathilde's he saw his old friend carelessly dressed and reverting to absinthe, a horror in which concern and jealousy each played a part; for though not neglecting his friends, actually seeing more of them in fact, Verlaine was obviously rapt away by the boy from Charleville. Lepelletier conscientiously asked them both to dinner. But if he disapproved of Rimbaud, Rimbaud detested him on sight—to him Lepelletier symbolized the bourgeois playing at politics—and did not trouble to hide his feelings before this "excreter of ink" as he publicly called him.

"He never opened his mouth during the first half of the meal," said Lepelletier, "except to demand, coldly, as if he were in a restaurant, bread or another glass of wine. Later, under the influence of a strong Burgundy which Verlaine liberally helped him to, he grew aggressive, shooting off volleys of paradoxes and sweeping generalizations. In particular he tried to mock me by calling me 'saluter of the dead' because he had seen me lifting my hat to funeral processions passing along the street. As I had lost my mother two months earlier I forbade him to continue in this strain and gave him such a severe look that he took offense and approached me menacingly. Impulsively and foolishly he had grasped a dessert knife which he no doubt thought to use as a weapon. I caught hold of his shoulder and forced him back into his seat, telling him that as the Prussians had not frightened me, a mischievous child wasn't likely to. And I warned him, almost more in joke than anger, that if he didn't take care and persisted in irritating us I would help him downstairs with a hearty kick or two on the behind. Verlaine broke in, excusing his friend and begging me not to be angry. Rimbaud then kept quiet, drinking heavily and surrounding himself with clouds of tobacco smoke, whilst Verlaine recited poetry."

Leaving aside the heroics from Lepelletier, Rimbaud would have been the first to agree that he baited his host; it was becoming a question of principle. To Lepelletier the affair did not appear in that light; the last thing he would think of in connection with Rimbaud, apparently his antithesis, was a sense of principle. The falsity in his account is not in the facts but in the manner; he was not paternally admonitory as he would have the reader believe, he was furious. He did not forget that evening and his chance for revenge soon came. In the middle of November the young poets thronged to see a one-act play by Glatigny at the Odéon. Under a pen name Lepelletier wrote an account of it in a journal, adding: "The fair Catulle Mendès was to be seen here and there arm in arm with the pale Mérat. Elsewhere Léon Valade, Dierx, Henri Houssaye talked together. The saturnian poet Paul Verlaine was observed arm in arm with a charming young person, Mlle Rimbaud."

The "Mlle Rimbaud" was all over the interested section of Paris within a few hours. At rue Nicolet, Lepelletier, questioned by a mystified Mathilde, explained that he had written it "to teach them a lesson."

If the gossip reached Rimbaud he would simply add it to the mounting account of a degenerate Paris and take a savage pleasure in providing fresh ammunition for the gossipers. For by this time he was in revolt, not simply against his old heroes, Banville, Leconte de Lisle, Coppée, but the rank and file, and had begun deliberately to antagonize many of them. Delahaye describes him at the Café de Cluny, one of the poets' cafés, lying along a bench grunting loudly with disapproval during the reading of a poem and airing communard views so extreme as to outrage most of the company. This became a common form of protest. His behavior at the cafés changed the character of Fantin-Latour's group portrait *Hommage à Baudelaire,* intended as a companion to his *Hommage à Delacroix.* Verlaine had insisted that Rimbaud be invited to sit as a follower of Baudelaire and this insistence led first to the withdrawal of Leconte de Lisle, who disliked Verlaine, then of Banville, who had not forgiven Rimbaud, and, most significantly, of Verlaine's friend Mérat who, disgusted by the boy's obscenities and insults to other poets, said that one of the two must go. Rimbaud would not budge, and the picture, a mere rump by this time, was completed without Mérat and named *Coin de Table*.

Rimbaud's now unconcealed hostility, coupled with the whispers of scandal, alienated all but the handful of wilder spirits, anti-social themselves, Richepin, Ponchon and Forain chiefly. Towards the end of the year, at a *Vilains Bonshommes* dinner, he made certain of ostracism. As usual after the meal a poet was declaiming one of his new poems. "That evening," said Verlaine, "much poetry had been read after dessert and coffee. This poetry-reading was not the least fatiguing part of the dinner, particularly when the poems were more than a little declamatory." Rimbaud agreed; he had heard more than enough and cared least of all for the poem then being remorselessly dinned into the company by its author. He began to punctuate the end of each line with an unmistakable *merde*. He ignored every attempt to stop him. The declaiming poet was a friend of Carjat who, annoyed, told the "brat" to be quiet or he would box his ears. At this Rimbaud caught hold of Verlaine's sword stick, drew the sword and wounded Carjat in the hand before he could be caught and disarmed. He was carried home, put to bed, and Verlaine was told that he would not be allowed to attend the dinners in future.

Rimbaud's behavior has been put down to an inability to take his liquor. But the drinking was, after early and unsatisfactory experiments, effect not cause. He anticipates his attitude and gives the reason for it during a walk with Delahaye after his friend had found him at Cabaner's. "I asked him," says Delahaye, "what he thought of the new ideas in Paris. He replied wearily and briefly, showing that his hopes had collapsed, 'Nothing. Chaos. All kinds of reactions are possible and even likely.'" His reaction was to recline on a bench in a café grunting at expositions of modern poetry. For to him the poems he heard declaimed in the cafés and at the *Vilains Bonshommes* dinners were merely exhibitions of vanity, and the rapturous applause so much lickspittle. No one was serious, not even Verlaine, though Rimbaud intended to make him so; and the Parnassian movement he had worshipped from distant Charleville exposed itself on nearer acquaintance as a pleasant pastime, played by men with safe jobs or private incomes who discovered innocuous ways of evading the laws of French prosody. He looked for the ravaged face of the striving, suffering artist, he saw well-fed young men laughing over café tables; expecting to be inspired by the radiance of genius, he was distracted by the glitter of cleverness; he talked of his determination to penetrate the unknown by unexampled sacrifices of virtue, sobriety, reason, and he was offered a drink; his oaths were gleefully treated as the delightful novelty of blasphemy from a baby.

"It seems so strange to me that I should have to protest to you that I'm serious," he had written to Demeny a few months earlier. Now, in Paris, the experience was repeated. No one was serious but him; and his seriousness was treated as the latest amusement, as exhibitionism. And, final insult, even the amusement was palling; his audience was frankly bored.

So wounded vanity and a genuine disillusion allied to produce an anti-social demonstration. It was Charleville all over again, yet for him far worse than Charleville since his visions of a return to a gratified and even contrite mother had fallen to the ground.

Rimbaud had only one way of expressing disappointment and hurt—by a rudeness more or less calculated. Almost everyone took the rudeness to be rudeness unqualified, sign of bad breeding, swelled head, extreme youth, too much drink. Verlaine understood a little of his mortification because Rimbaud lowered his defenses sufficiently for an affectionate man to guess what he suffered, but Verlaine's opinion counted for little; he had identified himself with Rimbaud, defended him and went into isolation with him; Rimbaud was dismissed as a gifted ragamuffin— an important passerby, said Mallarmé—with an evil eye, and Verlaine was his victim.

In December Rimbaud achieved the near impossible and broke with Cabaner. Ostensibly he withdrew himself in disgust because Cabaner drank milk—his parting shot was to fill one of the bottles with urine—but the true reason was that the easy-going musician got on his nerves. He demanded an obviously earnest approach to life and Cabaner, dreaming his way through a dreary existence, pleased him no better than the prosperous poets.

The withdrawal from Cabaner was the last stage in Rimbaud's downward progression as far as free quarters were concerned. For the future he would have to fend for himself, or to be exact the one or two faithful would have to fend for him. Which they did: and in December "Rimbe" was installed with "Gavroche" (alias the young Forain, who wanted to launch into the life of the Latin Quarter) in an attic in rue Campagne-Première, a few steps from Cabaner's and within strolling distance of all the cafés.

Within a week or two—on January 15, 1872—the two became three. Verlaine joined them, a homeless Verlaine. Matters at rue Nicolet had gone from bad to worse. The departure of Rimbaud, so much longed for by Mathilde, had increased her husband's absences. Rimbaud had failed in Paris but he had not failed with Verlaine. He had picked him out as the great poet of the future as he had discovered Baudelaire as the great poet of the past, but Verlaine had to be trained to his eminence. An essential part of this training was separation from philistine surroundings. Up to a point Verlaine abandoned himself to the training with a will—Rimbaud was merely saving him the trouble of making a decision—but he lent a less obliging ear to disparagement of his wife and mockery of the father-son relationship. He had no wish to leave Mathilde, stupid and vain though he knew her to be; on the contrary the violent restlessness of Rimbaud called for precisely the counterpoise which Mathilde provided. But Verlaine's attempt to oscillate harmlessly between Rimbaud and his wife, taking the good from each and none of the trouble, was foiled by absinthe. "Rimbe" had not nicknamed his companion "Verlomphe" for nothing; absinthe made nonsense of everything, good resolutions included; one could not indulge during the evening in cloudy dreams of greatness with Rimbaud and then go home sober and loving to Mathilde; absinthe followed after in the form of violent-tempered reaction to the rosy glow of an hour or two earlier; and Verlaine's bedroom behavior became so bad that Monsieur Mauté, discovering belatedly what was afoot, at once sent Mathilde into the country, denied his house to his son-in-law and refused to give her address.

For two months the *ménage-à-trois* in rue Campagne-Première persisted, yet perhaps not in complete unanimity; Forain had dreams of a studio of his own, Rimbaud was not convinced of the wholeheartedness of his companions and rightly enough in the case of Verlaine who, guilty and conscience-stricken, was negotiating with Mathilde. Her terms for a return were the dismissal of Rimbaud from Paris; and when her father threatened a legal separation (divorce not then existing) Verlaine's protestations died away. In March he sent Rimbaud back to Charleville and returned to rue Nicolet.

CHAPTER NINE

Exile and Return

1872

RIMBAUD's feelings were those of a child who has been sent out of the room; the same impotent rage, the same fury of self-justification. He was being sacrificed, he said, "to a caprice." True, Verlaine had assured him that he should come back as soon as relations with Mathilde were put on an amicable footing, but this, considering what Rimbaud thought of Mathilde, was a dubious consolation. The whole incident was, however he looked at it, a falling away, and the most painful part was yet another humiliating return to a mother whose pursed lips showed what she thought of his precious literary career. It must have seemed to him that he was absolutely dogged by his chubby face. To him, a ferocious egoist, the barrier between adult and adolescent caused special bitterness: what had age or appearance to do with one who felt superhuman powers? Yet the would-be god was wrapped in swaddling clothes; his cleverness, poetic gifts, vision were either praised because he looked a mere child or ignored for the same reason. In Charleville he had gained more amusement than notoriety; in Paris he gained the last kind of notice he wanted; the "brat" of Carjat was the measure of his final standing with the poets.

He went back to Charleville disgruntled but nevertheless he went. It was a significant choice because for the first time he had a choice; staked by Verlaine or, to be exact, by Verlaine's mother, he could have gone to Douai, to the relatives Verlaine was anxious for him to meet at Arras or at Paliseul and Jehonville the other side of the frontier just above Charleville; but he chose Charleville as he was always to choose it. All complaints about his home were exposed for what they were whenever he was faced with a decision; the blood tie remained decisive, and Madame Rimbaud without a rival.

He tried to convince his mother that the Paris setback was temporary and meaningless: he was and must be a poet. She "could not see anything practical" in the poetry he was still writing but which no one would pay for. And his retort "It's got to be done," though it might strike a chord of a kind in Madame Rimbaud's soul, did not earn him what he really wanted. So there he was, unacknowledged as the master poet of the future, unloved, standing first with none; even the admiring Verlaine had discarded him in favor of the vain and stupid Mathilde. The poems he wrote were cries of frustration:

> *Oisive jeunesse*
> *A tout asservie,*
> *Par délicatesse*
> *J'ai perdu ma vie.*
> *Ah! Que le temps vienne*
> *Où les cœurs s'éprennent.*

> Idle youthfulness,
> The slave of everything,
> Through delicacy
> I have wasted my life.
> Ah! Let the time come
> When hearts fall in love.

He had shot up in Paris—Delahaye comments on the way in which he had outgrown his clothes—but his face had not changed, nor had something even more prejudicial to intimacy with women, his idealism: a normal girl objects to a younger and smaller escort, an intelligent girl shrinks from worship. Whether Rimbaud could worship any living person but himself or his mother may be doubted, but this did not save him from the hunger and thirst he talks about so much at this time. "He who doesn't find his *Sœur de Charité*, either as woman or idea, is one of the wretched," he had told Demeny, and he was wretched. To be the King of men implied a Queen of women.

But where was he to find her? In Charleville? Yes, unhappily, at 5, Quai de la Madeleine. He remained unsatisfied.

Nevertheless he had grown up in Paris; the Charleville bourgeois were no longer adequate game, and he made no attempt to work out his unhappiness on them; he mooned about the country, wrote his poems, talked with Delahaye, Bretagne and the rest of the small literary band. Once, unbearably restless, he went to see Verlaine's aunt at Arras and wrote to Verlaine from there. He wrote frequently to Verlaine and Forain, letters eventually destroyed by Mathilde because they were "so queer that I thought they must have been written by an idiot." Mathilde's opinion is unhappily without interest and it is a pity she did not allow better qualified judges to read them; one or two of Verlaine's letters have been kept, and very revealing they are: so silly, filled with conspiratorial plans to outwit Monsieur Mauté (who had been cast as the villain of the piece) and come together again, as to give a very different face to the intimacy about which the Paris cafés were chattering. Verlaine writes like the schoolboy he so often reverted to in those days; he and Rimbaud were having huge fun embroidering the legend; if their little world persisted in seeing them as degenerate devils they intended to give it a helping hand.

Verlaine was more than usually silly because of circumstance: he had become respectable once again but with increasing effort, and let off steam to Rimbaud. Under the combined pressure of Mathilde and her father he had taken a clerical job, and was driven by exasperation to suggest that his friend might do likewise instead of accepting all the money he chose to send. This tactless reminder of Rimbaud's dependence produced an outburst from the high-minded poet in Charleville; Mathilde quotes a few lines of the reply, lines which read in character—a row of eight *merdes*, a blunt refusal to soil his soul by grubbing for money, and a "When you see me actually eating *merde* you won't think any more that I cost too much to feed."

This brought an immediate collapse from Verlaine; he had

begun to see his friends through the boy's stern eyes; Paris turned insipid, the mental and moral stuffiness of rue Nicolet became hard to breathe, and his own life appeared a humbug and waste. Boring too: so in May he took a room for him in rue Monsieur-le-Prince (Forain had moved to a studio on the Quai d'Anjou) and, saying nothing to Mathilde, summoned him back.

2

This new and short stay in Paris was more satisfactory than its predecessor. One of Rimbaud's great merits—Verlaine was to comment on it frequently—was that he would not endure what is known as a false position. Having given up hope of dominating a brilliant society of poets, he accepted with a kind of joy his exclusion from it. Not in the Parnassian cafés or salons would he develop the poetry of the future.

In other directions his mind had grown clearer. He had already abandoned, if he had ever seriously contemplated, the use of magic to enfranchise his imagination; even the derangement of the senses had dwindled to occasional bursts of liquor available to all; as his chief stimulant he had come round to the company of that second great poet in embryo, Verlaine, and one or two occasional satellites. So he got to work for the first time in Paris, got to work after and in the midst of interminable discussions with Verlaine, Forain, Richepin, Ponchon and Cros of the nature of poetry, the technical problems, the aims.

These discussions took place in the lesser cafés, in the streets, in Forain's studio and in Rimbaud's room. Verlaine, still working in his office, did not join his friends until evening, and he and Rimbaud often stayed up half the night in the attic high above the street trying to thrash out the new poetry. Rimbaud's satisfaction in having a room of his own in Paris blossomed into his "Jeune Ménage," written on the back of a letter from Forain:

La chambre est ouverte au ciel bleu-turquin;
Pas de place: des coffrets et des huches!
Dehors le mur est plein d'aristoloches
Où vibrent les gencives des lutins.

The bedroom is open to the slate-blue sky;
No room: chests and bins!
Outside the wall is full of aristolochias
In which the gums of the elfs are vibrating.

Here too he continued to write prose poems which were to take their place in *Illuminations*. In these, as in everything he attempted, he built on foundations begun by other men—in this case Gautier, Baudelaire and Cros—rather than constructing a form peculiar to himself, but the experiment gave him the exhilarating sensation of treading new ground. One of the poems began

O *mon* Bien! O *mon* Beau!

O *my* Good! O *my* Beauty!

and these high spirits were carried into his caricatures and his contributions to Cros' *Album Zutique* which included the delightful parody of Verlaine's *Fêtes Galantes*

Rêveur, Scapin
Gratte un lapin
Sous sa capote.

Colombina
Que l'on pina!—
Do, mi,—tapote

L'œil du lapin
Qui tôt, tapin,
Est en ribote.

Musing, Scapin
Scratches a rabbit
Under his overcoat.

Columbine
Who was . . . !
Do, mi—pats
The rabbit's eye
Which soon, hidden,
Goes on a spree.

Another kind of joke was his "Voyelles" sonnet with its

A noir, E blanc, I rouge, U vert, O bleu

Black A, white E, red I, green U, blue O

a sonnet which was to produce an agitated literature in the years after his death, playing much the same part with his imitators and worshippers as Verlaine's jeux d'esprit "Art Poétique" and "Langueur" were to play with the Symbolists and Decadents of his day. Verlaine was to say the last word on "Voyelles" with his "I know that he didn't care two sous whether A was red or green."

A letter to Delahaye, dated Parmerde, Juinphe 72, gives a fair picture of his life with its absurdities and its satisfactions. He has his reputation to keep up as dissolute man-about-town: "Yes," he says, "life is wonderful in that Ardennes peepshow. I don't regret the provinces where one eats flour and muck and drinks raw wine and country beer. You're right to black-guard it day in and day out. But this place! . . . The heat isn't unbroken, but when I see that the beautiful weather is to everyone's interest and that everyone is a pig, I hate summer, which kills me when it begins to make itself felt. I have a thirst as fearful as a gangrene: the rivers and caves of Belgium and the Ardennes, those are what I miss.

"All the same they have my favorite drink here. Long live the academy of Absomphe, in spite of the ill will of the waiters! To get drunk by means of this icy wormwood, absomphe, is to wear the most delicate, the most evanescent of garments! But afterwards one sleeps in *merde!*

"Always the same old moan, eh! One thing is certain: *merde* to Perrin. And to the bar of the 'Univers' whether it faces the *Place* or not. I won't curse the 'Univers,' however. I very much hope that the 'Ardenne' will be filled to bursting more and more intemperately. But all this is very small beer. . . . I do my work at night now. From midnight to five in the morning. For the past month my room in rue Monsieur-le-Prince looked into the garden of the Saint-Louis school. There were some enormous trees under my narrow window. At three o'clock in the morning the candle began to grow dim; all the birds in the trees began to sing at the same time. This was the end. No more work. I had to look at the trees, the sky, thrilled by this indescribable hour, the first of the morning. I could see the school dormitories, absolutely dead. Already the jerky noise had begun, sonorous, delightful, of the dustcarts on the streets. I would smoke my square-headed pipe and spit on the tiles, for my room was an attic. At five o'clock I went down to buy bread; this is the time for it. Work has begun everywhere. For me this is the time to get drunk in the wineshops. I came back to eat and then lay down until seven when the sun brings the woodlice out from under the tiles. December evenings and early morning in summer, these are what always ravish me here.

"But at the moment I have a fine room on a bottomless court built of stone three meters thick. Rue Victor Cousin is on the corner of the Place de la Sorbonne next to the Bas-Rhin café and looks into rue Soufflot at the other end. There I drink water all night, I don't see the morning, I don't sleep, I suffocate. And there you are . . .

"Don't forget to sh . . . on that literary and artistic journal *La Renaissance* if you come across it. Up to now I have managed to avoid those pests of emigrants, the *caropolmerdis*. And *merde* to this time of year . . ."

His hard feelings about *La Renaissance littéraire*, which was edited by Emile Blémont, were scarcely justified; in September one of his poems was printed in it, the first time his work had

appeared in a journal of any moment. But long before then, in
fact only a few days after his letter to Delahaye, he had abandoned Paris.

The room no doubt had something to do with his abrupt departure, hating heat as he did, and another kind of climate,
the pervading air of intellectual dishonesty, was also becoming
more than he could bear, but the determining factor was
Verlaine who, terrified of another break with his wife, was behaving with indecent respectability, that is to say he refused
to drink heavily every night in the week, he stayed in his insurance office, he even spent some time at home. So correct
was he at rue Nicolet that Mathilde did not suspect that
Rimbaud had returned to Paris.

To Rimbaud's logical and inflexible mind this effort to enjoy
the best of both worlds was inadmissible. He began to wonder
more than once whether he was not wasting his time on Verlaine;
the man scarcely seemed worth it. He was fond to the point of
foolishness but was he serious? He enjoyed his drink, that disgusting ascent to olympian heights, as drink; he enjoyed discussions on the poetry of the future no less than he enjoyed naughty
stories and wrote one or two poems with which his companion
could find no fault. In fact he seemed tiresomely able to produce a fine poem without unheard-of sufferings.

But Rimbaud had put his hand to the plough; he had, he
said, "in all sincerity of mind pledged myself to restore him to
his primitive state as a Son of the Sun" and he would carry it
out. Besides, Verlaine was likable when he was not irritating,
he had money which saved his friend from distracting work
and in his better moments he still promised relief from his
obsession.

He and Rimbaud had become well known for their inces-
sant bickering—it was this which had led to Mérat's withdrawal from *Coin de Table*. Often earnest below the surface,
they hammered out much of value; in this way they arrived
at a theory of poetry; but real explosions began to appear
when summer heat, overmuch absinthe and doubts of the *fils*

du soleil had broken down Rimbaud's temper. This came to a head in the "aberration" of the "Rat Mort." Sitting with Verlaine and Cros he asked them to put their hands face downward, on the table. "I want to show you an experiment," he said. They obliged. He whipped a knife out of his pocket and held it above the spread hands. Cros hurriedly snatched his hands away. Verlaine left his there. Rimbaud lost all control; even his disciple refused to take him seriously. In a sudden fit of rage he stabbed downwards with the knife and slashed Verlaine's wrists. The expected and hope-for chastisement did not come. Verlaine, hurt and startled, jumped up and ran into the street. Beside himself, Rimbaud followed and hacked his leg twice before he could get away.

Verlaine's pretense at rue Nicolet that he had been wounded whilst fencing did not soften the hard young avenger of weakness. Verlaine had given up his worldly friends, he had stuck to Rimbaud against the advice of the *Vilains Bonshommes* crowd, but he had not given up Mathilde. On the 7th of July came the supreme test. Mathilde had a sore throat and Verlaine was walking to the doctor for a prescription when he saw Rimbaud approaching. Rimbaud said curtly that he was leaving Paris that day; was Verlaine coming?

What about my wife? asked Verlaine, playing for time.

To hell with your wife, said Rimbaud.

Verlaine knew that tone; after no more than a moment's hesitation he turned and went off with the boy.

CHAPTER TEN

Annus Mirabilis

1872–1873

THEY sat at the cafés until dark, discussing plans. Verlaine, who had already decided (since he dare not decide anything else) that this was to be a lark, settled the matter by the innocent proposal that they visit the aunt in Arras already known to Rimbaud. They went off lightheartedly by the night train and their high spirits carried into the station bar at Arras where they ate a leisurely breakfast before calling on Verlaine's aunt. A station bar in the early hours does not encourage liveliness, and when an old man began to listen to their conversation "with an air not so much stupid as malicious" they decided on the spur of the moment to give him something worth listening to; putting on their best criminal manner they muttered audibly of breaks from prison, thefts and even a murder. Effectively; for the old man soon departed unostentatiously and returned with the police.

Their blood up, Rimbaud and Verlaine kept the game going and to the horrified delight of the customers at the bar were carried off to the police station. There Rimbaud, weeping, complained of being forced into crime by his brutal companion and Verlaine, examined in his turn, took a high and mighty line; born in Metz, taken into Germany since the 1870 war, he had the right to opt for citizenship: "And upon my soul if this is the way honest Frenchmen are treated, I am not likely to choose France."

The magistrate began to suspect a hoax and told the policemen to take the couple back to the station and put them into the next train for Paris; but Verlaine, well in his part, demanded that they should be allowed to finish their interrupted breakfast. He had his way and, well fed and triumphant, he and Rimbaud arrived back in Paris that evening.

They crossed at once to the Gare de l'Est and took the train for Charleville where they spent the next day talking and drinking with Bretagne. At midnight Bretagne saw them off in a hired cart which took them across the frontier by one of the unguarded lanes and left them safely in Belgium.

The affair at Arras revealed a new Rimbaud, consciously youthful in the first flush of triumph, having rescued Verlaine from a fate worse than death and gained a companion in spiritual adventure. Physical adventure too, for he felt twice the being in the open air, all the Cuif in him panting for the country. In this mood he was irresistible and Verlaine made no attempt to resist him. As they walked the road to Brussels both were "intoxicated to the point of frenzy, talking art and living art" and one at least found the life "atrociously delicious."

This was Verlaine, talking in retrospect after Rimbaud was in his grave. The "atrocious" can be waived as an afterthought of middle age; the only feeling of that kind possible at the time would be caused by the daring flight of Rimbaud's imagination as they walked and talked in the sunshine or sheltered during the rain. Looking into those blazing blue eyes and listening to the queerly attractive Ardennais burr of the voice that had only just found its feet, anything seemed possible to Verlaine. Others had felt the fascination, others would feel it; and if Verlaine ever doubted, the doubt was not of his companion but of his own fitness to stay the course. He was over-modest as to his poetic gifts but correct in the occasional fear that he was not made of the stuff of heroes. Rimbaud, for instance, could throw off the past with apparent ease when he had his eye on the future; Verlaine threw, in secret, many a backward thought, to his wife, his child, his comfortable companions in the cafés, even to that long lost office seat in the Hôtel de Ville; but Rimbaud had only to smile, to speak, to give a prance on the road or leap a stile with airy confidence and joy, and the world was again well lost. Not that Verlaine ever seriously intended to lose the world; he was merely setting it aside whilst he played the boy with this wonderful poet, not the less wonderful for the laughs which he had from time to time at his little meannesses, his mangling of the French language, his habit of complaint which he had brought almost to a fine art.

Mathilde said that her husband dropped her a note via his mother saying that he would come back one day. If this is true, the note was written on one of the days when Rimbaud missed his mother, suspected that Verlaine was halfhearted, or was annoyed because his companion had failed to obtain another remittance from Madame Verlaine. But these days were infrequent, and to the end of his life Verlaine was to remember that leisurely tour of Belgium and the weeks in Brussels as a time of miraculous well-being.

As for Rimbaud, his poetry, always an index to his feelings, portrayed faithfully and in one instance magically this one blissful period when, free, in funds, in health, in congenial company, in the open air most of every day, he believed that his great powers were on the eve of realization; no more bitter, blasphemous verses echoing frustration in a pretentious vocabulary but an unfamiliar geniality of mood, culminating in a glorious hymn to carefree happiness.

> *O saisons, ô châteaux,*
> *Quelle âme est sans défauts?*
>
> *O saisons, ô châteaux,*
>
> *J'ait fait la magique étude*
> *Du Bonheur, que nul n'élude.*
>
> *O vive lui, chaque fois*
> *Que chante son coq gaulois.*
>
> *Mais! je n'aurai plus d'envie,*
> *Il s'est chargé de ma vie,*
>
> *Ce Charme! il prit âme et corps,*
> *Et dispersa tous efforts.*

Que comprendre à ma parole?
Il fait qu'elle fuie et vole!

O saisons, ô châteaux.

O seasons, o castles,
What soul is faultless?

O seasons, o castles,

I have made the magic study
Of Happiness which no one eludes

Hurrah for it, every time
That its Gallic rooster sings

Indeed, I'll have no more longing,
It has taken charge of my life,

That Charm! It took soul and body,
And dissipated every effort.

What meaning to give to my words?
It makes them flee and soar!

O seasons, o castles.

2

The vagabondage was interrupted by the apparition of
Mathilde and her mother. Verlaine was summoned to their hotel
where his spirit of escapade vanished the moment he saw his
wife again—saw her in the pose best calculated to recapture a
susceptible man. He agreed to return to Paris that evening.
But he refused to leave without saying goodbye to Rimbaud.
For some hours they sat together at a café. Rimbaud's sarcasms
had their effect; Verlaine kept his appointment at the railway
station but he had been drinking and the women could not get
a word out of him. At the frontier station they had to leave
the carriage for a customs examination. When Mathilde and her
mother got back again there was no sign of Verlaine; he did not

appear until the train was moving and then only shook his head when Madame Mauté called to him to get in.

Verlaine ended this decisive day—he was never to see his wife again—by writing an angry note to Mathilde from the frontier station; he was, he said, "going back to Rimbaud if he'll have anything more to do with me after the way you've made me betray him."

Rimbaud took him back, but the relationship had changed its character or, rather, increasingly took on its true character; from this moment Rimbaud knew that Verlaine had not been "saved" but remained a man subject to every wind of emotion, a man constitutionally unable to set his face against any form of love; when with Rimbaud he loved Rimbaud, when with Mathilde he loved Mathilde. To Rimbaud this was unpardonable weakness; he could neither forget nor forgive. But Verlaine's gift remained—already his poetry had become stronger and deeper—and so did Verlaine's money which the practical Rimbaud could not overlook; without it, since he would not look for or could not find work, he would have to return once more unsuccessful to Charleville. And to dislike Verlaine was practically impossible; one could despise him, which Rimbaud did more and more with all the implacability of dedicated youth, but the elder man's affectionate and unselfish amiability again and again won over his stern critic.

But there it was, Rimbaud no longer had a companion in arms, he had a weaker brother. The savagery which had seized the boy in the "Rat Mort" came back again and again, not in the form of knife-slashing but in contemptuous sneers and practical jokes which were crueller to a man like Verlaine.

After one of these incidents Verlaine, hankering after Mathilde and dismissing realities, invited her to come to live with them both at Brussels, assuring her that Rimbaud was "doing very well" there. How Rimbaud was doing well he did not say—perhaps nothing more had happened than Blémont's promise to print the poem in the *Renaissance littéraire*—and the assurance was insufficient to drag a reply from Mathilde or to prevent him and Rimbaud from leaving for England soon afterwards.

There were reasons for Verlaine to attempt England. His fears of arrest as an ex-communard had disappeared since he left France, but the Belgians were persecuting communard refugees by making work difficult for them to find. He was in theory anglophile, proud of his scanty hold on the language, tolerably well read in English literature and nourishing an indestructible if flimsy belief that he could immediately make a living there. Rimbaud had not lost his romantic passion for strange countries and, ever practical too, welcomed any chance to learn a new language. He could scarcely be expected to endure for long a prim Brussels, mild copy of Paris. He knew that Vermersch, his old hero, was living and working in London with other communard refugees; and, as he was soon to write in *Illuminations:* "fed by wine from cellars and road biscuit we rambled, I in a hurry to find the place and the formula." He had not found the formula in Charleville, Paris, Brussels; perhaps he would find it in London.

So for various reasons—among which must be counted the sense of spree which had shot them up to Arras and back again a few weeks earlier—both were found on the Ostend-Dover ship one rough night early in September. The next day they called on Régamey, one of the *Vilains Bonshommes* artists, in his Langham Street studio. Régamey sketched them, remarking with an inward smile that they "didn't exactly sparkle with elegance," and helped them practically by the information that Vermersch, on the point of marriage, was leaving his rooms off Tottenham Court Road. After a night or two in Soho, they installed themselves in Howland Street. Andrieu, Verlaine's old associate at the Hôtel de Ville, was tutoring the precocious Oliver Madox Brown just round the corner in Fitzroy Square. The exiled communards' headquarters were only a few minutes' walk south, in Old Compton Street. So they were not short of company, and were soon attending the communard club lectures, lending Vermersch a hand with his communard paper *L'Avenir*, and patronizing the French restaurants round about Leicester Square where most of the exiles gathered to eat, drink and gossip.

But they were in a great foreign city for the first time and, being tireless walkers and curious young men, set themselves to know London. They explored Limehouse and the docks, Hyde Park with its orators, Kew, the Crystal Palace, and the medley of main streets and side lanes from the City to the West End, Rimbaud slouching the pavement with long strides and a top hat, bought for a shilling, perched incongruously on his head. They became ardent theatergoers, impartially hearing Shakespeare, Sheridan, Offenbach, Hervé and the latest craze, the Minstrels, from the dizzy and smoky heights of the gallery. They sampled opium in Limehouse after a reading of De Quincey. They tried to master the language by talking to all and sundry. They visited the picture galleries and discovered in one, the French Gallery, a sight not reckoned on by tourists, themselves as large as life staring out of *Coin de Table*. Nor did they merely admire; they had a critical word or two to say: "What beauties!" Verlaine cried to Blémont of the Bellinis in the National Gallery and the Reynolds in the Wallace Collection; but "*zut* for that *farceur* of a Turner. A bad Monticelli!"

What Rimbaud thought of London he kept to himself, to Verlaine and his mother. Verlaine had plenty to say, and in general their view of London coincided; the first shock of dirt, drabness, the hideous and the sordid over, both agreed that it possessed a special charm of its own. Rimbaud had his own way of expressing this charm as in the "City" section of *Illuminations:*

"I am a temporary and not too greatly discontented citizen of a metropolis believed to be up-to-date because all known taste in the furnishings and exteriors of houses as in the plan of the city has been evaded. Here you would not distinguish the traces of a single monument of superstition. At last morals and language are reduced to their simplest expression! These millions of people who have no need to know one another like-

wise conduct education, business and old age in such a fashion
that the course of their lives must be many times less long than
that which a crazy statistic invents for the people of the Continent."

Whether this was written then or the next year is beside the
point, since Rimbaud's views did not change. He spent his
eighteenth birthday in London, and no doubt celebrated it in
a theater that evening. But during the day he was likely, the
first exploratory fever over, to be found reading in the British
Museum, for he and Verlaine were doing more than merely
enjoy themselves in the obvious ways, they were still experimenting in poetry which Verlaine said was becoming "more and
more *modernistic.*" Rimbaud was working out prose poems for
Illuminations (though he was far from thinking of publication
as a book) and, not less important, was making Verlaine into
the great poet that *Romances sans paroles* was soon to proclaim.

As companion too Verlaine gave satisfaction during these
autumn weeks to a Rimbaud rendered slightly less morally
rigid by the strangeness of London and the English. But in
November Verlaine fell from grace; hearing from Lepelletier
that Mathilde was about to begin proceedings for a legal separation and that one of her grounds would be his immoral relationship with Rimbaud, he panicked, and Rimbaud was reminded
with disgust that the weak brother had tenacious affections and
an apparently unquenchable thirst for bourgeois home comfort.
Nevertheless Rimbaud could not remain absolutely unconcerned
by the news, though he never made clear whether his concern
was for the insult or the fact that some of his manuscripts were
in the hands of the Mautés. And after Verlaine had protested at
length but to little purpose to Lepelletier (who had some training in law) with an offer to submit to a medical examination
and a threat that he would defend and demolish the case, Rimbaud took a hand: he wrote to his mother and explained the
position.

Madame Rimbaud had met Verlaine the previous December
(when he made a short visit to Charleville) and perhaps during

the July day when he and Rimbaud were waiting to cross the frontier. He regarded her with a sort of incredulous awe, this form of womanhood being outside his experience. Outside his comprehension too, had not Rimbaud prepared him in advance. But the preparation was not as in the cafés of Charleville; for once Rimbaud, influenced by his friend's affection, had allowed himself some expansive moments. Verlaine, whose sense of humor remained lively, promptly nicknamed her "La Mère des Gracchi." For her part, Madame Rimbaud was impressed by his enthusiastic forecasts of her son's great future as poet and, like most people who met Verlaine in those years, she appreciated his good nature. She did not see the departure from Paris as a desertion of Mathilde and the baby; after all, she had had much experience of men and boys leaving home. Her son's news came as a shock; she was angry and immediately agreed to approach the Mautés.

The démarche was no more successful than the formal visit already paid to rue Nicolet by Verlaine's mother; Monsieur Mauté was polite but non-committal and refused to hand over any papers; the manuscript of "La Chasse Spirituelle"—according to Verlaine, Rimbaud's finest poem—was never seen again.

The one positive result was a getting together of the two mothers. Monsieur Mauté had hinted that the affair might be overlooked if Verlaine and Rimbaud separated and the women took the hint; as Madame Verlaine supplied the money on which they lived, pressure was easy; by December Rimbaud was back in Charleville and Verlaine remained in London hoping that his mother would join him there.

Of the boy's short stay in Charleville only the obvious was allowed expression, his boredom and restlessness. It was his dilemma that he could neither be happy at home, intellectually stifled (*"ô canot immobile!"*) and kept at arm's length emotionally, nor away from it. Not for long at any rate; he had only to be in the company of others for sufficient time to realize that they could not back their affection with the strength he demanded.

As for Madame Rimbaud, she was spending her life trying to be reconciled to her lot; to go the whole way in self-sacrifice was beyond even this strong and devout woman, hence the appeals to heavenly justice which Arthur had adopted in his own fashion. But she believed in deeds not words; always the peasant, she sought practical consolation in the material and social success of the children she had not wanted. This accounted for her increasingly hostile attitude to Frédéric, still selling newspapers, showing no sign of making money or a name for himself and every sign of becoming another Uncle Auguste. But Frédéric presented no problem; he was a cross she had to bear, not silently. The girls presented no problem; they had taken to the life respectable like ducks to water and were undemanding in their affections, finding satisfaction in each other. Arthur was another matter; the most stupid philistine is uneasily aware of the exceptional and Madame Rimbaud was not stupid; when her second son looked at her with those disturbing eyes, when he talked largely of fame in some unpredictable future, she covered her perplexity by authoritarian gestures but at heart she remained uncertain and her actions did not match her gestures. She, the last person in the world to entertain maternal delusions, had been presented with one proof after another that he was extraordinary—the career at school, the tributes of friends, the praise of Verlaine—but the sight and sound of him was proof enough. How to pin this restless, brilliant child to a desk in Charleville's Hôtel de Ville, or to any desk? How to meet the emotional demands of this positive child? To this there was no answer. Unable to give in one direction she gave in another; Arthur must do as he pleased. Under protest, ungraciously, time and again she compromised.

So within a month, soon after the new year, Rimbaud was in London again. Verlaine had caught influenza and, persuaded that he was not long for the world, scattered messages in all directions: "I am *dying* of grief, of illness, of boredom, of loneliness. Excuse this brevity from a very sick man. Goodbye, perhaps forever." Madame Verlaine, sent a telegram, rushed over

to her son and, unable to deny him anything, at once provided
the fare for Rimbaud to rejoin him, Rimbaud who had received
his deathbed message with a "Verlaine is like a child left in a
room without a light, sobbing with fear. If I come back to him
our talks and long walks will quickly cure his body because
they'll cheer his mind."

This second stay in London lasted little more than two months.
Verlaine, convalescent, could at first say no more of Rimbaud
than that "his good nursing will perhaps help to prolong my
poor damned existence less painfully," but by the beginning of
February he was up and about again, his mother went back to
France and the round of work and pleasure began again. "Every
day we take enormous walks in the suburbs and the country,
Kew, Woolwich etc.," Verlaine told Blémont, "for we have
known the whole of London for a long time now." They resumed
their theater-going and their seats in the reading room of the
British Museum. Verlaine completed the poems for *Romances
sans paroles,* Rimbaud wrote more prose poems for *Illuminations.* And in preparation for "earning a few sous" by giving
French and Latin lessons they were, as Verlaine was telling
the same correspondent in March "hard at work learning English, Rimbaud and I. In Edgar Poe, in the collections of popular
songs, in Robertson, etc., etc. Still more in the shops, public
houses, bookshops, etc. where we try out 'posers' from the point
of view of pronunciation."

Verlaine was enthusiastically planning a revival of the previous
year's carefree weeks in Belgium: "This summer we shall probably go to Brighton, and perhaps to Scotland, to Ireland!" But
in the event the stay in London closed abruptly. Verlaine was
being insistently advised by his mother, Blémont and Lepelletier
to come back to France, publish his book, see Mathilde and
effect a reconciliation. He saw the sense of this, declared as
early as February "I intend to return to Paris soon," and at the
beginning of April actually set foot on a cross channel steamer
at Newhaven. There he overheard a discussion about himself
between two men whom he believed to be plain-clothes police—

as far back as the death of Louis Napoleon in December he had prophesied a new anticommunard drive—precipitately abandoned ship and returned to London. He really was being watched by the police and his movements reported to Paris, and, made fearful of both London and Paris, left the next day for Ostend, this time in the company of Rimbaud.

Verlaine's intention was to walk through Belgium to his aunt at Jéhonville, where he thought to lie low for a time, enlivened by Rimbaud's company. But at Namur he "had a kind of cerebral attack from which I recovered only after taking medicinal water in bulk." The description is unlikely to have deceived Blémont, to whom it was given; the "cerebral attack" was nothing more mysterious than the aftereffects of a drinking bout. Verlaine's solitary drinking bouts were always caused by a hurt he had not the strength or the coldness to face in soberness. And this particular hurt was Rimbaud's departure for Roche. The abrupt flight from London, tailing behind a panic-stricken Verlaine whose money dictated every movement, had brought the boy up short. The moralist joined forces with the realist to denounce the life he was leading and the man he was leading it with. Verlaine was just tolerable as companion and general provider in a lively city; in a Belgian hamlet like Jéhonville where life was virtually extinct and money valueless his emotionalism and weaknesses were not worth bearing. No future there; rather Roche until something better turned up. So in the second week of April a Verlaine much the worse for wear arrived dispiritedly and alone at his aunt's house whilst fifty miles to the south Rimbaud walked unheralded into the farm at Roche on Good Friday, 11 April.

3

The Rimbaud family had moved to Roche a few days earlier and was beginning what was to become the custom of spending the summer there. The farmhouse, though partly gutted during the war, was habitable, and if the farm did not prosper as in the days of old Monsieur Cuif, it was workable and even profitable. Madame Rimbaud had never lost her appetite for farmwork and reckoned thriftily that she and her children would all save the cost of hired labor whilst the country air set up her elder daughter. For unlike her brothers, her mother and Isabelle, the young Vitalie was delicate.

Then nearly fourteen, Vitalie was tall for her age with soft fair hair and the large hands and feet and long oval face of the family. As with so many children destined to die young, she was devout, affectionate and saw good in everything. She began to keep a journal with the move to Roche—her first train journey—and faithfully set down the exact distance from Attigny railway station, 4 kilometers, 1 hectometer, and her joy when she first spied the tall mansard roof covering the granary and the dovecot over the wagon house through the trees which sheltered the Cuif farm on three sides. She and Isabelle lovingly explored the house (seen by them only once before, three years earlier) with its great shuttered living room, stone-floored kitchen, lofty bedrooms and enormous granary filling the entire roof. Then they went further afield by moonlight, into the grassy, high-walled court with its noble gateway opening on to the road and its fire-blackened walls, through the ruined outhouses into the gardens, orchard, fields and paddocks.

It was Vitalie who recorded the arrival of Arthur. "This day," she writes, "made an epoch in my life, for it was marked by an incident which particularly touched me; without being given previous notice, the arrival of my second brother put a crown on our joy. I still see myself in the room where we usually sat occupied in putting our affairs in order; my mother, brother and sister were near me when a discreet knock sounded on the door. I went to open it and . . . imagine my surprise, I found myself face to face with Arthur. The first moments of astonishment over, the newcomer explained the purpose of this occurrence; we were very joyful and he was well content to see us satisfied."

This inside view shows that the charm of Arthur had its

victims in the Rimbaud home as well as out of it. Many years later Isabelle—then twelve years old—said that her brother looked ill, walked much alone, lay on his bed by the hour, ate badly and insisted that he simply needed to be left in peace. And he was left in peace; the harmony of the family was sufficient for that. The four of them went to church, worked on the land and in the house. The fifth had other work to do and was allowed to do it; "for him the pen" as Vitalie was to put it; he would take himself off to the granary day after day and write. Vitalie could not in her wildest dreams have imagined what the admired brother, only four years her senior, was writing in the midst of this calm pastoral existence which gave her such delight, nor for that matter could any other of the four. A few lines written during this April and May explain what was the matter with Rimbaud at Roche and how right he was to insist that no one could help him. He who at sixteen boasted of attaining the infinite decided at eighteen that the infinite—the version of it conceived in pride—was not worth attaining. But he had his own way, as always, of describing disillusionment:

"Once, if I remember rightly, my life was a feast at which all hearts opened, at which all wines flowed.

"One evening I seated Beauty on my knees. And I found her bitter. And I reviled her.

"I armed myself against justice.

"I ran away. Oh witches, oh misery, oh hate, my treasure has been confided to you!

"I managed to drive all human hope from my mind. With the secret spring of the wild beast I strangled all joy. . . .

"Ah! I've had enough:—But, dear Satan, a less incensed eyeball I beg you! And whilst waiting for the one or two little despicablenesses still to come, let me tear out for you who love the lack of instructive or descriptive talent in writers these few frightful pages from my notebook of the damned. . . .

"I have the blue-white eyes of my Gallic ancestors, their narrow skull and their clumsiness in battle. I find my clothes just as barbarous as theirs. Only I don't grease my hair. . . .

"From them too I get idolatry and love of sacrilege; oh! all the vices, anger, lust—magnificent lust; above all, lying and laziness.

"I have a horror of all trades. Vile, all peasants, masters and workers. The hand that guides the pen is worth the hand that guides the plough. . . .

"But who gave me such a treacherous tongue that it has guided and safeguarded my indolence up to now? Without even using my body to earn a living, I have lived everywhere, more idle than the toad. . . .

"My day is finished; I'm leaving Europe. Sea air will blow out my lungs; lost climes will tan me. To swim, to trample the grass, to hunt, above all to smoke; to drink liquors as violent as boiling metal—just as my dear ancestors did round their fires.

"I'll return with iron limbs, dark skin and furious eye; I shall be judged by my appearance as one of a strong race. I will have gold; I shall be idle and brutish. . . .

"When still a child, I admired the intractable convict on whom the prison doors are always closing; I visited the inns and lodgings he had consecrated by his sojourn; I saw *with his eyes* the blue sky and the work in the countryside in bloom; in cities I scented his fate. He had more strength than a saint, more good sense than a traveler—and he, he alone! witnessed his glory and his right . . .

"Do I know nature yet? Do I know myself? *No more words.* I bury the dead in my belly. Shouts, drums, dance, dance, dance, dance! . . .

"Quickly! are there other lives? To rest in wealth is impossible. Wealth has always been common property. Divine love alone provides the keys of knowledge. I see that nature is only a show of goodness. Goodbye, chimeras, ideals, errors! . . .

"Boredom is my love no more. Rages, debauches, madness —of which I know all the outbursts and the disasters—all my burden is laid down. Let us contemplate undazed the extent of my innocence. . . .

"I am not prisoner of my reason. I said: God, I want freedom in salvation: how can I find it? Frivolous tastes have left me. No further need of devotion or divine love. No more regrets for the age of impressionable hearts. Each of us has his reason, contempt and charity; I reserve my place at the top of that angelic ladder of common sense. . . .

"I have devoured a mighty mouthful of poison. Thrice blessed be the advice which was given to me! My entrails are burning. The violence of the venom twists my limbs, deforms me, lays me low. I die of thirst, I suffocate, cannot cry out. This is hell, eternal punishment! See how the fire blazes up again! I burn well. Get on with it, demon! . . .

"And this is life still! If damnation were eternal! A man who wants to mutilate himself is well damned, isn't he? I believe I'm in hell, therefore I am in hell. It is the fulfilment of the catechism. I am the slave of my baptism. Parents you have created my misfortune and your own. Poor innocent! Hell has no power over pagans. . . .

"And to say that I hold by truth, that I understand justice, that my judgment is sound and decided, that I am ripe for perfection . . . Pride. My scalp is shriveling. Pity! Lord, I am afraid. I am thirsty, so thirsty! Ah, childhood, the grass, the rain, the lake over the stones, *moonlight when the bell was chiming twelve* . . . The devil is in the belfry at this hour. Mary! Holy Virgin! . . . Horror of my stupidity. . . .

"I am going to unveil all the mysteries: religious or natural mysteries, death, birth, the future, the past, cosmogony, nothingness. I am a master of phantasmagoria.

"Listen! . . .

"I possess all the talents! There is no one here and there is someone: I don't want to squander my treasure. . . .

"This makes me regret the world very little. I am lucky not to suffer more. My life was only sweet follies, it's a pity.

"Bah! Let's make every imaginable grimace.

"Decidedly we are out of the world. No more sound. My sense of touch has disappeared. Ah! my castle, my Saxony, my willow wood! Evenings, mornings, nights, days . . . How tired I am!

"I ought to have my hell for anger, my hell for pride—and the hell of laziness; a symphony of hells.

"I die of lassitude. This is the tomb, I go to the worms, horrors of horrors! Satan, you fraud, you want to dissolve me with your charms. I protest. I protest! a prick with the prongs, a snatch of fire . . .

"My God, pity, hide me, I behave too badly! I am hidden and I am not.

"The fire flames up again with its damned."

In the midst of this work he wrote to Delahaye. The letter and what was to become *Une Saison en Enfer*, written at the same moment, contrast oddly, the one adolescent, the other beyond age; the letter could be paralleled by thousands written by spirited young men wishing to convey world-weariness; the work was unique in form and expression; the boy of eighteen had leapt out of his generation. He headed his letter Cabbage (Roche) and began "Dear friend, you can see my life in the sketch below. Oh Nature! Oh my mother!"

The sketch showed a little man in the sky holding a spade as the priest holds the chalice. Out of his mouth come the words "Oh Nature! oh my sister!" On the ground in the midst of flowers, grass and trees stands a big man wearing clogs, a cotton cap on his head and a shovel in his hand. In the grass is a goose with the words ballooning out of its beak "Oh nature! oh my aunt!"

He continued: "What sh . . . ! and what masters of innocence, these peasants. In the evening it's necessary to walk five miles or more to drink a little. The *mother* has put me into a sad hole."

Here he made another sketch entitled "Cabbage, my village" showing Roche as seen from the Rimbaud farmhouse.

Then: "I don't know how to get out of here; I will get out, however. I regret the frightful Charlestown, the 'Univers,' the Library, etc. Still I work pretty regularly; I'm writing little prose tales under the general heading of *Pagan Book* or *Negro Book*. It's stupid and harmless. Oh innocence! innocence, innocence, inno . . . curse!"

He ended the letter: "I've nothing more to tell you, the contemplation of Nature absorbing me completely. I'm yours, oh Nature, oh my mother!" but opened it to add, having received a letter from Verlaine, that "he is going to propose to you a meeting at Bouillon on Sunday the 18th. I can't go there. If you go he will probably hand you some prose fragments, of his or mine, to return to me.

"Mother Rimb. will be going back to Charlestown sometime in June. This is certain and I shall try to stay in that lovely town some time.

"The sun is overwhelming and it freezes in the morning. The day before yesterday I went to see the Prussmars at Vouziers, a sous-prefecture of ten thousand souls seven kilometers from here. That revived me a bit.

"I am abominably restricted. Not a book, not a tavern within reach, not an incident in the street. What a horror this French countryside is. My fate depends on this book for which half a dozen atrocious stories have still to be invented. How invent these atrocities here? I won't send you these stories although I already have three of them, *it costs so much!*"

He ended finally by a postscript asking Delahaye to send him a popular edition of Goethe's *Faust*. The request is instructive; the *Livre Païen* which was to become *Une Saison en Enfer* is Faustian in thought and language.

As for the "horrible French countryside," Roche was then a hamlet of rather more than one hundred people, and the Rimbaud farmhouse stood at the junction of the roads looking down the "Main Street" and over to rolling, wooded country. Nothing sad, nothing ugly about this outlook; but mortally quiet it certainly was, and for an intellectually vigorous young man to be shut up in a Roche with empty pockets, a bad conscience and too much time to think is punishment indeed.

Not long after this letter, written early in May, he was released; released after overcoming misgivings only too well founded that he was exchanging bad for worse.

4 ~~~~~

Verlaine was the agent of release; Verlaine with a fresh supply of money from his mother, Verlaine conscience-free for the moment, an attempted rapprochement with his wife having been repulsed. He protested his innocence— "Alas! I have been *chaste* since I left Paris!!" he assured Lepelletier—and proved it "in very vivid terms"; in fact, in eight unprintable words. Above all, he was "bored to death . . . without books, without anyone to talk to . . . seeing only at long intervals the friend to whom I have pledged my whole affection and who does me so much good." He began to talk of a return to London with this friend: his departure from "the great city," he had told Blémont from the beginning, was "provisional only."

The friend, though equally bored at Roche, was far from being of the same mind as to the direction of escape. He had not forgotten Namur or, for that matter, his decidedly ambivalent feelings towards Verlaine in Paris, Brussels and London. He refused the first suggested meeting but his scruples did not survive the letter Verlaine wrote after walking through the rain to the frontier town of Bouillon and finding neither Rimbaud nor Delahaye there. Verlaine made another appointment, for May 24 at the same place, and this time Rimbaud was there, Delahaye too. For once Verlaine took charge of the future; he had already told Lepelletier that he proposed to go from Bouillon to Liège and Liège to Antwerp where he would take ship for "Leun'-deun," and that is what he and Rimbaud did. After a fifteen-hour sea trip of "unforgettable beauty" they arrived in London on the morning of the 27th and found new lodgings at 8 Great College Street, Camden Town, "a gay district" Verlaine told Blémont "which remind one of Brussels."

A month later, on June 21 and again four days afterwards,

Verlaine was still writing optimistically to the same correspondent and to Lepelletier. Camden Town remained "gay" with Vermersch in Kentish Town near by and with fine country for walking at Hampstead: "I go there often when I don't go to the Reading Room of the British Museum." And "I am a *tutor.*" After advertising in several papers he had found a pupil for lessons in French at three shillings a lesson; he was negotiating for a post as French master in a school; he and Rimbaud were learning English rapidly by the help of evening conversations with Englishmen: "every evening, or nearly," Verlaine explained, "I have 'tea parties' in which I force myself at a *slow* pace to understand the subtleties of spoken English." They were enjoying themselves too; at the Alhambra was *Faust,* at the Princess Theater Desclée and his French company, at the St. James' the Alcazar company of Brussels in Offenbach, Hervé, Lecocq. "I go there almost every evening when I haven't a lesson," said Verlaine. He and Rimbaud had seen the Shah of Persia make his state ride through London; a fat Charles de Sivry, Verlaine wrote as complete explanation. More: "My drama is finished—in my head. My novel likewise. My next book of verse also." In brief: "I have refound my health and courage."

As before, Verlaine alone reported progress. Rimbaud was mute. And to a point, on the surface, all was as Verlaine said: He and Rimbaud were reading, walking, theater-going vigorously, picking up English and even a little money and seeing much of Vermersch, Andrieu and the communard band in London. They were generally busy and enjoying life. Yet within two weeks of Verlaine's last letter they had separated.

The break was sudden only because for their first month they were protected willy-nilly from each other by the presence of Verlaine's mother. Madame Verlaine had followed her son to London, perhaps to settle him in comfort, probably to try to make the new venture appear respectable in the eyes of Monsieur Mauté, certainly to warn Verlaine that he must spend less (he had gone through thirty thousand francs since first meeting

Rimbaud, she estimated) and try to earn something; it was she who provided the money for the advertisements as for everything else.

On June 25 she left for Paris and the precarious harmony between Rimbaud and her son began to collapse. Rimbaud was nursing a guilty conscience. He had come to London against his better judgment and in defiance of his somber mood, and no amount of gaiety, drink, talk, reading or work could change that judgment or soften the mood. He was seeing *Faust*, reading *Faust*, his writing was Faustian, his thoughts too. He too had sold his soul. But he had none of Faust's compensations; he had not acquired knowledge or power; he had not even dealt with the devil, a little flirtation excepted. His devil, he was coming to think, was nothing more dignified than the despised Verlaine; for this sensual buffoon he had imperiled and perhaps lost his dignity and honesty if not his immortal soul. And when Verlaine showed that he had the measure of his friend intellectually or, worse, when he laughed at him, Rimbaud could not endure the insult of such an attitude from such a man. But the worst of his crimes was that he had money. Why had Rimbaud agreed to return to London? To the ferociously clear-minded boy the answer was inescapable: for Verlaine's money.

A sad Faust indeed! Rimbaud did not spare himself; the savage mood of Roche persisted. He did not spare Verlaine either: he was Faust, no doubt, but he could ape the devil too: "Pitiful brother!" he was writing in *Illuminations* "what atrocious nights I owed to him! 'I wasn't taking our enterprise seriously. I made fun of his weakness. We should go back into exile, slavery, and it would be my fault' . . . I replied by laughing at this Satanic doctor and . . . would lie down on my mattress to sleep. And almost every night as soon as he slept the poor brother would get up, mouth putrid, eyes starting from his head—as he had dreamed!—and drag me into the room howling his dream of idiotic grief."

This was from the life. But if Verlaine had nightmare after

nightmare it was not without cause. His friend's "aberrations" had been turned against him from time to time ever since the affair of the knife at the "Rat Mort" but were as nothing to the attacks which began almost as soon as Madame Verlaine had turned her back. Rimbaud knew, none better, how to hurt a physical coward who was also a fond man with an uneasy conscience; his attacks ranged from verbal scourging—Verlaine's weaknesses, moral, physical and spiritual being pitilessly exposed—to bodily "ragging"; he would pounce on him from dark corners, threaten to commit unmentionable assaults. He also renewed his tactics practiced at the Charleville cafés, telling horror stories and making blood-curdling prophecies.

He watched the struggles of his friend with sardonic satisfaction; he suffered, so why should not the man whom in this mood he named his evil genius; and, ever the artist, why should he not write these comical flounderings into his work? As he did, putting the hapless Verlaine into *Une Saison en Enfer* as well as into *Illuminations;* and the man he was pin-pointing innocently drew a sketch of him, bowler-hatted, pipe smoking, in a public house with the scribbled caption: "Rimbaud writing *Saison en Enfer.*"

There seems little doubt that the savage analysis of Verlaine in *La Vierge Folle et L'Epoux Infernal* must have been in Rimbaud's mind at Roche. He had told Delahaye that three of his "stories" were written there and that six remained to be done. The one on Verlaine was the first of the six. No wonder that he had hesitated to rejoin Verlaine; no wonder that, having given way, his conscience rebelled and he turned against the man who had persuaded him. For this new section of *Une Saison en Enfer* was diabolically clever, true in essence but with sufficient exaggeration to give the necessary bite; it revealed a quite horrifying comprehension of his companion's mind: the irreconcilable pictures of a fiend Rimbaud, a Rimbaud not of this world, a pathetic child Rimbaud, a matchless and rather alarming prodigy Rimbaud; the spasmodic regrets for lost friends and lost innocence, the fear of damnation, fear of earthly tor-

ment, the infirmity of purpose and the efforts to escape responsibility—all is there. It is brilliantly done and without
mercy.

Matters came quickly to a crisis. When Rimbaud adopted his
satanic tactics Verlaine immediately felt tenderly towards
Mathilde and wondered why he had ever left her. Thoughts
of a reconciliation and a renewal of home life, thoughts never
far from his mind, returned. He threatened to leave the boy.
Rimbaud ignored the threats; he could not believe that Verlaine would ever leave him; how could the weak leave the
strong?

Possibly Verlaine could not believe it either—he was the
kind of man who speaks in anger and almost immediately
regrets—yet by the first days of July he was gone; gone, it
seems, because of a remark thrown at him as he returned laden
from the shops: "What an old c . . . you look with that herring!"
The remark was not out of the ordinary, but served that particular day as the final straw. Both lost their tempers, Verlaine
walked out of the house and boarded the next ship for Antwerp.
He was followed by Rimbaud who reached the docks just as the
ship cast off. The ship sailed away leaving Rimbaud on the dockside beckoning frantically to Verlaine on deck shaking his head—
the second time within the year that he had shaken a head more
fatefully than he knew.

This was July 3. Rimbaud returned to the lodgings, a little
boy once more. He collapsed as he had collapsed in Mazas
prison, during his stay in Paris, and when faced by the bill
at the Charleville bookshop. The next day he pulled himself together sufficiently to write an hysterical letter:

"Come back, come back, dear friend, only friend come back.
I swear to you that I'll be good. If I was unpleasant to you it
was only a joke I obstinately persisted in; I'm more sorry than
I can say. Come back and all will be forgotten. What a pity you
took the joke to heart. I haven't stopped crying for two days.
Come back. Be brave, dear friend. Nothing is lost. You have only
to make the journey again. We will live here again bravely,

patiently. Ah, I beg you. It's for your own good too. Come back, you'll find all your things here. I hope you've realized by this time that our argument was meaningless. Frightful moment! But when I signaled you to leave the ship, why didn't you come? Fancy living together for two years only to end up like this! What are you going to do? If you don't want to come back here, do you want me to join you? Yes, I was in the wrong.

"Oh say you won't forget me.

"No, you can't forget me.

"As for me, I think of you always.

"Speak, reply to your friend, aren't we to live together any more?

"Be brave. Reply to me quickly.

"I can't stay here much longer.

"Listen only to your heart.

"Quick, tell me if I'm to join you.

"Yours for life."

The facts did not warrant the panic. Verlaine had left no money but had abandoned all his books, papers and clothes, some of which Rimbaud turned into cash. The communard group were within reach—Rimbaud had already seen Vermersch —and were good for a loan if he had behaved tolerably well with them. In any event Verlaine had written at once from Brussels asking one of the group to look after him.

The turning of the worm was no bad thing and might have taught the boy a lesson. Unhappily, Verlaine, incapable of more than momentary unkindness, had already repented in a letter written on board ship and couched in such terms as to surrender all the initiative he had seized.

"I want to tell you" he said, "that you must *at heart* understand *at last* that it was absolutely necessary for me to leave, that this life of violence and *scenes* with no better excuse than your whim couldn't go on any longer. As I have loved you tremendously (*honni soit qui mal y pense!*) I also want you to know that if I'm not reconciled in full amity with my wife in three days I shall blow out my brains! My last thought, my friend, will be for you, for you who were calling to me from the pier recently and whom I didn't want to rejoin *because it was necessary for me to make an end of myself*—AT LAST! Will you accept my dying embrace?"

The heroics brought Rimbaud up sharp. He shed no more tears. He wrote again, in character:

"You are in the wrong this time, very wrong. To begin with, there's nothing positive in your letter. Your wife won't come or will come in three months, three years, how do I know? As for dying, I know you! Whilst waiting for your wife and your death you'll be flinging yourself all over the place boring everyone. What? you have not yet understood that our anger was as false on one side as on the other! But it's you who are wrong in the end because when I called you back you persisted in your false feelings. Do you think your life would be pleasanter with others than with me? *Think!* Ah! absolutely not! You can only be free with me, and as I've sworn to be very kind in future, as I'm sorry for all the wrong I've done, as I've at last got my mind clear and as I love you very much, if you don't want to come back or for me to rejoin you you are committing a *crime for which you'll suffer* MANY LONG YEARS *by the loss of all freedom and by miseries more atrocious* perhaps than those you've already endured. After all, remember what you were before you knew me!

"As for me, I'm not going back to my mother. I shall go to Paris. I shall try to leave on Monday evening. You have forced me to sell all your clothes, I couldn't do anything else. They aren't sold yet; they are not going to be taken away until Monday morning. If you want to write me in Paris address to L. Forain, 189 rue Saint-Jacques. He will know my address.

"Certainly if your wife comes back I shan't compromise you by writing—I shall never write.

"The only true word is: come back. I want to be with you, I love you. If you pay attention to that you will show courage and a sincere mind.

"Otherwise I pity you.

"But I love you, I embrace you and we shall see each other again."

This letter came on Verlaine at an unfortunate moment; he had regretted his suicide announcement almost as soon as made; a spate of telegrams to his wife and friends had brought only the arrival of his mother and a letter from Madame Rimbaud. He hoped, no doubt, that she would order her son to Brussels. This she did not do; but she gave him excellent advice, understanding that he was wretched and remembering her own wretchedness. Her letter was kind, direct, wise; it would have shown the perceptive Verlaine in a less emotional moment why her son was always talking about her.

"By the time you receive this I hope that your mind will have grown calm and reflective. Kill yourself, wretched man! To kill oneself when one is overwhelmed by unhappiness is an act of *cowardice;* to kill oneself when one has a tender, godly mother who would give her life for you and who would die of your death, and when one is the father of a little creature who holds out its arms to you today, who will smile at you tomorrow and who will one day need your support, your advice—to commit suicide in such conditions is an *infamy:* the world despises a man who dies thus, and God Himself cannot pardon him so great a crime and casts him from His breast.

"Monsieur, I don't know why you have fallen out with Arthur, but I have always seen that the relationship could not end happily. You will ask me why. Because whatever is not authorized and approved by good and respectable parents cannot turn out happily for the children. You young people, you laugh and jeer at everything, but that does not alter the fact that we have the experience, and every time you don't follow our advice you will be unhappy.

"I don't flatter you, you see: I never flatter those whom I like.

"You complain of your unhappy life, poor child! How do you know what the morrow will bring? Hope, then! What do you think earthly happiness is? You are too sensible to think that happiness consists in the success of a plan, the satisfaction of an impulse or a whim. No, a person who saw all his wishes granted, all his desires satisfied would certainly not be happy for the

moment the heart holds no more aspirations it could not have
any more feelings and so no more happiness. The heart must
beat, and beat at the thought of good—of some good which one
has done or which one intends to do.

"I, too, have been most wretched. I have suffered much,
wept much, and I have been able to turn all my afflictions to my
advantage. God has given me a strong heart, filled with courage
and energy. I have struggled against all adversities; then I reflected, I looked round about me, and I became convinced, quite
convinced, that each of us has at heart a wound more or less
deep. To me my wound appeared much deeper than those of
others. It's only natural; I felt my own hurt and couldn't feel
the hurt of others. Then I said to myself—and I see every day
that I am right—: true happiness consists in fulfilling all duties
however painful they may be!

"Do as I do, dear Monsieur: be strong and courageous in the
face of every affliction; drive from your heart all bad thoughts.
Struggle, struggle without ceasing against what is called the injustice of fate, and you will see that unhappiness will stop pursuing you and you will become happy again. One must work
hard and give one's life an aim. You will no doubt still have
many bad moments, but however wicked men may be, never lose
hope of God. He alone can console and heal, believe me.

"Madame, your mother, would give me great pleasure by
writing to me. I greet you and will not say goodbye; I very much
hope to see you again some day."

The advice to Verlaine to forget his resolution at once under
pain of eternal damnation was much to his liking. As he told
the friend in London whom he asked to look after Rimbaud:
"My wife refusing to come after my threat to kill myself, I am
waiting until midday tomorrow but SHE WON'T COME and I'm
beginning to find it too c . . . ish to kill myself like that, and
prefer—for truly I am dreadfully unhappy—to join the volunteers
for the Spanish republicans. Tomorrow I shall go to the Spanish
ambassador here and I count on leaving very soon after that."

This sounded tolerably definite, but to Verlaine, drinking hard to keep up some sort of courage, it was merely a delaying action. Then came Rimbaud's letter and all his plans dropped away; he wrote at once to his landlady in Camden Town: he was coming back and he enclosed a week's rent. He did not move, however, because he had given Mathilde until the next day and he still hoped against hope that she would arrive.

The next day was a Sunday. Verlaine was perhaps too fuddled to have thought of this; in any event, the Spanish Embassy being closed that day and no steamer sailing from Antwerp, he decided to give Mathilde the benefit of the doubt—four days instead of three.

His letter to the landlady arrived in London on the Monday morning. She showed it to Rimbaud who at once replied: "I have seen the letter you sent to Mrs. Smith." He wrote, then crossed out, "Unhappily it's too late." He then went on: "You want to come back to London! You don't know how everyone would receive you! And the looks Andrieu and the rest would give me if they see me with you again! All the same I'll be very brave. Tell me your idea honestly. Do you want to come back to London for me? And on what day? Did my letter make up your mind? But there is nothing in the room any more. Everything is sold except an overcoat. I got two pounds ten. But the sheets are still at the laundry and I have kept a heap of things for myself: five waistcoats, all the shirts, some pants, collars, gloves and all the boots. All your books and manuscripts are safe. In short, the only things not sold are your black and grey trousers, an overcoat and waistcoat, the bag and hat box.

"But why don't you write to me?

"Yes my dear chap I'm going to stay another week. And you'll come back? Tell me the truth. You would show a sign of courage. I hope that it's true. You can be sure of me, I shall behave very well.

"Yours. I wait for you."

Had this letter reached Verlaine early the next morning, or had he held his hand for another day, Rimbaud's future might have been greatly changed. As it was Verlaine, after drinking his way undecidedly through the Monday, telegraphed a few minutes after the post offices opened the following morning: "Volunteering Spain. Come here, Hôtel Liègeois. Laundry, manuscripts if possible."

That same day after he had discovered that the Spanish would not accept foreign volunteers, he wrote a letter to Mrs. Smith (whether he posted it is uncertain) saying that he was going to Paris, giving an address there and asking for his things to be sent on to him.

Rimbaud, in amenable mood, not having recovered completely from the shock of Verlaine's departure, left for Brussels immediately; the mention of volunteering for the Carlists must have come as an exciting surprise, though whether he could seriously imagine Verlaine as a soldier is another matter. He arrived that evening.

He found Verlaine in a state of hysteria; Mathilde had not answered his telegram, the Carlists did not want him, his friends in London would apparently make a mock of him if he returned there. He was left with the alternative of staying in Brussels or going to Paris and for a great part of the evening dithered between them: he wanted to go to Paris to see Mathilde but was afraid of arrest as a communard, afraid also that if he went with Rimbaud his chance of a rapprochement with his wife would be gone forever.

Rimbaud had made up his mind to go to Paris. The sight of Verlaine chaotically undecided had revived all his contempt. He wanted to go to Paris and demanded money to get there.

They argued in the cafés that evening and in the connecting hotel bedrooms that night with Madame Verlaine as a bewildered witness. They argued all the next day in hotel and café. Stalemate: Rimbaud was adamant, Verlaine vacillating but obstinate. On Thursday morning Verlaine went out alone to the café. He sat there drinking, trying to cloud a mind become intolerably clear. This was another Namur; Rimbaud was determined to leave him. But it was worse than Namur; Rimbaud was not simply declining to follow him to a sleepy Belgian hamlet, he was saying in so many words that he had done with him. No love in those blue eyes, no affection even, nothing but a bored contempt. Life in a European capital could tempt him no longer. He was interested in money for one thing only, to get away from the man who gave it. For him the affair was over; he had made a mistake, and when Rimbaud acknowledged a mistake he threw the cause of it to the devil. In the last resort he had only one criterion, the standards of his mother. In the past year he had departed from these standards again and again, and for nothing; he had not won fame, earned a penny. And the author of this wasted year still tippled, procrastinated, supplicated.

It was no quarrel this time but finis. Verlaine had never in his life been able to endure a withdrawal of affection, whether by death or design; now, desperate, he drank, to dull his brain and give him courage. He returned to the hotel an hour or two later, drunk. There was more talk, and as the warmhearted always do, he floundered deeper with every word he spoke. Neither would give way, Verlaine begging Rimbaud to stay in Brussels, Rimbaud, demanding the fare to Paris.

At last Rimbaud walked disgustedly out of the room into the street. Verlaine went after him and brought him back, locked the door, and put a chair against it, sat down, drew a revolver from his pocket and aimed it at Rimbaud, demanding that he stay if he did not want all three of them shot.

Rimbaud, leaning against the wall, ignored the threat contemptuously. He repeated his demand for money. Verlaine fired and hit him in the wrist.

When he saw what he had done Verlaine, immediately sober, threw himself on to his mother's bed, handed the revolver to Rimbaud and begged him to put him out of his misery.

Rimbaud told him not to be a fool. When Verlaine had quieted down, his mother pointed out that Rimbaud's wound ought to be properly dressed. All three walked to the nearest hospital where the wound was dressed, then came back to the hotel.

Another discussion began. Verlaine still appealed to Rimbaud to stay in Brussels, Madame Verlaine advised him to wait with

them at least until the bullet could be extracted. Rimbaud refused; he would go that evening, he declared; not now to Paris
but to Roche. He demanded the fare.

Eventually, Madame Verlaine, seeing that the boy's mind
could not be moved, gave him twenty francs to buy a ticket
home. In the early evening the three of them walked out again,
this time to go to the railway station.

As they walked Verlaine continued to beg Rimbaud to stay
with them in Brussels. Rimbaud refused curtly.

Before they reached the station Verlaine put a hand in his
pocket, stepped ahead of the other two, turned to face them
and told Rimbaud that he would not allow him to go further.

Rimbaud afterwards declared that Verlaine threatened to
shoot him, Verlaine said that he threatened to shoot himself.
Whatever the truth, Rimbaud took no chances. He turned, ran,
and demanded protection from the first policeman he met.

The policeman took all three to the nearest police station,
statements were taken from them, Verlaine was locked up for
the night and the others warned not to leave the city. Rimbaud,
a little feverish, went back to the hospital and was put to bed.

During the next week Verlaine in the Petits-Carmes prison
and Rimbaud at the Saint-Jean Hospital were interrogated more
than once. In a long deposition Rimbaud said that Verlaine had
asked him in the previous year to leave Paris with him; that
their quarrels in London concerned Verlaine's laziness and his
unfriendliness towards the communard group; and in his account
of Verlaine's hesitations about returning to Paris he did not mention that his friend wished to go alone.

These statements, all of which blackened the case against
Verlaine, may have been the result of fever; at that time the
bullet had been lodged in his left wrist for three days. They may
have been caused by resentment; he had received a severe shock
and may have thought that Verlaine should pay for it by a few
days in prison. But the trend of the questions put to him after
he had made his statement perhaps stuck in his mind. The police
inspector asked if he knew the cause of the differences between

Verlaine and his wife. He replied that Verlaine did not wish his wife to continue to live in her father's house.

"Doesn't she also say that your intimacy with Verlaine is one of her complaints?"

"Yes," Rimbaud replied, "she accuses us of having an immoral relationship, but I won't give myself the trouble of denying such calumnies."

This contemptuous dismissal of Mathilde's accusation was, from Rimbaud, a remark worth attending to, but the inspector, with something much more important in his mind than a mere case of assault, saw the boy only as a junior partner in indecency. Rimbaud, hearing from Madame Verlaine that Verlaine had been examined by police doctors, began to realize that he had involved his friend in difficulties, and, worse, that he himself might become involved. The dread that had driven the distraught Verlaine to fire the revolver was well founded: disgust with the "pitiable brother" was a familiar emotion which Rimbaud could balance by practical profits; conflict with authority, and on such shameful grounds, was unacceptable either to the *bourgeois malgré le poète* or to the frightened boy. At this moment Madame Rimbaud's son made his first motion towards echoing her scandalized distrust of French literature; he washed his hands of Verlaine.

Four days later the bullet was extracted. The next day Rimbaud made another statement of an altogether different tone from the first.

"I persist in the declarations which I have already made to you that before shooting me Verlaine had tried in every kind of way to keep me with him. It is true that at one moment he showed an intention of going to Paris to try to become reconciled to his wife and that he wanted to prevent me from accompanying him; but he changed his mind every moment and did not keep to any one plan. Therefore I cannot discover a genuine motive for his attack on me. Moreover, his mind was completely deranged; he had drunk in the morning as it was his custom to do when he let himself go, and was in a state of insobriety."

The cool reception of this statement was such that Rimbaud,

now seriously worried, visited the police station the next morning and insisted on making an act of renunciation. He had left the hospital, the doctor having said that his wound would be healed completely in three or four days, and was on his way home.

The new statement said:

"I the undersigned Arthur Rimbaud, nineteen years of age, man of letters, living usually at Charleville (Ardennes, France) declare, to do homage to the truth, that on Thursday the 10th of the present month, about two o'clock, at the moment when Monsieur Paul Verlaine, in his mother's room, fired a revolver shot at me which wounded me slightly in the left wrist, Monsieur Verlaine was in such a state of drunkenness that he had no knowledge of what he was doing;

"That I am absolutely certain that in buying this revolver Monsieur Verlaine had no hostile intentions against me and that there was no criminal premeditation in his act of locking the door on us;

"That the cause of Monsieur Verlaine's drunkenness was simply the thought of his differences with his wife, Madame Verlaine;

"I declare, moreover, that I willingly offer him and consent to my renunciation pure and simple from all action, criminal, correctional and civil, and I withdraw from today from the benefits of all proceedings which would or may be intended by the Public Prosecutor against Monsieur Verlaine for the act he has done."

Having signed this statement, Rimbaud took the first train to Roche.

CHAPTER ELEVEN

End of a Poet
1873–1875

HE arrived at Roche on July 20, the day after leaving Brussels. We are told that he found the family eating lunch in the kitchen, that he entered, arm in sling, face pale, manner distrait, sat down, burst into tears and with a despairing cry of "Verlaine! Verlaine!" buried his head in his arms on the table and sobbed aloud. We are also told that in succeeding days and weeks he hid himself in the granary with his writing and that Madame Rimbaud, listening at the door, heard moans, sobs, cries of rage, oaths, blasphemies, jeers from within.

These recollections of the twelve-year-old Isabelle, passed on to her husband twenty-four years later, are not supported by Vitalie who was actually keeping a journal then. Vitalie says only that when the rest of the family harvested, "my brother Arthur did not take any part in our agricultural work; for him the pen provided work so serious that it did not permit him to take part in manual labor."

That Rimbaud's arm was in a sling, that he looked tired and unhappy and spent most of his time in the granary completing *Une Saison en Enfer* are the only certainties. If he had shown wretchedness in the dramatic forms described by Isabelle, her sister would have said so. But Vitalie's journal, which is a frank little document, is a record of happiness; everything pleases her that summer; she says what she sees, and the implications of her words are plain: for Madame Rimbaud to permit one of her children to sit writing when a harvest was being gathered in is yet another sign that this particular child stood apart in her mind. No listening at the granary door was needed to show her that this son was troubled; Verlaine's suicide message was not

165

then three weeks old, and the arm in a sling, adequately explained or not, told its tale.

So he wrote *Une Saison en Enfer* undisturbed; and when, some time in August, he finished it, he showed it to her. She read it and asked him what it meant. He answered: "It means what it says, literally and in every sense." It is easier to say what this remarkable work is not than what it is. It is not a farewell to literature; Rimbaud was to disprove that within the next few months. It is neither an affirmation of atheism nor a return to catholicism. It is not a confession written in humility. It is a cri de cœur.

Isolation emphasized the tone of what he wrote. Before that April he had always had the run of Charleville, the sense of movement, talk in the cafés, busy shops. At Roche he was alone with his thoughts. In July he faced the same isolation and uglier thoughts; he had left for London against his better judgment and returned shocked, self-sick, cynical. He was indeed in hell, the hell reserved for the clear-sighted. He looked back over the years of search, few in number but a lifetime to him, and saw one mistake after another, one lowering of principle after another. He had long since abandoned hope of purposefully deranging the senses, yet, weakly submitting to Verlaine and the communard group, had continued to drink like any stupid sot. He could find no comfort anywhere. He had nothing to show for his wasted years. One return home followed another, penniless, inglorious. Again and again he had to play the prodigal son, he who longed to play the conquering hero. The accommodating mood of his mother aggravated his humiliating position. He had failed himself and failed her. His superb mental equipment remained, his confidence in himself even if the confidence was shored up by desperation. He renounced Rimbaud the seer, renounced him in a splendid flourish of language. He greeted with savage irony the new Rimbaud: "Peasant!" He even forecast his future. Baudelaire and Leconte de Lisle, to mention only two of the poets he had studied for years, both wrote with sensuous longing of the simple life in the French outpost of Réunion; Leconte de Lisle and Gautier evoked highly-colored images of the ancient sources of culture, Greece and the Near East, India and China. And to these influences was added the feeling that western civilization was played out and that a return to the primitive was essential to progressive inspiration—the belief which was to encourage Gauguin, a few years later, to leave his thankless struggle in France.

But for the moment he was concerned with his own degeneration, and after he had put the finishing touches to his pitiless picture of Verlaine, he turned an eye inward:

"Now me. The story of one of my follies.

"For a long time I boasted that I was master of every imaginable landscape and found laughable the celebrities of modern painting and poetry . . .

"I invented the color of the vowels—*A* black, *E* white, *I* red, *O* blue, *U* green—I settled the form and movement of every consonant, I prided myself on inventing a poetic speech with intuitive rhythms which would one day be within reach of all the senses. I reserved the translation rights.

"At first it was an investigation. I wrote of silences, I wrote of nights. I wrote down the inexpressible. I arrested vertigoes. . . .

"Outworn poetic ideas played a large part in my alchemy of the word.

"I accustomed myself to elementary hallucination; in place of a factory I readily saw a mosque, a school of drums beaten by angels, barouches on the heavenly ways, a drawing room at the bottom of a lake; monsters, mysteries; a vaudeville title would set up terrors in front of me.

"Then I would explain my magic sophisms with the hallucination of words!

"I ended by considering the disorder of my mind as sacred. I was idle, the prey of a sluggish fever. I envied the happiness of beasts—caterpillars who represent the innocence of second childhood, moles the slumber of virginity!

"My temper soured. In specific kinds of songs I said farewell to the world . . .

"I became a fabulous opera; I saw that all beings have a fatality of happiness; action is not life but a mode of dissipating strength, a nervous irritation. Morality is the weakness of the brain.

"It seemed to me that several *other* lives were owing to every being. . . .

"My health was threatened. Terror came. I would fall into sleep for days, and rising would continue the saddest of dreams. I was ready for death and my weakness led me along a road of perils to the ends of the world and Cimmeria, home of darkness and whirlwinds.

"I had to travel to distract the spells gathered in my brain. On the sea which I loved as if it were about to wash away impurity, I saw the comforting cross arise. I had been damned by the rainbow . . .

"Ah! that life of my infancy, the high road in all weathers, supernaturally sober, more disinterested than the best of beggars, proud of having neither country nor friends, what stupidity that was. And I only realize it now! . . .

"Having recovered a ha'porth of sense—it soon goes!—I see that my discomforts come from not having understood soon enough that we are in the Occident. Occidental swamps! . . .

"Yet I was scarcely thinking of the pleasure of escaping modern sufferings. I had not in mind the bastard wisdom of the Koran. But is there not real torment in that, ever since that proclamation of science, Christianity, man *humbugs himself,* proves the obvious, puffs himself up with the pleasure of reiterating these proofs, and can only live that way! Subtle, inane torture; source of all my spiritual digressions. . . .

"It is not because we cultivate fog? We eat fever with our watery vegetables. And drunkenness! and tobacco! and ignorance! and self-sacrifice! Is not all this far from the thought, the wisdom of the Orient, the primeval fatherland? Why a modern world if such prisons are invented!

"Churchmen will say: That's understood. But you mean Eden.

There's nothing for you in the history of Oriental peoples. That is true; it is of Eden I was dreaming. . . .

"Had I not *once* an attractive boyhood, heroic, fabulous, to be written on sheets of gold, too much good fortune! By what crime, what fault have I deserved my present weakness? You who assert that beasts sob from grief, that the sick despair, that the dead have bad dreams, try to recount my fall and my slumber. As for me, I am no more able to explain myself than the beggar with his everlasting *Pater* and *Ave Maria, I no longer know how to speak!* . . .

"I created all fêtes, all triumphs, all dramas. I tried to invent new flowers, new heavenly bodies, new flesh, new languages. I believed it possible to acquire supernatural powers. Well! I must bury my imagination and my memories! . . .

"I! I who called myself seer or angel, exempt from all morality, I come back to the soil with a duty to seek and rugged reality to embrace! Peasant! . . .

"Let us welcome all the flowing in of vigor and real tenderness. And, at dawn, armed with an ardent patience, we shall enter magnificent cities . . . and it will be permissible for me *to possess truth in one soul and one body.*"

These are fine words coming to a magnificent conclusion. Imprecise words also; what he had abandoned or is about to abandon is patent enough, what he intends to take on is less clear. "No more words!" he says; and *"I no longer know how to speak!"* These for the moment were poetic licenses; the writer wrote and planned on. But "Peasant!" was true enough. And with peasant practicality backing the writer's ambition he tried to get *Une Saison en Enfer* printed as soon as he had finished it. "My fate depends on this book," he had told Delahaye a few months earlier.

This he managed to convey to his mother—a measure of his influence with her—for Madame Rimbaud paid for the printing, paid too for her son to travel to Brussels to find a printer and settle terms.

The printing was done that autumn, five hundred copies, and Rimbaud received his six free author's copies at Roche. He sent off three: to Delahaye, to Millot, to Verlaine in the Petits-Carmes under sentence of two years' imprisonment. The other three he took with him to Paris, to give one to Richepin, one to Forain and with the last to try to interest a publisher.

In November he was seen by another poet sitting alone at the "Tabourey" where he had once been listened to with attention. He had failed to find a publisher. The merit of a work was not, in the Paris of that time, the only or even the chief requisite for publication as Verlaine was to discover when he came out of prison even though he was regarded as the injured party, a weak man led astray by a satanic youth. The satanic youth therefore had no chance; he had a bad reputation before he left Paris with Verlaine in the summer of the previous year; by the time he returned all the literary cafés knew that Mathilde had just been awarded a separation from Verlaine and that one of the grounds was the immoral relationship of Rimbaud and her husband. This was enough to damn any man, let alone a boy who had gone out of his way to show his scorn of contemporary poets and their work. Rimbaud saw something of Forain and Richepin; for the rest, he was ignored; no publisher would consider his work, none of the poets would speak to him.

He returned, unsuccessful once more, to Charleville, where the two girls had entered a convent school. Delahaye, then working in the Hôtel de Ville, said that Rimbaud took to walking about the town in the top hat of his London days; he had grown tall and the choir-boy face had begun to lose its chubbiness; he remained extraordinarily goodlooking.

The top hat was a pathetic gesture. He spent a wretched winter; he had had to confess to his mother that his Paris journey had served no purpose and Madame Rimbaud refused to throw good money after bad. The printer in Brussels, left with a bad debt, stowed the five hundred copies of Une Saison en Enfer in his basement. They were discovered there by accident twenty-eight years later.

But Rimbaud was not prepared to let his first book die the death in a printer's basement. He believed that *Une Saison en Enfer*, once published, would make his name and prove in the only terms understood by Madame Rimbaud that he was an important poet. He would not give up without a struggle.

His earnestness won the day. Early in the new year of 1874 he returned to Paris. Again his mother provided the money, again he failed to get a publisher, again he is found sitting alone at the "Tabourey" with a group of hostile poets at the far end of the room, and again he is seen and spoken to by a young poet.

On the first occasion, in late autumn, a young poet had walked up to him and offered him a drink. Rimbaud did not answer and he went away. The second occasion, in March, was more productive. A young man, who had been sitting with the group of poets, got up, shook hands all round, then walked not to the door as expected but over to the solitary figure slumped in his chair, a rather clumsy figure, he thought, with brick-red face, wavy fair hair, piercing blue eyes and large hands and feet.

The young man was short, stocky and wore his black hair almost to the collar; his large auburn eyes were shielded by long and silky black lashes and from the midst of a brownish face protruded an impressive nose with a slight Arabic curve. It was a figure that shouted Midi. Germain Nouveau came from the hill town of Pourrières rising out of the plain of Aix-en-Provence. He had taken his baccalauréat at Aix, dabbled in poetry and painting and, encouraged by Richepin, traveled up to Paris to try his luck as soon as he came into a small inheritance on his twenty-first birthday. That was a few months before the meeting in the "Tabourey." In those months Nouveau had scattered his legacy throughout the cafés and brothels of the Latin Quarter. He had been taken up by Cros and his group but had been too much occupied by spending to do more than dabble ineffectually in verse and make one or two indifferent paintings. He was well thought of, not so much for his work as for a scatterbrain unexpectedness in his reactions to life: "His charm," said Delahaye, "consisted of a nonchalant stubbornness and a quaint vivacity, the one chasing the other and dominating in turn; the conflict could be seen clearly in the eyes . . . at one moment dark with a sultry melancholy, soon afterwards shining with a caressing gaiety." He gave the impression of "making up his mind as he went along, and showed a perpetual tendency to search for the unusual aspect of things; at first because of a natural fear of error, then and dominantly because he felt that new ideas were likely to be more amusing than old ones. He soon discovered that a little bittersweet helped in this work of intellectual subversion."

This was Nouveau, a simple contrary creature. When his companions in the "Tabourey" shunned Rimbaud, he was immediately interested. So over he walked with a jaunty step and resolutely placed himself in front of the solitary whom he accosted with the battery of southern charm fully charged, thick lips open in an ingratiating smile, eyes glowing, head and shoulders whimsically rocking from side to side, lightly bearded brown face inclined at a slight angle, one short arm thrust out in an appealing gesture, the hand half open, having the air "of showing some rare jewel or of emphasizing the end of some precious and learned strophe he had just been reciting." And in a soft, rather nervous voice and with an accent veering comically between the south of his birth and the parisian he had picked up in the last few months, he declared that he had read Rimbaud's poetry, that he admired it and that it had inspired his own work.

He spoke of the poetry but looked at the poet. For Rimbaud could not even slump in a chair ordinarily; he was as distinctive as creative people always are—and as hopeful. He allowed himself to be bludgeoned into accepting a drink; who could say what might come of it? His instinct was to postpone for as long as possible yet another confession of money spent with nothing to show for it. They sat themselves before glasses of beer. After the second, Rimbaud moved the discussion from poetry to travel. He was, he explained, just about to leave for London—an idea which may well have come to him since Nouveau's arrival. He spoke at some length of England: it was the greatest of the civilized countries, its people had a more liberal outlook and were more intelligent than elsewhere, and life there, organized with a logic and vigor superior to any other country, offered a greater variety of satisfactions to the foreigner.

This homily by a young man of nineteen who had visited only one other country apart from England was immediately decisive. Rimbaud possessed "a prodigious skill in finding the convincing detail without apparent effort." So Delahaye; but conviction rested not so much in what Rimbaud said as the way he said it. As soon as he paused, Nouveau, who had certainly never thought twice in his life of England or the English, jettisoned his natural spirit of opposition without a backward glance and cried: "When are you going?"

"Tomorrow," said Rimbaud.

"We go together!" announced Nouveau enthusiastically.

Rimbaud, possibly slightly startled by the speed of his new disciple's conversion, possibly caught by a twinge of conscience, said, "That won't inconvenience me at all, but I ought to warn you that we might have rather a hard time."

Nouveau dismissed the warning with a toss of the dark head, a squaring of the already square shoulders and a defiant gesture of the arms. "We'll get a job."

The compact was sealed on the spot and Nouveau became (though Rimbaud was surely speaking lightly for once in his life) a "son of the Sun." As it was then evening and they were due to leave early the next morning it is possible that they went direct from café to station; legend has it, not improbably, that the impetuous Nouveau carried off, forgotten in excitement, the key of his lodgings and left his belongings to the landlady; Rimbaud always traveled light.

2

The two surviving sons of the Sun are next found working in a cardboard box factory in the land of promise; they were paid by the day and the cost of every bungled box was deducted

from what was at the best of times barely a living wage; and as
Nouveau at least was not deft with his hands the profits were
pitifully small. They shared a room in Stamford Street near
Waterloo Station, not the most salubrious of quarters, and it
may safely be assumed that they did so on the remnant of Nouveau's legacy; it is impossible to imagine the penniless Rimbaud
enduring Nouveau for long on any other terms.

As they were doing piece work in their Holborn factory they
were free to leave at any time for the British Museum, a ten-
minute walk. For by the beginning of April both had readers'
tickets on which they threw an extra Christian name or two
for good measure, this being a penchant of Nouveau. They went
to the Museum less for the purpose of intellectual improvement
than of studying the daily papers for vacant jobs. The flood of
Frenchmen into London after the fall of the Commune had
caused a glut of those wishing to teach French, as Rimbaud and
Verlaine had discovered earlier. Nor were scholastic agencies,
at which both registered, better able to help. They could, however, and did try to speak the language, by reading in the
Museum, airing English of a sort in the cafés, shops and pubs,
and by exchanging lessons with their landlady's son. Nouveau,
because he knew nothing, was dependent on Rimbaud who, he
told Richepin, "though knowing enough for our common needs,
wants to perfect himself."

Rimbaud's reactions to this new spell in London are lost with
the disappearance of letters to his family, but Nouveau was
voluble enough for two. Soon after their arrival he wrote to
Richepin from the Café de l'Etoile in Leicester Square and
confessed that his first impression of London had been one of
"physical and moral suffocation: light eclipsed, smell of musk
and coal in the streets, expressionless heads of Englishmen, great
bustle without sound of a voice."

This was a reasonable first view from someone plunged into
the Waterloo area eighty or more years ago, but even in that
early moment Nouveau had one pleasure—"Charming, the cabs!"
—and as Rimbaud painstakingly and unsentimentally took him

over the ground already trodden by himself and Verlaine, the theaters, galleries, riverside, the southerner began to melt. They heard *Mlle Angot* at the Pavilion, and the Minstrels who pleased Nouveau as they had pleased Verlaine. And Nouveau, standing before the Turners, echoed Verlaine with his "empty . . . not up to much" and excelled with his "Tell Forain to come here— ye Gods, would he sell some pictures!" Rimbaud's knowledge of the shops at which they could buy food cheaply also impressed his companion: "magnificently good bargains."

For they were soon hard up. The factory work did not last long, no teaching job appeared, theaters and drinks cost money. Their movements after the beginning of April are lost in the kind of mystery which seems to afflict Rimbaud and those who accompanied him. Rumor speaks of both at last finding posts in schools, but the next time Nouveau is traced with certainty he is in Brussels in the spring of the following year, earning a living of a sort by writing love lyrics to a Belgian actress on behalf of a wealthy Russian. His ways and Rimbaud's were not to run together, but Nouveau at least never forgot his London companion.

Rimbaud comes back into the picture much earlier, at the beginning of July, and with a kind of drama, for on July 6 his mother and Vitalie arrived in London. To prise Madame Rimbaud from Charleville or Roche, let alone from France, was a feat that only her second son could have accomplished, and even with him a crisis of some magnitude must have arisen to make her part with two return fares to London. He is said to have fallen ill and sent for her, but as he met her and his sister at Charing Cross and showed them round London in the next week or two, and as Vitalie, whose journal is the sole source for the events of this time, says nothing about his health, the likelihood is that he ran out of money and panicked as he had panicked before. And somehow he persuaded Madame Rimbaud that with her help he could get himself profitably established in England.

He showed a revealing consideration of what was due to his family; no mean room in Stamford Street for them but a large

double room in the clean and respectable Argyle Square. Vitalie
was impressed by the room, but it was understood that Arthur,
in London at least, was particular. Madame Rimbaud had
brought her best dress with her, a grey silk one with a chantilly
cape, but did not wear it for a week or more; until, in fact, her
son said "that when we went out with him it was necessary for
us to appear well dressed to bear witness to his respectability."
A notable remark, as notable as the fact that he had been careful
not to take up with Andrieu, Vermersch and company since returning to London.

    Madame Rimbaud and Vitalie came for two weeks and stayed
three. It was not a happy time for any of them despite the strong
family feeling. They made many excursions under Arthur's
proud guidance: to the House of Parliament, Leicester Square
and the Alhambra, the Thames, the City, Saint Paul's, the parks,
the British Museum (where Rimbaud showed his sister in great
detail the remains of Theodore, Emperor of Abyssinia) the Albert
Memorial, the underground railway, the Tower, the docks, the
picture galleries. Mother and daughter were duly impressed,
touched too by Arthur's solicitude, but the excitement of sight-
seeing merely gave a temporary gloss to a difficult period. The
heat was killing, the delicate Vitalie felt unwell most of the time,
was homesick and missed her confidante Isabelle, left behind in
the convent; she and her mother, unable to speak a word of
English, had to spend most days in their airless room, Arthur
usually going off to the British Museum until six o'clock in the
evening. Much more serious, mother and brother were plainly
worried. Through the whole of Vitalie's journal runs the blighting
effect of suspense: her brother was advertising for a post and
replying to advertisements, he had offers but mysteriously refused them; he became irritable, her mother puzzled and stern,
and she unhappy as always when the family unity was threatened.
The morning post tried them all. After five days Vitalie announced joyously that "a letter has come in which three different
places are offered him." But her joy was premature: "Nothing
for Arthur, no news"; this was the theme after ten days, with a

significant "Mama is so sad, so unapproachable." Another week and it became: "We and Arthur are much troubled and perplexed. The places he has had! If he had wanted he could have been settled and we could have gone. If he had wished we could have gone today."

This was Vitalie, who could not reconcile herself to the English: "What coldness, what stiffness!" But that same day she continues later with a "After all, could I really have felt great pleasure in leaving after having been a witness to Arthur's grief and entreaties?" For Madame Rimbaud had put her foot down— their two weeks had passed, money was being poured out like water and nothing had been settled—and her son, not for the first or the last time, collapsed. Not in vain; as Vitalie adds: "Mama has said: another week."

Six days pass: "This morning, about nine o'clock, I was putting my things in order when Arthur, gloomy and excitable, said suddenly that he was going out and would not be coming back at midday. But at ten o'clock he came back and told us that he would be leaving tomorrow. What news!"

Vitalie and her mother do some hurried shopping, for themselves and Isabelle, and collect a little wardrobe for Arthur. But on the morrow he did not leave, his shirts not having come back from the laundry. There was more shopping.

The next day, July 31, he left at half past four in the morning. "He was sad." Vitalie and her mother went back to France that afternoon, but Vitalie could not feel the joy she had been anticipating those last three weeks: "I think of Arthur, of his sadness; of Mama, who weeps, who writes . . ."

Madame Rimbaud wept as she wrote to the son she had just seen off. She wept because he reminded her of other, earlier farewells to his father whom he resembled so much. This perhaps; yet she was not a woman who wept easily; she could not avoid intimations that the brilliance of this favored son would come to nothing. How could she dream that he had already done his life's work? She had watched the enthusiasms flare and fade, she had waited in vain for the success in Paris, she had paid for *Une*

Saison en Enfer to be printed and found that the copies never even left the printer; she had read it, understood nothing and understood all, that it was the work of an unhappy and undecided boy. And had he made up his mind now? He sought a post at school, talked of mastering languages so that he could travel; to what end she was unable to grasp and he to convey. She was a peasant and shrewd: was it anything more, this talk of his, this life he had led for the past four years, than the restlessness of his father? But she had loved his father. "My poor Arthur"—this was to be her epitaph for her son, and on that summer morning in London a premonition of the future moved her.

3 ⟞

Rimbaud was supposed to have gone off to his job the day before, so he caught the earliest possible train and, like any peasant, left the house in absurdly good time. Where he took the train to is another matter. Delahaye says that he went to a school in Scotland, and as he was to see much of Rimbaud that winter he may be right. But by November he was in Reading, giving French lessons in the house of a M. Camille le Clair who had private pupils and held classes in that language. And from there he sent an advertisement to *The Times* which appeared twice, on the 7th and 9th. It read:

> A PARISIAN (20) of high literary and linguistic attainments, excellent conversation, will be glad to ACCOMPANY A GENTLEMAN (artists preferred) or a family wishing to travel in southern or eastern countries. Good references. A. R. 165, Kings Road, Reading.

The wish to leave Europe had been forecast in *Une Saison en Enfer;* this was his first attempt to carry it out; he was beginning to feel enough confidence in his command of English to take advantage of the habits of those inveterate travelers. But his "artists preferred" was a mistake. There were no answers, or none to the purpose. And as he did not wish or was not asked to remain at Reading, Christmas found him at home again and making no move to return. He had seen England for the last time.

The check in England did not weaken his determination to leave France, France which had not acclaimed him. So he looked naturally to the nearest country, Germany. He would soon have looked no further than the French army had not Frédéric, then doing his military service, saved him from it. Rimbaud, whose brushes with the police in Paris and Brussels had fixed in his mind a lifelong fear of authority, could never persuade himself that he was exempted; he realized only that the law which allowed a widow or wife living apart from her husband the benefit of one son at home—to support her—allowed him for the moment to pursue his course with the aid of his mother's money. He arranged to stay en pension with a family in Stuttgart so that he could improve his German, and by January was living just outside the town in the house of a Dr. Wagner and giving French lessons to the children. These lessons provided him with pocket money, Madame Rimbaud, refusing to do more than pay for his keep, provided him also with another grouse, and he remained discontented and unhappy.

He was distracted from the insistent question—what he should do and where—and from the equally familiar frustration of gifts running to waste, by a brief but exhilarating encounter with Verlaine. Much had happened to the Vierge Folle in the eighteen months since he had last seen his Epoux Infernal. The period with Rimbaud followed by the shock of the parting and the rigors of prison had turned him into a great poet; during the early part of his eighteen months of solitary confinement, first in Brussels then at Mons, he had written poems of which the pre-Rimbaud young Verlaine-about-town was incapable. Then came the news that Mathilde had been awarded a legal separation; a collapse; and a revival as reborn Catholic which, as it was sustained, astonished everyone in the prison where conversions were familiar but ephemeral. He began to write religious poetry.

He saw nothing of Rimbaud and heard only the few scraps of news that his mother and Lepelletier—his two visitors—were able to give him. By them he sent copies of his recent poems to Roche and Charleville; without effect, for Rimbaud used the religious poems as lavatory paper.

Happily ignorant of this gesture, Verlaine emerged radiant from prison in January, 1875, about the same time as Rimbaud went to Stuttgart; released six months early because of impeccable behavior. He made tentative advances to his wife and was rejected out of hand; rebounded into a Trappist monastery from which he retired hastily at the end of a week, having discovered the limitations of asceticism; then, panting for converts, turned his attention to Rimbaud. Not knowing his whereabouts he sent a letter to Delahaye and begged him to forward it. The letter was earnest and pious and ended with the exhortation "Let us love one another in Jesus!"

Apart from an astringent reference to "that muck heap," Rimbaud had never spoken about Verlaine since leaving Brussels eighteen months earlier. If he thought the two-year sentence was savage he said nothing. If he wrote to Verlaine the letters have not been kept nor did Verlaine mention them. He did not try to visit his old companion in prison. All the signs are that he determined to dismiss Verlaine from his mind and succeeded.

Now Verlaine, as affectionate as ever, had set his heart on redeeming the friend he had led astray: that was his simple argument. Rimbaud did not reply to him, but made play with the whimsies of "Loyola" in what Delahaye, the intermediary, described as "a page of sneers." Verlaine had assured him in the letter that the return to the faith had been neither facile nor hurried: "I have meditated on the subject these last six months." On which Rimbaud commented: "Some meditation!"

Delahaye, realizing that if Rimbaud had ever had any wish to take up the friendship again, Verlaine's religiosity had successfully extinguished it, tried to fob off the eager proselytizer. Each rebuff merely inflamed Verlaine's ardor. Finally, Delahaye asked Rimbaud if he might give Verlaine his address.

To his surprise Rimbaud, bored with his Dr. Wagner and the heavy Germans and scenting fun, replied, "It's all the same to me. Yes, if you want to, give 'Loyola' my address."

Three days later Verlaine was in Stuttgart, and Rimbaud was telling Delahaye with sarcastic pleasure: "Verlaine arrived here the other day with a rosary between his paws . . . Three hours later he had denied his God and had made the ninety-eight wounds of our Savior bleed afresh."

To unmask the hypocrite: that was, naturally, Rimbaud's first impulse; he could not conceive that his friend's conversion might have been genuine, and thought he had proved his point when, after a series of arguments aided by plenty of liquor, he knocked down the by then drunken evangelist and left him lying insensible on a bank of the Neckar.

He was all geniality when Verlaine, succored by peasants, reappeared shamefaced and bearing no malice; and this meeting of the two poets—their last—was sober and friendly. Though his reception of Verlaine had been in the less pleasant vein of old times, Rimbaud had changed; in appearance he was, said Verlaine, "very correct" and he was working hard "prying into libraries in the full flush of the *philomath* as he called it." For his part Rimbaud spoke kindly of Verlaine: "He stayed two and a half days, was extremely reasonable and on my advice has gone back to Paris after which he will finish his studies *là-bas dans l'île*."

So after visiting Paris Verlaine returned to England (Rimbaud was quoting Banville on Hugo in the days of the exile in Jersey) to improve his English as Rimbaud had done. He did not return empty-handed. "At Stuttgart," he said, with the touch of mystery he loved, "the manuscript of *Illuminations* was handed to someone to take care of." The mystery was not profound since Verlaine was Rimbaud's only visitor at Stuttgart; and a month or two later he explained to Delahaye from the snug teaching post he had found in Lincolnshire: "This is why I asked you for particulars of Nouveau. Rimbaud having begged me to send his 'prose poems' to this Nouveau, then in Brussels, to be printed (this was two months ago) I sent them (postage 2 fr. 75!) immediately and naturally accompanied them with a polite letter to which he replied no less politely."

4 ~~~~

This was Rimbaud's last effort to get himself into print. He may have hoped that Verlaine could do something with these poems in Paris and thought of Nouveau as a second string. In any event neither Verlaine nor Nouveau managed to get them printed; the poems had to wait eleven years before they were published in Paris prefaced by a Verlaine since become famous.

The story of *Illuminations* has been told many times. It is enough to say here that, most of the forty-two poems being undated, no one can prove when they were written. It is probable that Rimbaud began them in Paris in 1872 and wrote the last in England two years later.

Nor is that the end of the *Illuminations* mystery, a mystery very much in the Rimbaud manner. For not only is there no agreement as to the dates of the poems or their order, there is no certainty as to their meaning; there have been innumerable guesses and the guesses are likely to continue as long as Rimbaud interests the literary critics.

It is easier to say what he was trying to do than to guess what he meant, if he meant anything more than the registering of passing moods. In *Illuminations* he was trying to demonstrate what he had long since talked of, in his "seer" letter to Demeny, as "the new forms that inventions of the unknown demand"; what he actually did was to make words, juxtaposed in a certain fashion, illumine one "lantern-slide" picture after another in the mind of the reader. But he did not intend to stop there; he wished to make the word all-sufficient, and the picture presented by his words at once seen, heard and smelled.

A droite l'aube d'été éveille les feuilles et les vapeurs et les bruits de ce coin du parc, et les talus de gauche tiennent dans

leur ombre violette les mille rapides ornières de la route
humide. Défilé de féeries. En effet: des chars chargés d'ani-
maux de bois doré, de mâts et de toiles bariolées, au grand
galop de vingt chevaux de cirque tachetés, et les enfants et les
hommes sur leurs bêtes les plus étonnantes;—vingt véhicules,
bossés, pavoisés et fleuris comme des carrosses anciens ou de
contes, pleins d'enfants attifés pour une pastorale suburbaine;—
même des cercueils sous leur dais de nuit dressant les panaches
d'ébène, filant au trot des grandes juments bleues et noires.

On the right, the summer dawn rouses the leaves and the mists
and the sounds of this part of the park, and the slopes on the
left hold in their purple shadow the thousand swift ruts of the
wet road. A procession of fairy scenes. Yes indeed: wagons
loaded with gilt wooden animals, poles, and many-colored
canvas, with the full gallop of twenty dappled circus horses,
and the children and men on their most extraordinary beasts
—twenty vehicles, embossed, beflagged and beflowered like
carriages from old times or out of stories, filled with children
dressed up for a suburban pastoral—even some coffins under
their black canopies raising ebony plumes, disappearing with
the trot of the big blue and black mares.

He succeeded well enough to influence modern poetry pro-
foundly, though it may be doubted whether any of his followers
in after years was able to carry the process further. Rimbaud
certainly thought that he had reached the end. With a return
of the hard common sense inherited from his mother and with
his customary intellectual honesty he realized that he was merely
being clever like any other gifted boy fascinated by words. Very
clever, he being what he was, but clever nevertheless. And he
was no longer interested in intellectual games.

But he was not content simply to abandon the prose poem,
and for this there was another and more important reason.
All his life he had put his faith in the power of the imagination.
He had begun, as so many children do, by using the imagination to escape from the limited intellectual atmosphere at home.

As he moved into his teens, however, he discovered that he had not merely to escape from the imaginative limitations of his mother but from the whole world of Charleville. Even Izambard, even Demeny, Delahaye, Bretagne, Deverrière—his intellectual companions of those years—revealed themselves in his idealistic view as fundamentally down to earth; they not merely came to terms with ordinary life, they enjoyed it. Paris taught the same lesson. Finally, his chosen companion, Verlaine, made no secret of his immense pleasure in all sensual excursions; he drank because he enjoyed drinking, not because drinking might waft him to another and purer world of thought and feeling; his voracious appetite for food and women followed the same earthy course; his poetry, fine though it might be, was no more than a synthesis of the pleasures of the senses and emotions common to all.

To Rimbaud the world had been a place to escape from; the only realities were to be found in the imagination. Yet by trying to live the life of the imagination he found himself involved in the shocking fracas at Brussels and discovered that there were no cash compensations. Poet he might be, but he was innately conventional and demanded tangible rewards; the imaginative life had alarmed the first without providing the second—no publisher would take *Une Saison en Enfer*, no publisher would take *Illuminations*. This last rebuff was decisive.

The poet had fought a long fight against odds. Ever since his fifteenth year he had dreamed his dreams, written his poems in the teeth of his mother's disapproval. The battle between poet and son was unequal and the poet had to die. Imagination dismissed, the realist took control without difficulty. His verbal experiments now appeared to him not only unprofitable but childish. "Je hais maintenant les élans mystiques et les bizarreries de style." He possessed an excellent memory and could take a hint. It was four years since Izambard, faced by "Le Cœur Supplicié," had written, "Take care that you don't end in a bottle yourself, a museum monstrosity." Rimbaud's answer, when he made it, was prompt. Ruthless with others, he was now ruthless with himself. He stopped writing.

CHAPTER TWELVE

Winged Feet

1875–1880

RIMBAUD was an impatient young man as well as a purposeful one. This and a wish to see the world were to obscure the purpose so thoroughly during the next five years as to give him the appearance and reputation of one who did not know his own mind. Yet he had never in his life acted without design and he did not do so then; there was no uncertainty in what he wanted to do, only in how to do it; there he was at a loss, inexperience, haste and vanity all leading him astray. But behind every seemingly hare-brained adventure was the wish to return home famous and wealthy. Fate, envy, bad luck—call it what he pleased—had ordained that Madame Rimbaud was not to be swept off her feet by a very god of literature, was not even to be impressed by handsome profits from her son's books. Some other way had to be found. "Se peut-il," he had asked himself not long before, "qu'elle me fasse pardonner les ambitions continuellement écrasées—qu'une fin aisée répare les âges d'indigence—qu'un jour de succès nous endorme sur la honte de notre inhabileté fatale?" He was strong, healthy, clever; the world, filled with fools, was wide open to him; he had only to find "le lieu et la formule" and success would fall into his lap.

He could not wait. "Moi, pressé . . ." The urgency is sensed in the letter to Delahaye in which he announced Verlaine's coming and going, a letter distinguished by the drawing of a large figure down the left side of the page spitting, in German, from a weird mouth "May Wagner be forever damned!" He says: "I only have another week of Wagner and I regret this money paid grudgingly and all this rotten time for nothing. By the 15th I shall have found a cosy little place no matter where, and I shall whip up the language frantically so that I shall have done in two months at the most."

As with every other stopping place except the snatches of Douai and his room in rue Monsieur-le-Prince, he expressed discontent; he could find only a solitary item to praise: "Everything is inferior here. I except one thing: Riessling" and he draws a pile of wine bottles with a "Riessling, Fligende Blatter."

Ten days later he is telling "My dear family"—the first letter home to be preserved: "I didn't want to write before having a new address. Today I received your last 50 francs . . . I have a very large room, extremely well furnished, in the center of the town, for ten florins, that is to say 21 francs 50, service included, and I am offered board for 60 francs a month. Anyway I don't need it, these little combinations always concealing some trickery or tying one down however economical they appear. I shall try, then, to make do until April 15 with what I have left (50 francs) because I shall again need advances by that date: for either I shall have to stay another month to get myself properly ready or I shall have to advertise for jobs, the following up of which (the journey, for example) will call for money.

"I hope that you find this rational and reasonable. I try to steep myself in the ways of this place by every means possible, I try to teach myself; though one really has to suffer from their manner. I salute the army, I hope that Vitalie and Isabelle are well; I beg you to let me know if anyone wants anything from here, and am your devoted A. Rimbaud."

He writes affectionately, and discusses money in his mother's manner. To a point this was politic, but the manner fits him like a glove; it heralds the re-aligned Rimbaud, the "Peasant!" of his poem.

The key to the letter, however, is the bracketed "the journey"; for soon after throwing off this apparently casual remark he began a series of escapades which made his former life seem positively stable. The "man of letters" of the Brussels police court statement turned into Verlaine's "man with winged feet." A few weeks after he had written this calm and cautious letter

Stuttgart suddenly became unbearable and, selling his trunk for ready cash, he walked out of the town and headed south. A Dr. Wagner in the suburbs was, after all, he discovered, only a symptom of a general malaise from which no large room in the center of the town could protect him; he did not like Stuttgart, he did not like the Germans. And there was no sign that he would make money there.

Besides, he had a plan; to reach the island of Paros, where a man he had met for a moment had a profitable soap factory, and to pick up Italian and Greek on the way. The journey through southern Germany and Switzerland exhausted him— his money running out, he was forced to walk over the Alps— and by the time he came down into Milan he was ill. He is said to have been sheltered and cared for by a Milanese woman. If he was in fact befriended by her, she is of no moment in his history since he never saw her again and never mentioned her; all he did, apparently, was to try to reclaim the copy of *Une Saison en Enfer* given to Delahaye so that he could present it to her. More interesting is the evidence of Rimbaud the respectable in the shape of a printed card sent to Delahaye bearing his Milan address.

But it was the wanderer and not the white-collared Rimbaud who walked south from Milan as soon as he felt strong enough; walked into a sun so strong and unfamiliar that before he reached his goal of Brindisi, from which he hoped to take ship for Paros, he went down with sunstroke, was taken to hospital and when discharged, being penniless, was repatriated by the French consul at Leghorn.

At Marseilles where he was put ashore he did odd jobs. Then, as so often with Rimbaud, the accounts of his movements diverge. The most familiar story is that he met a Carlist agent in a bar, enlisted in the Carlist army and, with the handsome bonus in his pocket, hurried back to Charleville. Isabelle claims that this was a tall story he told his Charleville familiars and that in fact he joined his family in Paris that summer and took a temporary post in a suburban school.

Isabelle's account is suspect for several reasons: her mother, with two homes of her own, would not pay for three months' living in Paris without a very good reason—which her daughter does not provide; Vitalie was very ill; no schools are open in France until the middle of September, and by the end of that month or the beginning of October Rimbaud was home again.

He broke his journey in Paris. He was in savage mood. Nouveau, meeting him there, was disconcerted; Cabaner and Forain complained of his "intemperate speech and behavior." The "intemperate" is understandable: he was in the city of wealth and fame which had consistently refused him a chance of either, and he was en route for a provincial town to confess that his first effort to make money outside literature had failed.

He returned to a new home, an apartment in rue Saint-Barthélemy, and to a sorrowful one, for Vitalie was dying. His major plan for the winter was to learn more languages, but his impatient mind roamed over many possibilities; he thought of going through the Ecole Polytechnique with a view to taking up engineering and asked Delahaye, then in his first term as schoolmaster at Rethel midway between Charleville and Roche, how he could obtain a science "bachot." Nothing came of this, for Rimbaud had not the patience for a long course of instruction. Also, having become twenty-one on October 20, he was haunted by the delusion that he might soon be called up for the army. "Military instruction and 'Bachot,'" he wrote to Delahaye, uneasily assuming the devil-may-care air expected by this particular hero-worshipper "would give me two or three pleasant seasons!"

He began to learn Arabic and modern Greek. He also learned to play the piano. The fantastic story of Rimbaud, refused a piano by his mother, cutting dummy keys in the dining-room table, illustrates the credulity of his listeners at the cafés and his own persistence in publicly blackguarding his mother. He was using her, as always, as scapegoat for his own deficiencies; self-dissatisfaction was pushed on to shoulders which could bear it.

She, who knew nothing of the café talk, saw what all the world saw, that only unpractical ambitions and a distaste for the obvious prevented her clever son from taking well-paid work in Charleville. She no doubt told him so if he ever complained openly of being kept short of pocket money. The farcical collapse of the Paros plan solidified the doubts which had made her weep in London the previous year. Yet for all her threats and restrictions she could not command enough ruthlessness to act on them; indeed, she actually indulged him by hiring a piano and paying for a teacher.

As his prose poems show, his mind was turning towards the East. He had first heard talk of it at the Paris cafés: the poets busily writing hymns to the glory of the mysterious East and even speaking vaguely of reinvigorating their muse at this ancient source, the painters excited by the rediscovery of Eastern art and planning a return to their beginnings, as they chose to call it. The impressionable boy heard and remembered. But in the long run, down to earth as his elders were not, his longing for the East took a turn that would have disconcerted them; the romance still appealed but the opportunities stepped into first place. He was tolerably well read in history and drew his own conclusions. The primitive countries not only offered the artist a return to nature, they offered the adventurer a quick cash dividend. So he stayed at Charleville through the winter, preparing for a fresh sortie by learning eastern languages. To give himself pocket money, he taught German to the son of the proprietor of the house, and to fill in spare hours he practiced the pianoforte.

He had plenty of spare hours. He had never been one to drudge at a task. Once he had found relief at the Charleville cafés. Now all was changing. He had raised the wind too often at the expense of his old school companions. He considered that, as in the old days, he offered good value for money: who else in that benighted town had traveled half across Europe on next to nothing before his twenty-first birthday? But his sponging aroused some hard feelings, for he could not hide all his con-

tempt. The stay-at-homes began to treat him coolly, and
Delahaye wrote gloomily to Verlaine of Rimbaud's moral disintegration and predicted that the brilliant youth would end
his days in Charenton.

To Verlaine, because the Verlaine-Rimbaud comedy had
come to life again. Each in his way wanted something of the
other. Rimbaud reopened relations as he had reopened relations with Izambard and for a similar reason. Verlaine's visit
to Stuttgart had put ideas into his head. Thirty thousand francs
in one year, spent mostly on Arthur Rimbaud! And the fond
man was fond still, fond and at a safe distance. Emotional
storms were ruled out but money could be sent by post, and
in April, before leaving Stuttgart, Rimbaud demanded some, to
pay for piano lessons he said.

His letters have disappeared. Verlaine declared to Delahaye
—given the confidences of both sides—that Rimbaud had
threatened, if he did not pay up, to enlighten his employer in
England about the prison record, separation from his wife and
all the rest of the unrespectabilities of the sober French master
in the Lincolnshire school. "First he replied with impertinences
garnished with vague threats of blackmail, then with ridiculous
calculations by which he demonstrates that it would be good
business for me to lend him the money. Not to mention a letter
written in a kind of drunken gibberish amidst which I made out
the statement that future letters would include the demand that
I "fork out" or else—*zut!* In a word he is still banking on my old
foolishness, on my wicked stupidity not so long past of wanting
to live only through him and by him. Add the intolerable rudeness of a child whom I spoilt and who repays me—the logic,
the justice of it!—with criminal ingratitude. Hasn't he in fact
killed the goose who laid the golden eggs?"

He replied, concealing his address, with earnest recommendations of the good life and a right application of talents, and
"I explained in detail my arithmetical reasons for not sending
him money."

An irregular correspondence continued into autumn and

winter via Delahaye, neither of the two principals knowing the address of the other and all three enjoying themselves. In the middle of October Rimbaud is telling Delahaye "Received Verlaine's postcard and letter a week ago . . . I won't comment on these latest vulgarities of Loyola, and I've no more time to give to this business at present since it seems that the 2nd 'portion' of the 'contingent' of 'class 74' will be called up on November 3." Nevertheless, after a "Such pre-occupations absorb me," he cannot resist, "However please send on, when you can, any interesting 'Loyolas.' "

All this and more, with Delahaye's comments and advice, was passed on to Verlaine who, with time on his hands, gave good measure in reply, sending further "Loyolas" to Rimbaud and instructions and requests to Delahaye. He illustrated the power of the Rimbaud fascination to the final degree; although he had learned some wisdom and was not free from pique, eighteen months of prison could extinguish neither affection nor curiosity. "Send news of Homais," he was demanding in November, the apothecary of *Madame Bovary* who knew a little of everything being one of his many nicknames for Rimbaud. But he was wary of getting into the toils again: "You can tell him that his letters addressed to rue de Lyon aren't sent on to me (but by my instructions are read and kept by a devoted friend of mine). As for the *poste restante* in London, it is useless to encumber that institution with letters which are never called for. The day he becomes serious, he knows the way (you) to send me something sincere."

Warnings notwithstanding, he missed the boy; Lincolnshire might be safe, respectable and good for a damaged self-esteem, but stimulating it was not. So:

Malgré moi je reviens, et mon lett' s'y resigne,
A cet homm . . . ais qui fut si philomathe, hélas!

In spite of myself I come back, and my letter is resigned to this
    fact
To this man (Homais) who was so philomathic, alas!

is followed by fond mimicry of Rimbaud replying to a Delahaye suggestion that he shall begin his studies: "And who is the creature more stupid than a dog and more boring than a wild beast who advises the Ecole Polytechnique? (this is most unjust, most unjust, and I become bitter, etc.)"

Against all the evidence he clung to his romantic picture of the bohemian Rimbaud: "Where is HE staying? I imagine some angelic mother or father awakened every night by returns on all fours, spewing (I know that!) and other anti-bourgeois exploits. And the mother, the *daromphe*, what does she say of all this? Is it still my fault? Does she still live at 5 bis quai de la Madelomphe? Because I seem to remember (you too perhaps) that it will be necessary some day, perhaps in a year, perhaps later (I don't know yet) for me to communicate with this Mother of the Gracchi on the subject of my separation case!"

He accepted reluctantly the picture of a young man who despised literature, sneered at religion and mulcted his friends; Rimbaud, he thought, was confusing insolence with strength and deceit with cleverness and was behaving, if Delahaye heard aright, like a cad who might turn into a nasty piece of work. He preferred to believe in the brilliant promise of yesterday, and, if he could see a change of heart, friendship and good feelings were "Christianly available, that goes without saying."

The "Christianly" was scarcely the way to win Rimbaud back; Verlaine had not yet thrown off the convert's irritating exhibition of piety, but he plunged on and towards the end of the year made a final appeal:

"Despite my promise (if I remember rightly), I haven't written to you earlier because I was waiting for a satisfactory letter from you. Nothing received, nothing answered. Today, however, I break my long silence to confirm all that I wrote you some two months ago.

"I remain the same always. Strictly religious because this is the only good and intelligent thing to be. Everything else is trickery, wickedness, stupidity. The Church has made modern civilization, science, literature: she has made France particularly, and France is dying because she has broken with her. That's clear enough. And the Church makes men too, *creates* them. I'm astonished you don't see this, it's so strikingly obvious. I had plenty of time during those eighteen months to think again and again on these things and I assure you that I cling to it as my only plank. And seven months spent among Protestants has confirmed me in my catholicism, my legitimism, my resigned courage.

"Resigned for the good reason that I see and feel myself as justly punished, justly humiliated, and know that the severer the lesson the greater the pardon and the obligation to respond to it.

"How can you think that this is a pose or a pretext? Why write such things as (I can't remember the exact words) 'modifications of the same sensitive individual,' 'rubbish,' 'tommyrot'—all bunkum and a nonsensical hotch-potch . . . ?

"So I'm always the same. The same affection (modified) for you. I greatly wish I could see you enlightened, reflective. It's a great grief to me to see you following such idiotic paths, you so intelligent, so *ready* (however much this may surprise you!). As proof I point to your own disgust with everything and everybody, your perpetual anger against all things—reasonable enough at bottom, this anger, though you don't know *why*.

"As for this matter of money, you can't really fail to recognize that I am *generosity itself*: this is one of my very rare virtues —or one of my very many faults, as you please. But, this granted, and the need to repair, by little economies, the enormous breaches made in my tiny capital by *our* absurd and shameful life three years ago—and bearing my son in mind also, and also my new and firm principles, you must understand perfectly well that I can't support you. In any case, where would my money go? On drinks and pub owners! Piano lessons? What *humbug!* Hang it all, wouldn't your mother agree to pay for them?

"In April you wrote me letters so revelatory of your base and wicked plans that I can't risk giving you my address—although any attempts to harm me would be ridiculous and powerless from the outset, and besides I warn you that they would be answered *legally*, with evidence. But I pass over this odious hypothesis. It's some fugitive *caprice* of yours I'm sure, some unhappy brainstorm which a little reflection will drive away. However, prudence is the mother of safety, so I won't give you my address until I'm certain of you . . .

"Come, confound it, show a decent impulse, a little heart, some consideration and feeling for one who remains always, as you know, your very cordial P. V.

"P.S. I'll explain my plans—very simple!—and the counsels I should like to see you follow, religion apart, though this would be my great, great, great counsel, when you have replied *properly* via Delahaye."

This letter reached Rimbaud a day or two before the death of Vitalie on December 18. He was in no mood to reply to it through Christmas and New Year, and when that unhappy time had passed he still had nothing to say. The "blackmail" threat —a joke very much to his taste—had evidently given Verlaine some uneasy moments, but had not managed to frighten money out of him. The remark "Wouldn't your mother pay?" showed that he could no longer be fooled.

The affair was finished, comedy, drama and all, so the realist closed the books. He did not reply. Less than ten years later Verlaine was to "make" Rimbaud as poet, beginning a process which continued with a fervor into the next century; but as far as Rimbaud was concerned he was more than ten years too late.

2 ⟨⟨⟨⟨

1876

The next that is heard of him is on May 18 at the colonial recruiting station of Harderwijk on the Zuyder Zee, where he offered himself as a recruit in the Dutch East Indies Army.

The next day, after his papers had been examined and he had passed a medical examination (his height was 5 ft. 10 in.) he signed a six-year engagement. He was paid a bounty of 300 florins less ten, the official deduction to cover the cost of damages by recruits while they spent their money. On June 10, wearing his blue and grey uniform with its orange-bordered képi, he sailed from Den Holder in the Prins van Oranje with a detachment of 216 men.

This apparently sudden decision was explained later by Isabelle: her brother, she said, met in London a man from the Dutch East Indies army who persuaded him to join and traveled east with him. The last part of this account is certainly untrue; the Prins van Oranje did not carry any man who had been in London at the same time as Rimbaud. But he wanted to go East and this was perhaps the only way of getting there short of paying the fare or working a passage.

The ship passed through the Red Sea, Rimbaud's first sight of that sweltering area which was to become familiar to him, and disembarked the troops at Batavia, capital of Java, on July 22. After a week in barracks Rimbaud, posted to the first infantry battalion, embarked on another ship. He was put off at Samarang three days later with a number of men destined for various inland military centers. From there he and fourteen other recruits took the train to the terminus of Taungtang and marched the ten miles to their headquarters at the barracks of Salatiga. They arrived on August 2 and Rimbaud was allocated to the fourth company of his battalion.

Thirteen days later he did not answer the roll call. He had deserted.

If he needed examples of desertion he had had them in plenty on the voyage out; the day after they left Holland a French recruit dropped himself overboard; off Port Said seven Italians followed suit; in the Red Sea a German did likewise; all but one got away. But unlike these early deserters Rimbaud wanted the free trip as well as the bonus. Yet having reached the longed-for East he had second thoughts. Salatiga was an insalubrious spot, unromantic and offering no chance of making money; dangerous too; on the day after their arrival one of his companions, a young man from Tours, died of fever.

This death was perhaps decisive. For the moment, Rimbaud, shocked, abandoned the goal he had taken so much trouble to reach. At Samarang, thirty-five miles from Salatiga, a British ship called in for a cargo of sugar on August 17, two days after he had deserted. The comings and goings of ships at Samarang, the men's one life line with Europe, was common knowledge in barracks. He gave himself ample time to reach the port on foot and managed to get a passage.

The ship, bound for Marseilles, made several trade calls on the way and, her captain falling mortally ill, put into Aden for some days to arrange for his funeral and for a successor. Had Rimbaud wanted to try his luck in another hot country he could have done so without difficulty; he could, for instance, have left the ship at Aden which he was to know only too well in the future. But after the shocks and disillusionment of Java he could think only of his usual refuge. Marseilles was familiar to him; there he could earn the fare home. As he did. The ship docked at Marseilles on October 19; some two months later Rimbaud walked into his mother's apartment in Charleville.

3 ⟨⟩

1877

The first three months of the new year were spent in the same way as the early months of the previous year, in studying languages. He studied languages, which is in another world from learning them; and in these winter months of 1877 he was most interested in Russian, though it is said that he had only a Russo-Greek dictionary to work with. He had not forgotten the offer from St. Petersburg which Izambard refused. Now he would go to Russia and do what Izambard had failed to do. And he persuaded his mother, by heaven knows what arguments—or perhaps merely by the expression of his eyes and the sound of his voice—to send him off in April well provisioned.

This new venture ended quickly and in disaster. He got no further than Vienna. There he was robbed of his money and all his clothes except those he stood up in, robbed by the driver of the cab he had hired.

The victim was not yet the man of the world he liked to affect; the scornful mouth could not disguise his still youthful appearance and ingenuous expression. The aftereffects made this clear, for, his morale once again collapsing, he was bundled out of Austria, through Germany and deposited on the French frontier at Montmédy, fifty miles from Charleville.

He walked home to a reception which could scarcely have been enthusiastic. His friends were amused, not sorry to see the mighty brought low, and Delahaye made a caricature of a dandified Rimbaud in Vienna bemoaning his loss in terms made familiar by Verlaine, the long complaint including the inevitable "c'est trop injuste!." His mother was not amused. That was one reason why he set out again almost immediately, the alternative being a summer of farm work at Roche.

He went for the second time into Holland but only en route to Hamburg where he hoped to pick up a ship sailing south or east. He did not succeed. He is said, on the one hand, to have acted as interpreter in a circus which eventually made a summer tour through Scandinavia, and on the other hand (Isabelle) to have found work in a sawmill in Sweden. He could have done both. By September he was home again. He is generally supposed to have been repatriated by the French consul at Stockholm but there is no record of it if he gave his real name. It may be that he paid for a passage from his own earnings.

He was soon off again and traveled down to Marseilles with the intention of taking ship to Alexandria. At Marseilles he did odd jobs about the port, to earn his fare east or keep himself whilst waiting for a ship which would employ him. Eventually he found a ship, only to fall ill soon after it had sailed. He was put ashore at Civita Vecchia, the port of Rome, and taken to his second Italian hospital. He had contracted gastric fever caused by inflammation of the stomach due, the doctor said, to too much walking. When fit to travel, being without money, he was repatriated. He was home once more before the end of the year.

4 ⁓

1878–1879

"Courage and patience": these were Madame Rimbaud's watchwords through the vale of tears that was her world. She had to draw heavily on both by the time Arthur returned yet again jobless, penniless, futureless. Since his last visit to Roche —the unhappy time of *Une Saison en Enfer* five years earlier— her son had traveled in Holland, Germany, Austria, England, Italy, Scandinavia and Java, many thousands of miles, without apparent reward beyond some knowledge of foreign languages. His confident promises of good jobs and quick money had all proved hollow. How long? demanded the sorely-tried woman who had paid one railway fare after another; and dug in her heels. This time her son did not escape a summer of farm work; he could not risk long walks after his enfeebling illness and he could not raise the fare. So he stayed where he was, but not happily; a caricature "Sunday in the Village" savagely satirizes the absence of privacy, the absurdities and ugliness of life in the country. And life in the home was little better. The religious Isabelle, then eighteen, was still subdued by the loss of her sister; his mother's habit of bemoaning her lot did not make for liveliness and her authoritarian attitude to a dependent galled his pride as much as her coolness to a costly "failure" wounded his feelings.

He tried to escape. He went once more to Hamburg but once again failed to get work on a ship sailing east and had to return to Roche. But, the harvest safely gathered in, Madame

Rimbaud began to relent; she inclined an ear to the importunate boy; grudgingly she gave way; he could even, if one thought along such uncongenial lines, be said to have earned a few francs on the farm. In the third week of October he set off once more with money in his pocket and wrote from Genoa a long letter home, a letter beginning "Dear friends," a greeting which carries greater meaning in French than English. It was dated November 17, a notable date, for on that day his father died in Dijon; it was affectionate, and was written with the serious sense of purpose of one who has been sent off with a warning. "I arrived at Genoa this morning," he said, "and received your letters. A passage to Egypt must be paid for in gold; so there's no advantage there. I leave on Monday the 19th at 9 o'clock in the evening. I ought to arrive by the end of the month.

"As to the manner in which I came here, it was varied and refreshed from time to time by the weather. On the direct route from the Ardennes to Switzerland, as I wanted to join the German connection at Remiremont for Wesserling, I had to cross the Vosges; at first by coach; then on foot, no coach being able to pass because of at least two feet of snow and a warning of storms to come. But the feat to tell you about was the crossing of the St. Gothard which could not be made any longer by coach at this time of the year and which in conse-quence I couldn't do on four wheels.

"The St. Gothard pass begins at Altorf, at a point south of the lake of the Four Contours which I skirted in a mist. At Amsteg some ten miles from Altorf the road begins to climb and twist in alpine fashion. More valleys; only now do we get a view of the precipices below the milestones on the road. Before arriving at Andermatt one passes a scene of remarkable horror called the Devil's Bridge—less beautiful however than the Via Mala du Splügen which you have an engraving of. At Goeschenen, a village which has turned into a town because of the wealth of the workers, one sees at the bottom of the gorge the mouth of the famous tunnel, the workshops and huts of the company. However all this country which looks so wild is very hard-worked. If one can't see the steam threshing machines in the gorge, one hears a little, specially the mattock and the saw on the invisible heights. It goes without saying that the industry of the country shows itself above all in tree trunks. There are many mining excavations. The innkeepers offer you rather extraordinary mineral specimens which the devil, they say, buys at the top of the hills and sells in the town."

After this introduction he describes the crossing of the pass in company with other men, a difficult crossing because of sleet and snow storms. Late in the afternoon: "A pale shadow behind a cutting; it is the St. Gothard Hospice, a private and hospitable establishment, a wretched stone and pine building. We ring the bell. At the sound of it a squinting young man receives us: we step up into a dirty, low-ceilinged room where we are regaled free of charge with bread and cheese, soup and a drop of liquor. We see the big beautiful yellow dogs of the well-known story. Soon those held up on the mountain arrive, half dead. By evening there are thirty of us who are spread out after soup on hard mattresses and with insufficient coverings. During the night we hear our hosts breathing out in sacred songs their pleasure in robbing for yet another day the governments which contribute to their hovel.

"In the morning, after bread, cheese and a drink we leave, strengthened by this free hospitality which can be prolonged whilst a storm lasts. This morning the mountain looks wonderful in the sunshine; no more wind, all downhill, by cross paths with jumps and slides for hundreds of yards, until we come to Airolo, the other end of the tunnel, where the road again takes on an alpine character, twisting and obstructed, but always going down. This is Ticino.

"The road is under snow for more than twenty miles from the Gothard. Only after that, at Giornico, does the valley spread out a little. Vines begin to appear and little meadows which they manure carefully with leaves and other debris from the fir trees which they use like straw. Goats, grey oxen and cows, black pigs walk on the road. At Bellinzona there is a big animal market. At Lugano, twenty leagues from the Gothard, we take the train and go from the pleasant lake of Lugano to the pleasant lake of Como. From there I know the way.

"I am yours ever, I thank you, and in three weeks or so you will have another letter. Your friend."

There had been intimations—the insistence that his mother and sister wear their best clothes in London, the cards printed in Stuttgart—that Rimbaud was shedding the past; he now divested himself of literary skill. The imaginative boy, the would-be seer, the bourgeois-baiter, the poet, the inventor of new literary forms, the fastidious user of words of earlier years could never have thought let alone written "the industry of the country shows itself above all in the tree trunks" or "we take the train and go from the pleasant lake of Lugano to the pleasant lake of Como," nor could he have accepted the middle class view of nature running throughout the letter. Yet, thinking as he now thought, the letter was not uncharacteristic; he was not writing down to his mother—his comment on the monks of St. Bernard would not please her—but showing her the businessman on his travels.

Two days later he set sail, and early in December wrote again to his "Dear Friends," this time from Alexandria: "I've been here for two weeks and this is the first time things begin to look better. I shall have a job soon, and I already earn enough to live on, meagerly it's true. I shall either work on a big farm project some ten leagues from here (I've already been there but there will be nothing for some weeks); or, I shall soon join the Anglo-Egyptian customs with good prospects; or, more likely, I shall soon leave for the English island of Cyprus as interpreter in a gang of laborers. In any case I am promised something; and it is a French engineer—a talented and obliging man— who has helped me."

He did not specify the manner in which he had been earning "enough to live on," which was looting a wrecked ship off Suez. He did, however, make a request which united the Rimbaud of this time and the boy Rimbaud in his less idealistic moments:

"There's just one thing," he says, "that they want from me: a word from you, Mama, with the authority of the Mayor, saying this:

"'I, the undersigned, the wife of Frédéric Rimbaud, owner of Roche, declare that my son Arthur Rimbaud worked on my property until he left Roche of his own free will on 20 October 1878, that he conducted himself honorably here and elsewhere and that he is not at the moment subject to military law.'"

He adds the reminder "Don't forget the Mayor's seal which is most necessary" and continues, "Without this piece of paper I shan't be given a permanent job, though I believe that I should continue to get odd jobs. But don't say that I only stayed part of the time at Roche because they will then ask me for proof of longer residence elsewhere and the whole thing will fall through. Besides, if you do what I ask the company here will believe that I am capable of overseeing their workmen."

Fearing that his mother would jib at the evasion, he applied the only pressure he can think of to influence her: "I beg you to be good enough to send me this word as soon as possible; it is very easy and will lead to good results, at the least of insuring me a good job for the whole of the winter."

Madame Rimbaud did not make the statement, nor did the lack of it prevent her son from being offered the job; for the next that is heard of him is from Cyprus little more than two months later, on February 15, 1879, when he tells his family that he has been employed in the island for two months by a French firm with its headquarters at the port of Larnaca. "I am in charge of an isolated quarry by the sea; we are making a canal too. We also have to load the stone on to the Company's five ships and steamer. There are also a lime kiln, brickworks, etc. The nearest village is an hour's walk away."

He gave an unprepossessing picture of the conditions under which he worked. "There is only a chaos of rocks here, the river and the sea. Not a house. No earth, no gardens, not a tree. In summer it can be as hot as eighty degrees. It is often fifty now. This is winter. It rains sometimes. We eat turkeys, chickens etc. All the Europeans have been ill except me. There are twenty or more Europeans in the camp. The first arrived here on December 9. Three or four have since died.

"The Cypriot workmen come from surrounding villages; we employ as many as sixty a day. I am in charge of them; I allocate the day's work, dispose of the material, make reports to the Company, have all the money for food and all expenses, and hand out the wages. Yesterday I paid out the little sum of five hundred francs to the Greek workmen.

"I am paid at the rate of one hundred and fifty francs a month, I understand; so far I've received only twenty. But I shall soon be paid up to date and, I think, dismissed too, because I believe that a new company is going to take our place and do everything by piece work.

"It is this uncertainty which has kept me from writing. In any case my food costs me only 2 fr. 25 per day and, not owing much to the *patron,* it is always open to me to wait for other work, and there is plenty for me here, in Cyprus. They are going to make railways, ports, canals etc."

This matter-of-fact Rimbaud was not a little calculated; he had blossomed briskly into a hard worker under a broiling sun. Yet not contentedly; on the contrary, with a typically sulky-proud "Well, I've done what I said" and a demand for reward. For he ends with a "What is happening at home? Would you prefer me to come back? How are your little concerns going? Write as soon as possible."

"Would you prefer me to come back?" On the face of it this question comes incongruously from one who had spent nearly half his short life seizing every opportunity to leave home. Yet complaints of hardship, hints of danger, boasts of power and future success all had behind them one purpose, to wrest from home a word of praise, a cry of alarm, a confession that he was needed.

He had to wait a long time for the word; and when Madame Rimbaud did reply more than two months later it was to send him news of his father's death and to ask him for a power of attorney so that she could make sure of the money left to the children.

Chagrined and incredulous, he tried again. He was not making a fortune; he had had enough hard work in the heat, unused to one, detesting the other; he wanted to go home. He began to prepare for an honorable retreat. His welcomes had become progressively more frigid as he returned home defeated time after time. All his descriptions of the price he had paid for these attempts on fortune had not sufficiently impressed a mother whose somber philosophy made light of unsensational setbacks.

So he had first to make clear that in face of frightful hardships he had stuck to his job and made a success of it: "I am still head of the workmen at the Company's quarries and I direct the blasting and cutting of the stones." That said, he could deal with the hardships. His dislike of hot weather was well known at home; his "I'm jealous of you, I who stifle here" to Izambard from Charleville was simply an extension of grumbles in the family circle every hot summer. So he wrote meaningly "The heat is very great." And he pointed out that he had to put up with all the bugbears accessory to great heat: "The fleas are a frightful torture, day and night. Even more the mosquitoes. I have to sleep in the open, on the shore."

Yet Madame Rimbaud, who had toiled in the fields of Roche in all weathers, might think the less of him for giving way to the mere vagaries of climate. Some other, more compelling reason for retirement had to be found. The heat had, for instance, inflamed his temper. In consequence, he told her, "I have had disputes with the workmen and have had to ask for arms." But Madame Rimbaud was the widow of a soldier whose bravery she used to extol as an example to her children; and even the despised Frédéric had shown courage in the siege of Metz and the hazardous escape and journey home. Arthur could not be sure that his mother would react in the right way to his hint of danger; after all, he had the arms, not his workmen.

However this woman of iron had her weakness. Her son

knew it, shared it, attacked it succinctly. "I am spending a lot," he said; and summed up with: "May 16 ends my fifth month here. I think that I shall come back, but I would first like to have word from you. So write to me."

5 ～～～～

1879–1880

Before Madame Rimbaud replied he caught fever, the fever he had boasted of being the only one to escape, left Cyprus as soon as he was able, and, traveling by way of Marseilles, was back at Roche in June.

The fever left him weak, and he made no attempt to leave the farm. Delahaye came over from Rethel to see him and left what was to prove a final description. Rimbaud had changed greatly; when he opened the door Delahaye recognized him at first only by his eyes "so extraordinarily beautiful, the light blue iris surrounded by a darker circle of the color of periwinkle." For the rest: "The round cheeks of earlier days had fallen into hollows, leaving his face hard and angular. The fresh rosy complexion—like an English baby—which he had kept so long had given way to the duskiness of an Algerian, and on this brown skin, much to my amusement, grew the tawny blond beard which had been so slow to show itself."

His voice had changed too—the "rather excitable note had deepened and become grave"—and the old vivacity had disappeared: he was "very gentle, working obediently on the farm, gathering in the harvest with the calm and methodical intensity of one who had been a farmhand all his life."

Strolling about the farm, Delahaye admired the fields spread round them, each growing its own crop. "It would be much better if there were less variety and more strength," replied Rimbaud. "There are too many owners. The use of machines is restricted, almost impossible because of small holdings and the dispersion of land into lots. The cost of development by manuring, rotation of crops, etc. can't be borne by the small farmer; his means don't allow him to do things in a big way; he has more trouble for lesser returns. That 'great victory of 1789,' the breaking up of estates, was an evil."

From this prophecy of large-scale mechanical farming and the volte-face of the ardent communard of not so long past, the conversation moved to the climate as the evening drew in. He could not endure the winters of northern France, Rimbaud said; and when Delahaye reminded him of their schoolboy explorations in the snowy countryside round Charleville, he declared with a shudder: "The European climate is too cold for my constitution, which has changed. I can only live in hot countries."

To Delahaye the change was too sudden to be believed; he had not forgotten the joyful Rimbaud of winter or the listless, complaining Rimbaud of "I hate summer, it kills me" from Paris. He could not be expected to understand, since the speaker himself spoke in a mist of unknowingness, that he was listening to a notable demonstration of unconscious symbolism; Madame Rimbaud's increasing coldness could convey nothing to him. He passed the day in a daze; this young man who talked like an agricultural text book and an elderly hypochondriac was only a year or two removed from the intellectual white hope of Charleville. Evening after evening a little group, himself, Millot and Pierquin foremost, had listened to him at the cafés reviling and praising the poets, prophesying the coming of a new literature; day by day he had spoken of his literary hopes, had read his poems, asked Delahaye to copy them; eyes shining, hair tossing, voice soaring from bass to treble in excitement, he had been the very embodiment of the poet. Above their heads though much of his rhodomontade was, and some of it laughable, all three felt convinced that they were listening to a genius who would astound the world. The expectation died hard, and especially in Delahaye who, working at Rethel, had seen little of his friend recently. He was puzzled, and inevitably, at the end

of the day, brought the conversation round to literature; a thousand men could rove the world picking up a job here and there,
a million could work and discuss the land, but a Rimbaud . . .

Rimbaud was short with him. "I don't think of it any more."
He sounded so definite, so disgusted that Delahaye dropped
the topic.

He was short with Millot and Pierquin too that winter when
the Rimbaud family moved back to Charleville. He had, indeed,
been short with them for some time, and they were not pleased.
Neither was interested primarily in literature (Millot was to
become a judge, Pierquin a local antiquary) but the change in
Rimbaud from the eager young poet to the saturnine and penniless wanderer did not strike them as an improvement. Millot,
the more direct of the two, had long since, after the imprisonment of Verlaine, twitted Rimbaud sufficiently to bring him out
of his silence with a "Don't stir up that muck heap. It's too vile!"
But the outbreak died away into the usual moroseness and Millot
was soon saying sarcastically, "I can imagine meeting him one
day in the middle of the Sahara after many years of separation.
We are alone and are walking from opposite directions. He
stops for a moment: 'Hullo. How are you? Well? Fine? Goodbye.' And he goes on his way."

However, Rimbaud's fascination persisted even if it only
took the form of wondering what he would do next. And one
day Millot, meeting Pierquin in the street, told him that he had
invited Rimbaud to the Place Ducale for a farewell drink. "He
has bought a complete outfit," he said, "and has told the tailor
to send the bill to his mother. He's off again."

This was in the spring of 1880. The three met at the "Univers"
at 8 o'clock that evening. Rimbaud was "pretty taciturn"—
Pierquin is writing—"but when Millot congratulated me on
having bought a number of books [of poetry] published by
Lemerre, he broke silence brusquely to apostrophize me: 'It's
absolutely idiotic to buy books, especially that kind. You wear
a ball on your shoulders which ought to take the place of all

books. The only use of those things ranged along the bookshelves is to conceal the leprosities of old walls!' "

This Rimbaudian outburst cleared the air and "for the rest of the evening he overflowed with an unaccustomed gaiety. At eleven o'clock he left us—forever."

CHAPTER THIRTEEN

Trader

ADEN 1880

Rimbaud's advice would have impressed his companions
more if he had told them what he intended to do with
the "ball" on his own shoulders. He had spent the last
five years chasing about the world and as far as they could see
had nothing to show for them but a bronzed face. He did not
say a specific word about the future.

To Delahaye, whom he saw once again before leaving France,
he seemed scarcely less vague. He had, he said, done with a
life of wandering. He spoke of ambitions which he intended
to fulfil but did not name them. The one tangible piece of
evidence was his pride in the reference given by his employers
when he left Cyprus; he displayed it with "a faintly ironical
smile." Delahaye misunderstood the smile: that Rimbaud could
be content with or, worse, triumphant about the making and
amassing of money was as far beyond his imagination as his
friend's reason for the use of the "ball." Besides, Delahaye, like
the other old Charleville familiars, was too close to the events
of his time to realize what these events could do to a boy who
was emotionally insecure. At fifteen Rimbaud saw his country
invaded, his town besieged and occupied by enemy troops. Had
he been phlegmatic or even calm, had he possessed loving
parents and a home in which he was understood he might have
ridden the Prussian storm as untouched as his Charleville friends.
But a France defeated and divided reflected his own state: the
elation of unprecedented school triumphs crushed by suspicions
of affection unreturned, a striking poetic gift undermined by
what he most loved and by much in himself.

Peace came but there was no peace for Rimbaud. From the
year of the occupation of Charleville he never stayed in one

place for more than a few months. His restlessness was quickened
by the Parnassian cult of the East and by the belief, which
flourishes in a defeated country, that western civilization had
grown effete and materialistic—a belief which hardened in the
mind of the unsettled adolescent a few years later when France
and other western countries began to look outside national
frontiers for satisfaction. In 1876, the year of Rimbaud's abortive
journey to Java, Leopold of Belgium set up what became the
Belgian Congo, and Rimbaud's countryman De Brazza began
his daring explorations on the north bank of the Congo which
were to lead to the establishment of French Equatorial Africa.
The "scramble for Africa" had begun, the thought of Africa had
begun to appeal to men's imaginations; and to their greed: un-
dreamt of riches were there for the taking, it was popularly
supposed. And in this continent Rimbaud's attention, like that
of so many Frenchmen, was drawn particularly to Egypt and
Abyssinia; to the first because the French had felt a proprietorial
interest in it ever since the invasion of Napoleon; to the second
because it was there that, after being denied Egypt by England,
they were to look for compensation.

So Rimbaud, victim of war, heredity and history as well as
of the affections, set out in the spring of 1880, backed once more
by his mother. "He's off again!" Pierquin said jocularly; but the
familiar pattern disguised a vast difference; this departure was
not like its predecessors; Rimbaud, driven to lengths by indifference, had made up his mind to live out the prophetic lines
of *Une Saison en Enfer*. "I'm leaving Europe . . . I will have
gold," he had written eight years earlier; and as object: "I'll
return with iron limbs, dark skin and furious eye; I shall be
judged by my appearance as one of a strong race."

By April he was in Alexandria. Unable to find work, he crossed
to Cyprus in May. The English had taken over the island after
the Russo-Turkish war and were still making improvements;
and although Rimbaud's old employers had gone bankrupt, he
was soon employed. "I am overseer," he told his mother, "for the

palace which is being built for the governor general at the top of Troodos, the highest mountain in Cyprus (6000 feet).

"Up to now I've been alone with the engineer in one of the wooden huts which form the camp. Yesterday fifty workmen arrived and work begins. I am the only superintendent but so far I get no more than two hundred francs a month. It's two weeks since I've been paid yet I have many expenses; it's always necessary to travel on horseback; transport is extremely difficult, the villages far away, food very dear. And that's not all, for whilst one is very hot on the plains, at this height the cold is unpleasant and will be so for another month; it rains, hails, blows you down. I have to buy myself a mattress, blankets, overcoats, boots, etc.

"At the top of the mountain there is a camp where English soldiers will be coming in a few weeks when it will be hotter in the plain and less cold on the mountain. Then the delivery of provisions will be assured.

"So at present I am in the service of the English administration. I count on being given a rise in pay soon and on being employed until this work ends which will probably be about September. In this way I can get a good reference to help me to get a job in other work which will probably follow, and to save some hundreds of francs.

"I am not feeling well; I have throbbings at the heart which tire me a great deal. But it's better that I don't think of it. Besides, what can I do about it? However the air here is very healthy. There are only pines and bracken on the mountains."

He then asks his mother if she will buy two textbooks— including a book in English on the science of forestry and agriculture—and send them to him. There followed what was to become a familiar comedy. Aware of Madame Rimbaud's reluctance to spend money on what she considered to be inessentials, he explained at length, "I beg that you will pay for these books. It is necessary. *The post here won't accept money, so I can't send it to you.*" He promised to get the money to her later and wound up with a little bribery: "I'll try soon to send you a small sample of the famous Commanderie wine."

A week or two later, after news likely to induce mellowness, that he soon expected to begin cutting limestone "when I hope to make some money," he struck again with a "Please have the extreme kindness to reply and to send me what I've asked for."

Madame Rimbaud sent the books, but they did not reach him; soon after writing the last letter, in June, he left his job and the island, left it for reasons which were to hinder him wherever he went.

He had gone abroad to succeed and did not choose to tell his mother that he had moved, or why, until he had found other work, found it in Aden, at the other end of the Red Sea. Then she heard: "I left Cyprus nearly two months ago with 400 francs after disputes with the chief cashier and my engineer. If I had stayed I should have attained a good position in a few months. However, I can go back there."

He dismissed the following weeks laconically with "I looked for work in all the Red Sea ports, Jidda, Suakin, Massawah, Hodeida, etc. After trying to find something to do in Abyssinia I came here. I was ill when I arrived. I work for a coffee merchant from whom I only get seven francs. When I have a few hundred francs I shall go to Zanzibar where I'm told there are good prospects."

This letter evidently struck him as curt even for a Cuif to a Cuif, and he wrote again a week later, towards the end of August. He did not enlarge on his unsuccessful journey down the Red Sea; he was still preoccupied by his meager daily wage and plainly feared that his mother would think the less of him for accepting it. So he goes on "if I stay here (and I shall have to, for it is too far from everywhere for me not to stay quite a few months so as to earn several hundred francs as an insurance that I can go when I want), if I stay I believe that I shall be given a position of trust, and then I shall earn money a little more quickly."

The promise of managing a branch which his employer, Pierre

Bardey, made to him was kept. Bardey, who managed the Aden branch of a firm in Lyons, had at first taken pity on a fellow countryman sick and stranded, but he soon saw with a kind of bewildered admiration that he had to do with a very queer fish —not at all the usual type of beachcomber. "Sometimes he was morose and silent, sometimes animated, turning into an entertaining talker." The entertainment, like the man, was evidently new to Bardey. Rimbaud talked "with caustic verve, the object being to ridicule the acts and manners of those he was discussing. Naturally these stories, always cleverly told, made one laugh, even though one felt quite sure that when he was in other company one would be treated in the same way. And I must say that this little hobby of his was used more to express irony than malice."

Bardey, however, was a sensible man and not without insight. "I didn't attach much importance to these mental quirks. I put them down, with some reason, I think, to boredom and to a certain disgust for the world due to ordeals which he never spoke to me about but which his fine intelligence had obviously undergone . . . his rightful place certainly was not here but in the literary and artistic circles for which he had been born."

There he was, nevertheless, and seeking not literary or artistic renown but work that would earn the most money most quickly. He also showed himself efficient, sober and eager to get on, so that Bardey's kindness seemed likely to show profits. He was eager, too, to escape from Aden. He had come to one of the worst spots in the world and did not spare his family an account of it. His prominent bump of self pity or, to put it another way, his perpetual astonishment that justice did not reign in the world, was exploited with the usual purpose, to show his mother what he was undergoing to be the sort of man she admired. Aden was, he said "a frightful rock without a single blade of grass or a drop of fresh water; one drinks distilled sea water. The heat is excessive, especially in June and September. The normal temperature night and day in an airy, well-ventilated office is thirty-five degrees. Everything is very dear and so on. But what's the

use of talking; I'm like a prisoner here, and certainly it's necessary for me to stay at least three months before finding my
feet or getting a better job."

This brought a letter from Roche and he replied at once
towards the end of September. His mother was preoccupied by
her problem child, Frédéric, but Rimbaud first gave her an account of himself. He was "as well as one can be here. The firm
has a turnover of many hundreds of thousands of francs a month.
I am the only employee and everything goes through my hands,
I am now very well versed in the coffee trade and my employer
has absolute confidence in me. The only thing is, I am badly paid:
I get only five francs a day plus food, lodging, laundry, etc.,
etc., with a horse and cart, which amounts in all to about twelve
francs a day. But as I am the only intelligent employee in Aden,
I shall leave at the end of my second month, that's to say October 16, if I'm not given two hundred francs a month excluding
expenses. I'd rather go than be exploited. Besides, I have already
saved some 200 francs. I shall probably go to Zanzibar where
there are opportunities. Here also, however, there is much money
to be made. Many commercial houses are establishing branches
on the Abyssinian side of the Red Sea. This firm also has some
trade caravans in Africa, and it is still possible that I shall go
there. Then I should make more money and be less bored than
in Aden which, as all the world knows, is the most boring spot
in the world."

After more complaints of the heat and scarcity of water he
turned to Frédéric. His brother had come out of the army but
did not want to work on the farm at Roche. He preferred a
carter's job in Attigny. Worse still, he wanted to marry a dowry-
less peasant girl. Madame Rimbaud, who saw all her dismal
prognostications coming true, called for the moral support of
Arthur who had at last, however reluctantly, exotically and
temporarily, seated himself in the place she had struggled for
twenty odd years to fit him for, an office desk, who was saving
money and planning to make more. She obtained what she
wanted: "As for the idea of marrying when one has neither a

sou nor the prospect nor the ability to earn one, isn't that a
pretty miserable plan? For my part, whoever condemned me to
marriage under such circumstances would do better to kill me off
right away. But everyone has his own ideas. What he thinks is
none of my business and doesn't interest me at all, and I wish
him every possible happiness on earth and particularly in the
canton of Attigny (Ardennes)."

This last was not intended to save Frédéric from his mother
and did not. The days had long since gone by when Frédéric
looked up to his brother; he may well have thought that Arthur
was not distinguishing himself sufficiently to be able to spare
advice. In any event he remained a simple soul with no conception of the virtues of respectability, a white collar and a safe
job. To what extent he was the liar, hypocrite and cheat Madame
Rimbaud was to tell Isabelle (who disliked him for much the
same reasons as her mother) cannot be said; much of his dis-
simulation is traceable to the severity of his upbringing. At least
he found enough courage to fight his innate awe and affection
for his mother; when she threatened him with legal proceedings,
he announced that he would marry his penniless girl come what
might. Meanwhile he struggled along as the local carter's man.
Perhaps he had a sense of humor, for his round included the farm
at Roche.

In Aden Rimbaud was looking eagerly across the sea to
Africa. He was not mistaken in thinking that money was to be
made there; he heard of fortunes won by men who had no
objection to roughing it and who had the right mentality for
successful bartering. If he needed further confirmation, the action
of the western countries provided it; not many years were to pass
before the whole of the African shore of the Red Sea was in
European hands. But the good trader was always a step ahead
of his country, avoiding competition, regulations and other bugbears. Bardey was of this type. In the autumn he crossed to
Zeila in what was soon to be British Somaliland, and went up
country to the Abyssinian town of Harar with an assistant to
spy out the land. And in the first days of November Rimbaud

was telling his mother with the kind of businesslike detail that would appeal to her: "The firm has set up a branch in Harar . . . From there one exports coffee, skins, gums, etc. which are given in exchange for cotton goods and other things . . . I have been engaged from November 1 at the rate of 150 roupies per month, that is 330 francs or 11 francs per day plus food, all traveling expenses and 2 per cent of the profits . . . Naturally one must travel armed as there is danger of losing one's skin at the hands of the Gallas—however the danger isn't very great any more." And having made sure that she understood the mortal risk he was running, he left Aden with a three-year contract in his pocket and a final encouraging "I hope to save some money."

2

HARAR 1880–1881

In the middle of December he announced his safe arrival "after twenty days on horseback crossing the Somali desert. Harar is a town colonized by the Egyptians and dependent on their government. The garrison consists of many thousands of men. Here are our branch and storehouses. The marketable products are coffee, ivory, skins, etc. The country is high but not infertile. The climate is fresh and not unhealthy. All kinds of European goods are imported here by camels. There is much to be done in this country in other ways too."

He was in good spirits as always after a spell of activity and change of scene. Harar, primitive mud-built town though it was, seemed preferable to Aden in climate and opportunity, and two months later, in January, 1881, he was still declaring: "I shall try to make my work interesting and profitable"; this, partly because "I am soon going to make a big trip in the desert to buy camels. Naturally we shall be on horseback, with arms and the rest. The country isn't unpleasant."

In this mood he faced equally the prospect of being the only Frenchman in the town (Bardey's assistant going back to Aden as soon as he had settled Rimbaud in as temporary manager of the branch); he lived in the best house in Harar, he expected other Frenchmen to come— "We are going to have a Catholic bishop in this town who will probably be the only one in the whole country"—and he prepared against solitude by ordering many books. These, for which this time he paid his mother in advance, were mainly textbooks of the "mastered in three months" type: on steamships and shipbuilding, mineralogy, gunpowder and saltpeter, brickwork, artesian wells, ironwork, tanning, the wheelwright's trade, mining, pottery, gem making, glass making, masonry, metalwork, gunmarking, carpentry, house painting, telegraphy and exploration.

They led to an agitated and interminable correspondence with the family: why had his money not reached them, where were the books, why the delay? When he told Millot and Pierquin a year earlier to dispense with books and use their heads, he was speaking of imaginative literature; the literature of fact and practical purpose was another matter. He now proposed to master all crafts, all sciences in his spare, bored moments. That he equated this knowledge with the making of a fortune shows how little his travels had taught him. To get the most out of Africa in hard cash he had to keep his wits about him, employ his charm, have patience. The lesson was hard to learn; staying power was not his strong point, cleverness was far removed from business sense, and he was too proud and too little interested in people to exert his charm.

By February, after two months in Harar, complaints had begun: "I don't count on staying here for long; I shall soon know when I can go. I don't find this to be at all what I expected; and I live in a very boring way and without benefits. As soon as I have saved 1500 or 2000 francs I shall go and be very thankful. I expect to find something better a little further away. Give me news of the work on the Panama canal; has it already begun? I should be very happy to leave here right away. I have caught a disease, not very dangerous in itself; but this climate is treacherous for all kinds of illness."

The disease, a slight attack of syphilis, could account for his depression, but there was another reason; Bardey's brother, Alfred, had arrived to take charge of the branch. This was no surprise to Rimbaud, who knew his employer's plans, but to be subordinate in anything went against the grain. The complaints and the restlessness continued. His fancy soon veered towards an old eldorado: "In a month I shall know whether I have to stay here or pack up, and I may be on the way back to Aden when you receive this. I have had some preposterous troubles at Harar, and for the moment there's nothing to be done there as I had believed. If I leave this region I shall probably go down to Zanzibar and perhaps find work at the Great Lakes. I should much prefer to make my way somewhere by interesting work, and news doesn't arrive often here."

By the next month he was growing desperate and outlined a plan—vague, admittedly—which would have made Verlaine raise his eyebrows: "I am still in suspense. Business isn't brilliant. Who knows how long I shall stay here? Soon perhaps I shall make an expedition. A band of French missionaries have arrived and it may be that I shall go with them into country inaccessible to white men up till now." He ends with the somewhat twisted "I wish you stomachs less in danger than mine and work less boring than mine."

In his next letter a few weeks later, at the beginning of May, the rains had begun and his spirits were lower than ever. He asked again "has work begun at Panama?" ordered more books and a journal giving details of public works being undertaken throughout the world. He was still talking of buying a horse and going off into the little-known ivory country. The inhabitants were hostile, he told his mother, and "if things turn out badly" she must claim his salary from Aden, seven months' savings.

His satisfaction at this proof of industry and economy faded quickly; he did not go with the missionaries, and the news three weeks later that his mother had been unwell and was resting set him off on another bout of bitterness which was his way of showing concern. Madame Rimbaud was not young; time pressed.

"At your age it would be wretched to have to work. As for me, alas! I'm not at all in love with life; and if I live I'm used to a life of fatigue; but if I'm forced to wear myself out as at present and to feed myself in this atrocious climate on vexations as violent as they are ridiculous I'm afraid that my life will be shortened."

In his next breath he told his mother that in three months (still less than a year since he came to Harar) he would be able to send her 3000 francs. Not a bad beginning for one who had never before saved a sou, but impatience spoilt what could have been a triumph; misled by boredom and the discomforts of the rainy season he would not recognize that at Zanzibar or Panama, his two great delusions, he would be in the first case no better, in the second very much worse off than at Harar; he would not admit that the making of money in the way that suited him could be neither easy nor pleasant; he chafed against the mild surveillance of Alfred Bardey and yearned to be his own master; he was physically uncomfortable, without a friend except his servant or companions except the native prostitutes. Above all, worried by the news from home, he was haunted by the thought of wasted years. He was then only twenty-six but to him this was six years too old, the six years he had thrown away in the chase after literary fame. He panted to make up for lost time. So, reconsidering the destination of the 3000 francs: "I think that I shall keep them so as to begin a small business of my own in these parts, for I have no intention of passing all my life in slavery. So let us hope we are able to enjoy some years of real peace in this life; it's a good thing this life is the only one and that this is obvious, for it's impossible to imagine another life so frightfully boring!"

Unrebuked, he rewarded Madame Rimbaud in the next two months with notes—one cannot call them letters—even briefer than those that had gone before: he had twice been into the Galla country for ivory, once for skins, he had a slight fever and he proposed to make a six-weeks expedition into unexplored country at his own expense. This was all except a postscript re-opening a subject to become wearisomely familiar. "I'm not breaking the military law am I? I have never known where I am in this matter."

Before she had received both of these notes, Madame Rimbaud protested against his brevity. He replied at once, eagerly, towards the end of July: "I don't forget you at all, how could I? . . . I think of you and only of you. But what do you expect I should tell you of my work here which already disgusts me so much, or of the country of which I have a horror and so on? Should I tell you of the efforts I've made in spite of the most fearful fatigue and which have only resulted in giving me a fever which I've had for the last two weeks just as I did at Roche two years ago? But what do you expect?" The sense of triumph was unmistakable. "I'm all right now and I'm afraid of nothing."

Forget her! "I think of you and only of you." But words, in the Rimbaud family, were not acceptable as the criterion, so he went on immediately to provide practical proof. He had, he said, made arrangements with Bardey to pay his salary regularly to her—"what use is unproductive money to me in Africa?"

But more than this was needed; he had to show that he knew how to use money as well as make it. So Madame Rimbaud was to buy with it "immediately" good securities and lodge them with a lawyer or banker. "The only two things I wish are:

"1. That it shall be put in safety and *in my name;*

"2. That it shall bring in a regular profit.

"It's essential, however, to be absolutely sure that I'm not breaking the military law so that no one can in any way spoil the pleasure in store."

This was the business man and must win approval at Roche. Yet he was not satisfied; his mother was unwell, perhaps failing, Isabelle was not strong, the convention, as old as his memory, that money was always short in the home justified a gesture he was longing to make as the male support of the family. He added a brief rider to his instructions: his mother and sister were authorized to use the interest from his investments if they needed it.

At the beginning of September, having waited in vain for better news from Roche, he gave in his notice: "I continue to disenjoy myself strongly in this part of Africa. The climate is peevish and damp; the work I do is ridiculous and brutalizing and living conditions generally are also ridiculous. I have besides had unpleasant quarrels with the management and the rest and have practically decided to try a change of scene soon. I shall try to undertake something on my own in this country; and if it doesn't work out (and I should know quickly) I shall soon leave for, I hope, more intelligent work under pleasanter conditions. It may be however that in this case I shall remain with the firm—somewhere else."

And he repeated, with a further expression of hope "that in the matter of military service I am not in the wrong," what he believed to be the reasonable "All I ask in the world is a good climate and decent, interesting work; one day I shall find it! I also hope to receive only good news of you and your health. It's my chief pleasure to get your news, dear friends, and I wish you better luck and more cheerfulness than I have."

Quarrels with the Bardeys, Rimbaud feeling as he did and being what he was, were inevitable. For him and Alfred Bardey to be shut in a native town for days, weeks and months on end was an invitation to bickering. They were the only Frenchmen in Harar with the exception of a missionary; and as Rimbaud despised the Egyptians who garrisoned the town, the only chance of seeing a fresh face was when the rare trader passed through Harar en route for the coast or the interior of Abyssinia. He could not even escape by himself when work was done, for the town gates were shut at sunset.

Dissension under these conditions could be paralleled in all the commercial outposts of the world where Europeans were foregathering in their twos and threes to make money. But the main cause was different in Rimbaud's case; he was not irritable and touchy only through boredom, the trials of the climate and lack of variety in company. His trouble was fundamental; he had expected to find Africa a gold mine for a clever man, yet there he was, a paid employee, doing work which was an insult to his intelligence, his pride revolting against the day by day bargaining in the market place outside the Bardey store. He might almost as well have stayed in Charleville, he told himself, his savings mounted so slowly. Somehow, somewhere he had to find a means of making quick money. The first and obvious step was to be his own master so that all the profits went into his pocket.

Pierre Bardey believed, however, that in Rimbaud he had found a man of promise. The problem was to provide work that suited him as the bazaar exchange did not. He would not accept Rimbaud's resignation and shrewdly summoned his brother to a conference. The flattering move succeeded: Rimbaud, left alone, changed his tone at once and was soon writing home proudly: "I can't leave the branch here because this would at once put a stop to business, for I'm in charge of everything and provisionally director of affairs."

His mother, disliking the thought of investing his money in stocks and shares of which she knew nothing and in which she had no confidence, had suggested a better use for them, a suggestion which gave him the opportunity of displaying, with would-be carelessness, Rimbaud the capitalist. "I rely on you to do something about these wretched savings. But what the devil do you think I could do with landed property?" He had another 1500 francs to send her, he said, but would wait to hear that the first batch of money had reached Roche.

He still had a gesture to make. He had sent her all his savings, he had told her to use the interest from them for herself, but the ultimate proof of devotion remained unsaid. He added a casual, tempting "If you need it, take what I have; it's yours. I have no one to consider except myself and I want nothing."

As excuse for this, to a Cuif, almost naked display of feeling, he spoke of preparations for an expedition, longer and more dangerous than any he had yet made, into the Abyssinian province of Shoa. The excuse may have been accepted at Roche but to him the risks in these forays into the wild country beyond Harar formed a large part of their charm. Anything was preferable to the unbroken monotony of life in a native town. He scarcely knew what physical fear was; the possibility of a fight, the certainty of movement and the hope of gain and distinction at once excited and soothed. He directed everything, relied on his own wits, forced his body to do his will, and was first in the field entirely through his courage and exertions; almost everything he looked on was new to the eye of a European. No need, no time or energy to think, the effort to cover ever more virgin territory absorbed him. And no regrets; in these years he did not make a sign or suspicion of a sign that he regarded the life of the young Rimbaud with anything but disgust.

If he had disturbing backward thoughts, of which the waste of years was the worst, he did not have tempting ones as he rode, walked and forced a way into African fastnesses; the nearest he came to literature was a resolution to make use of that abandoned gift for strictly practical ends, an account, which he hoped would be profitable, of Harar and his explorations from it.

But the expedition to Shoa fell through. Alfred Bardey returned with an offer from his brother of a better job in Aden. A subordinate at Harar once more, he could think only of escape and a bigger salary. In Aden, however, which he detested; and it is an indication of his fanaticism that he accepted and was telling his mother and sister in December, almost exactly a year since he had arrived in Harar: "I leave very soon and it is unlikely that I shall ever come back here again."

3 ~~~~~

ADEN 1882–1883

The return to Aden was unproductive. Rimbaud had no intention of remaining with Bardey who was, he said, one of those "niggards and knaves, good only for exploiting the labors of their employees"; his real intention was to get another and better job. But although work was easier to find from Aden than the remote Harar, he had overestimated his powers. He found nothing. For the next fifteen months he stayed in the office at Aden, grumbling in familiar fashion to those at home, mimicking to Bardey the peculiarities of business acquaintances, and planning a future that should be rosier than the present.

Alfred Bardey's reports had shown his brother that the potentially brilliant young man was his own worst enemy in trade as in life. It was not simply that he despised the bazaar work and disliked being given orders; gossip traveled quickly in the business world of that vast area, and Rimbaud's "mental quirks" which a year in Harar had sharpened were already showing losses; irony or sarcasm at the expense of the absent man, however amusing, is a double-edged weapon: "His caustic and mordant mind made him many enemies. He never threw off the wretched and spiteful satirical mask which hid the true qualities of his heart. The repercussions of this cruel form of mockery did him a good deal of harm."

This considered judgment by one of the most experienced traders on the Red Sea coast did not affect Pierre Bardey's interest. His employee was an unusual man; he would not touch alcohol in a country where the heat tempted white men to drink heavily; he did not smoke; he spent next to nothing on himself; when he could be moved out of his customary taciturnity he proved an invigorating companion. He was plainly unhappy and divided in mind, destroying opportunities equally by his pride, witticisms and restless ambition which led him to one "get-rich-quick" folly after another. The close heat and the lingering syphilis—"he carried unmistakable marks of it on his mouth," said Bardey—affected his temper, and his employer, trying various remedies to help him, met with bursts of irritation. He put up with them, believing that Rimbaud, if he gave his mind to it, could outstrip everybody in Aden. This, he said, was generally admitted, even those who had "unhappy memories of his sarcasms . . . recognizing his superiority in practically everything."

So Bardey, in whom kindness, curiosity and hope of gain all played their part, remained patient whilst Rimbaud was writing home bitterly about "cursed interference" (he claimed among other things that Bardey opened his letters) and announcing, "I don't reckon to stay long in Aden, for I need more intelligent interests than I can find here. If I go, and I expect to go soon, it will be back to Harar or down to Zanzibar where I should have very good introductions; in any case, if I don't find anything I can always come back here where I should certainly find something better than the work I have now."

By this time Madame Rimbaud, who knew her son to be gullible and suspected that he would not settle to anything outside France, was beginning to take these assurances with native scepticism. She had shrewdly resisted the temptation to accept his money. "Take what I have; it's yours," he had said; she was prepared to soothe her conscience, even at the expense of doing violence to her nature, by making generous gestures to him; she was not prepared to be his debtor, knowing that nothing is given for nothing. But she indulged herself by buying land for him at Roche with his savings, hoping to give him security and something of his own to come back to. She demanded why, if he was so much dissatisfied, he did not return home where he would be made welcome.

His objections to the purchase of land fell away—"you have done well"—under the flattering sense of a common interest. He accepted her arguments against the dangers of stocks and shares with no more than the slightest parade of masculine dignity: "As for my interests, of which you speak, they are slight and I don't torment myself at all about them. Who can wrong me, a man who has only himself to think of? A capitalist of my sort has nothing to fear from speculations."

The return to Roche was another matter; he remained wary —"Thanks for the hospitality you offer me, my dear friends. This is understood on both sides"—and parried the question with a "As for coming back to France, what should I do there at present? It's much better for me to try to amass something here; then I shall see. For me the most important and urgent thing is to be independent, no matter where."

He had still to deal with his dissatisfactions: "Don't distress yourself on my account; there's nothing remarkable about my situation. I am, as ever, employed in the same box and I drudge like a donkey in a country of which I have an unconquerable horror. I move heaven and earth to try to leave here and find a better job. I certainly hope that this existence comes to an end before I have grown into a complete idiot. Besides I am spending a lot in Aden."

This, as his mother pointed out in her next letter, was not the "reassurance" he was supposed to convey. He tried again, half-heartedly: "I certainly hope to enjoy peace before I die. However I am very well accustomed to every kind of boredom and if I complain it's only a manner of speech."

Only a manner of speech; as he showed in his way when the women at Roche tried to pin him down. He was lonely, bored? Very well; Isabelle declared that she would like to join him. This proposal he rejected out of hand with a fearsome description of Aden, beginning: "It's the bottom of an old volcano, without a blade of grass." But he bewildered his readers by continuing "Personally I like this climate a great deal, for I have a permanent horror of rain, mud and cold. All the same it is likely that I shall be going back to Harar at the end of March. There it is mountainous and very high; from March to October it rains continually . . . Magnificent vegetation—and fevers."

This was January, 1883. He had spent a year in Aden. He was still in Bardey's office. But if immobile bodily, having no alternative, his mind soared over a world in which he made a name and money with unexampled speed. He put most store by the plan which, after his preliminary trading journeys into the interior from Harar, came naturally in an age of explorers. He explained: "I am going to write a work on Harar and the Gallas country, with maps and engravings, for the Société de Géographie . . . When the work is done and sent to them I shall perhaps be supplied with funds for other explorations. It's all very easy."

He explained a second time, even more confidently, "I can finish this job and then work at the expense of the Société."

This was said to Delahaye, a Delahaye who, following Verlaine, Nouveau, Izambard and the rest, had been dropped. Rimbaud's farewells in the Place Ducale three years earlier had been made in earnest. Since then, silence. Now he wanted something as he had wanted something from Izambard and Verlaine in the past; Delahaye seemed to be the best man to ask and without a qualm is asked.

The letter makes chilling reading. "Without further preambles," he says (the preambles consisting of a "I received your news with pleasure"), "you can do me a great service."

The service was to order for him, so that he could make maps for his proposed article, a theodolite, sextant, barometer, compass, surveyor's measuring line, box of architect's instruments, and textbooks on topography, trigonometry, mineralogy, hydrography, meteorology, industrial chemistry and astrology with two further volumes on exploration.

This letter, sent to Roche for forwarding, was read by Madame Rimbaud with horrified incredulity. "I'm not afraid to spend some thousands of francs which will repay me handsomely," her son blithely told Delahaye. So he was not content with the books he had been ordering at intervals for more than a year, books which after a struggle she had sent. She could just perceive that the clever Arthur might profit from them, although they had cost a lot of money, some three hundred francs in all. But sextants, barometers, theodolites! Thousands of francs pouring out of Rimbaud pockets! The poor woman's brain reeled. "Send them all off," her son commanded Delahaye, "add the postage to the cost and repay yourself from the money I have deposited with Madame Rimbaud at Roche." But there was no money; all he had sent her had been converted into land.

There was only one way of nipping this frightful folly in the bud; to withold the letter to Delahaye. But another and worse madness had already been perpetrated behind her back: "I have ordered from Lyons," he told her in his covering letter, "a camera; I shall take it to Harar and shall bring back views of these unknown parts. It is a very good stroke of business." There was nothing for her to do, he added comfortingly. "You have only to pay everything."

"Only!" The agitated mother suppressed the letter to Delahaye and replied at once to her son: she had no money, she would not pay a sou.

A confused interchange followed. Rimbaud canceled the order for instruments temporarily with a "But I really need them," and sent his mother a cheque for a thousand francs to pay for the camera. "If it costs more, another 500 or 1000 francs," he said as lightly as he was able, "find the money yourself and send all that is asked for."

The bill from Lyons arrived at Roche, and Madame Rimbaud —her tall, spare figure had been seen in all the photographic shops of Charleville and Vouziers anxiously inquiring the cost of cameras—dumbfoundedly, in as far as the mist before her eyes permitted, made out the figure of 1850 francs. Another distressed note went off to Aden; never would she pay such a sum. Nor did she until he sent a peremptory telegram, followed by a letter in which he gave her the not altogether adequate consolation of "I have a good 4000 francs here; but they are in an English savings bank and I can't get them out without expense. Besides I shall need them soon."

She paid. But when the 1850 francs had finally been wrenched away she wrote angrily: what did he mean by ordering goods he could not pay for? The thievishly expensive camera, costing many times the price of perfectly good cameras in the local shops, had not merely brought her close to ruin, it would never earn a sou, was a wicked folly; she refused absolutely to buy another thing for him.

This extracted a revealing reply from the money-spinner in Aden. "Naturally one doesn't buy a thing without knowing that one has the money to pay for it . . . You say I've been robbed. I know very well what a camera costs by itself—some hundreds of francs. But there are chemical products too, very many and very expensive, amongst which are gold and silver compounds priced at as much as 250 francs the kilogram; there are also mirrors, maps, pans, phials, the very expensive cost of wrapping everything, which push up the total cost. I have asked for enough of everything to last for a two-year expedition. I think I've made a good bargain. I have only one fear, that the things get broken en route, at sea. If they arrive intact I shall make a large profit and shall send you some curious things.

"So instead of being angry you ought only to share my pleasure. I know the value of money," he boasted, "and if I risk something it's in good earnest."

Knowing, however, as his mother did not, that 1850 francs was not the end of the matter—there was still the cost of carriage—he tried to reassure her by striking a bargain. "You have 2500 francs of mine that I sent you two years ago. Take over, from the land you bought with this, enough land to cover the sums you pay out for me."

But there was her threat to be dealt with. "What is specially sad is that you end your letter by declaring that you won't have any more to do with my affairs. This isn't a pleasant way of helping a man a thousand leagues from home, traveling amidst savage people and not having a single correspondent in his own country! I hope that you will modify this uncharitable intention. If I can't ask my family to do my commissions any more, who the devil can I ask?" He had got his way a thousand times by his sulky-charming "Who the devil . . . ?" technique, and was so certain of getting it again that he forthwith ordered more books with a "I beg you, don't throw my order to the devil! I'm going off again to Africa for many years, and without these books I should lack a crowd of references which are indispensable to me. I should be like a blind man; and the absence of these things would prejudice me greatly."

Madame Rimbaud sent the books and paid the 600 francs carriage for the camera as she had paid everything else. She knew, if only unconsciously, why her son was where he was, she knew why he grasped at every straw that might lead to money. But this time she paid not only unwillingly but unbelievingly.

Her fears were justified; most of the books were never read and the only return from the 2450 franc camera was a few poor photographs sent home, a few sold to the natives for a guinea a time.

Rimbaud's error was the naïve belief that the Société de Géographie would back him as an explorer. Exploration might have been the best use of his passion for novelty and movement; had he been able to turn himself into a Speke, a De Brazza, a Livingstone, the camera would have been a boon. It had been bought for use on the journey to Shoa which he had talked of a year earlier, before leaving Harar. To prepare for this he had kept his savings in Aden rather than send them home as before. The journey was intended as adventure and profit in one; he was convinced that there was much money to be made in Shoa by any man with the daring and ability to exploit this remote Abyssinian province.

Whether he would have proved to be that man was another matter; the test was postponed by events in Egypt which put Shoa and many other districts beyond reach for a time. How much he was to be affected by these events Rimbaud had no notion, he who was soon to tell his family (anxiously reading the newspaper and thinking of him) "You speak to me of the latest political news. If you knew how indifferent I am to all that! I haven't seen a newspaper for more than two years." Nevertheless he was sufficiently au courant with the talk of the town to say in the middle of 1882 "The disorders in Egypt are hindering all business on this coast."

The "disorders" were the massacre of fifty Europeans in Egypt a few weeks earlier by a nationalist mob encouraged by a certain Colonel Arabi Pasha, who had taken over command of the mutinous Egyptian army. The massacre led in July to the bombardment of Alexandria by the British fleet and to the landing of a British army under General Wolseley which two months later destroyed Arabi's army in the desert. That same month, September, Evelyn Baring was sent to Egypt nominally as Consul General, in practice as Governor General; Egypt had become a British protectorate.

"If the English occupation is permanent," wrote Rimbaud, "things in Egypt will go better." But "all the same, if the English occupy Harar a good time will have passed."

Despite this gloomy prophecy he announced soon afterwards, in January, 1883, that he would be going back to Harar in a month or two. He had, he told his mother, made a new contract with Bardey for three years (curtailable by three months' notice) at a higher salary "equivalent to 5000 francs net per year." He was "going to work seriously" and "I hope to have at least seven thousand francs in the bank at the end of the year not counting what I earn on the side." If anything went wrong "I can always start a small business of my own which would show a 60 per cent profit in a year." There was also that other seductive illusion, that he would be able to get, "in a year's time, funds from the Société de Géographie."

To sum up this recital of which any mother must surely feel proud: "In four or five years I should easily be able to make fifty thousand francs; then I could marry." The position was so favorable that he could say without a blush, having overlooked one small detail, "You will be asked, soon perhaps, from Lyons, for the sum of about 100 francs to pay for a graphometer I have ordered. Pay this and in future I won't ask you for anything without sending money."

And he anticipated comment and answered his mother's pessimistic prophecies with a triumphantly crushing: "I have 5000 francs here earning 5% interest; I'm not ruined yet."

Not one word of that black cloud on the horizon which was to drive him back to Aden the following year. Yet the whole Mediterranean world was talking of the Mahdi, the Holy War he had declared in the spring of 1881 and his staggering victories in the Sudan during the next eighteen months: 1500 Egyptian soldiers wiped out in December, 1881, 6000 in mid-summer 1882, 10,000 under the command of the English Hicks Pasha in

November. The Sudanese flocked to the banner of the new prophet; he had been divinely commanded, the Mahdi declared, to found a Mussulman Empire at the point of the sword; all unbelievers were to be destroyed or driven into the sea.

4 〜

HARAR 1883–1884

It may be that the return to Harar was forced on him, for at the end of January, 1883 he was involved in an affray with the firm's warehouseman, Ali Shamok. In a fit of anger Rimbaud struck him, and the attitude of Shamok and his fellow Arabs became so threatening that Rimbaud appealed to the French consul for protection. The rights and wrongs of the matter are not clear. Shamok, Rimbaud declared, was "very insolent." Nevertheless the Court at Aden would have imprisoned Rimbaud or expelled him from the colony "for brawling a little too violently" had not Bardey undertaken to be responsible for his future good behavior. Shamok, said Bardey, "was our oldest warehouseman and very useful to us. He adds, "It isn't good to have these people (the Arabs) against one. Commercially speaking, I mean." And to be on the safe side he offered the management of the Harar agency to Rimbaud.

Apart from this, the return, whatever Rimbaud may have said, was simply because he had to choose between Harar and Aden; and as he had just spent more than a year in Aden, the advantages of Harar shone out temptingly and its disadvantages (about which no man had been more eloquent than himself) shrank to pin pricks. There a new, determined Rimbaud, his head buzzing with plans, would make money quickly, return home, marry and settle down as the head of the family.

For marriage was very much in his mind; loneliness, his mother's wishes and the peasant instinct to preserve property all urged it. Soon after he had settled in his old job, the twenty-three-year-old Isabelle refused a suitor and declared that she would never marry. He commented sternly in his new role as prospective paterfamilias: "Isabelle is very wrong not to marry if someone serious, well educated and with a future presents himself. That is life, and solitude in this world is a bad thing. For myself, I regret not being married and having a family."

This echo of his mother, which could hardly fail to please, offered him an excellent pretext for reminding her, "for the present I am condemned to wander, tied up to a remote business, and every day I lose the taste for the climate, the ways of living and even the language of Europe. Alas! what use are these comings and goings, these labors and adventures amidst foreign races, these languages which one crams into the memory, and these numberless troubles, if one day, after some years, I can't rest in some part of the world that pleases me a little more, raise a family and have at least one son whom I can spend the rest of my life bringing up according to my ideas, armed and embellished with the fullest knowledge possible to attain in this age, and whom I shall see become a renowned engineer, a man made strong and rich by science? But who knows how much longer I shall live in these mountains? And I could disappear in the midst of these people without the news ever leaking out."

He ended by repeating: "The only thing that interests me is news from home, and I'm always happy when I can comfort myself with a picture of you at work in the fields."

Although his last remark was no more than the bare truth, the year he spent at Harar from 1883–1884 turned out to be one of the more endurable periods of his later life. Alfred Bardey had left the town and Rimbaud was undisputed master of the agency. He also had the feeling that this span of management was likely to be short; however much he had ignored politics in Aden, he could not ignore them in Harar; the Mahdi having driven the Egyptians out of much of the Sudan, there was a natural belief in Harar, as in all other Arab districts conquered by Egypt, that the time of the oppressor was running out. Rimbaud professed a philosophical detachment— "What will be will be and that's all there is to be said"—and possibly even felt it; but that he and the business were poised on a knife edge was clear, and this gave a zest to the despised everyday bargaining.

Another event sweetened his mood during this second period at Harar. He was a lonely man and virile; he took a local girl and lived with her in a manner suitable to his situation, she expecting nothing, he the absolute master.

Finally, he made during this year a journey which gave him great satisfaction, an exploration into the unknown Ogaden. The journey originated in Bardey's wish to discover new trading areas where he could be first in the field with offers for the local ivory, musk and gum and could dispose of his cotton goods. Rimbaud took with him his assistant, Sottiro, a man experienced in the ways of the Somalis. They went south from Harar as far as Babassa on the River Web, which no white man had seen before, and returned safely with plans to establish a trading post eight days out from the town.

Rimbaud's explorations had one aim, to make money. They called for physical endurance, courage, hard work, initiative, all his solid virtues. In one sense only the explorer remained the idealist of fifteen. A Verlaine, an Izambard, a Nouveau and now a Bardey had all been tested and found wanting. Revolting from the intolerable frailties of man, he turned to nature, an adversary who fought cleanly, was incapable of subterfuge, demanded respect and was worthy of a Rimbaud's attentions. This form of idealism apart, it was no romantic hero who rode into the plains of Ogaden but a man with his mind on the job and wasting no time on artistic irrelevances, as his dry, sensible and businesslike report on the unknown area and its trade possibilities showed. He wrote it in December for Bardey to read, note and forward to the Société de Géographie. It was an altogether different matter from the account he had so long meditated, of Harar and the Gallas who lived round about it—an account which could have been written by many men—and the Société evidently thought likewise, for they printed it in their Transactions for February, 1884, and asked him for a photograph to include in their "Albums of portraits of those who have made a name in the geographical sciences and in explorations."

By the time the request reached him, in March, he was closing the agency and on the point of returning to Aden. Business had continued to fall away— "Harar market has never been more worthless," he reports—and the action of Baring in Cairo was decisive.

The news from the Sudan had been steadily growing worse. To the south, General Gordon, sent to Khartoum, was cut off by the Mahdi's men early in March. More serious from Rimbaud's point of view was the report from Suakin, one of the Red Sea ports at which he had tried to find work on his way from Cyprus four years earlier. There, in February, an Egyptian army under the Englishman Baker was defeated by the Mahdists, a defeat which installed the rebelling Sudanese forces between Harar and Egypt and virtually isolated the Abyssinian town. Baring, chiefly concerned to put Egypt's finances in order, decided to begin by liquidating what remained of her conquests; Harar, which had been taken from the Abyssinians ten years earlier, was abandoned and an anti-European governor took the place of the Egyptian one.

As soon as the news reached Aden, Bardey realized that the Harar agency was doomed. He decided to cut his losses, and summoned Rimbaud back to Aden.

Rimbaud saw all his hopes vanish of making money or a name as explorer; no explorations, no trade would be possible with that part of Africa in chaos. Despairing, he sold his camera and could neither be bothered to send the photograph to the Société de Géographie nor to reply to Verlaine's letter.

For Verlaine, about to take the step which was to lead to the recognition of Rimbaud as an important literary influence, had tried to get in touch with him. Verlaine was then on the fringe of acknowledgment by the younger poets in Paris as the greatest living French poet. He remained short of money, however, and in the autumn of 1883 compiled for a literary journal selections

of the work of three men under the title *Les Poètes Maudits;*
the men were Tristan Corbière, Mallarmé and Rimbaud.

He had never lost his affection for Rimbaud and still had
many of his poems by heart. He used these, written down from
memory, to form the basis of his selection. But before actually
printing them he wrote to the address supplied by Delahaye,
telling Rimbaud what he proposed to do, asking for more poems
and for accurate details of his old friend's life during the past
eight years. As his introduction to the poems showed, his knowledge of Rimbaud's movements since Stuttgart was hazy,
Delahaye's information being of the sketchiest, and the whole
essay was careless and inaccurate. Nevertheless, journalism
though it was, his admiration for Rimbaud and his poetry rang
true. He repaid his debt handsomely; the boy had transformed
him from a promising poet into a great one; he now made
Rimbaud's name.

For the selections, reprinted in book form by Vanier early
the next year, caused a sensation in the advanced poets' cafés,
those from Rimbaud most of all. To the young men then experimenting with the poetry soon to be known under the general heading of Symbolism, Rimbaud had been no more than
the legend of a boy who appeared in Paris meteorically ten or
eleven years earlier, a gifted but unpleasant boy who afterwards
disappeared into space. Of his work they knew nothing. When
they read the poems printed by Verlaine, which included "Les
Assis," "Les Effarés," "Voyelles" and "Le Bateau Ivre," they were
astounded and immediately hailed Rimbaud as one of the main
precursors of Symbolism. From this moment his immortality was
assured. Had he had gone back to Paris from Harar—and by
that time he had twelve thousand francs saved—he would have
received the kind of welcome he had dreamed of in the early
seventies. He would have been a hero and leader of the young
poets. He might even have made money.

It was too late. His choice had been made long ago. "Maintenant je puis dire que l'art est une sottise." (Now I can say

that art is a lot of foolishness.) Leaving Verlaine's letter un-
answered, he returned to Aden for the third time.

5 〜

ADEN 1884–1885

Although he brought his native girl with him and set up a
house of his own, this did not save him, or the women at Roche,
from one explosion of bitterness after another. An attempt to
provide intellectual companionship for himself by sending the
girl to school was unsuccessful. That part of Africa facing him
across the Red Sea was for the moment out of bounds. The political turmoil which prevented him from staying there also
seemed likely to rob him of a livelihood; he faced the prospect,
appalling to the son of his mother, of being forced to live on his
savings; the fact that he had savings comforted him not at all.
Business was bad for all traders based on Aden; Bardey not
only had to close the branch at Harar but was in danger of losing his own job in the main branch; and after giving Rimbaud
the three months' notice required by contract he went off to
his firm's headquarters in Lyons to try to persuade them to
continue to trade in Aden.

Rimbaud was left to wonder what would become of him. All
was out of joint, he found; even his savings were proving a
nuisance: "I have from twelve to thirteen thousand francs here
and as no one in this place is to be trusted I'm forced to carry
this hoard about with me and watch it perpetually. And this
money, which ought to give me a small income sufficient to live
on without working, brings me in nothing because of these con-
tinual annoyances." Pondering on these "annoyances" of a Mahdi
and a Baring, he lashed himself into a frenzy of disappointment:
"What a desolating existence I drag out in these ridiculous cli-
mates and senseless conditions! With my savings I would have
had a small assured income; I would have been able to rest a

little after the long years of suffering; but not only am I unable
to remain one day without working, I can't even enjoy my gains:
the bank here only takes deposits without paying interest and
the commercial houses aren't at all safe!"

He summed up: "My life here, then, is an absolute nightmare.
Don't think I'm having a good time. Far from it. I have seen
time after time that it is impossible for anyone to live more
hardly than I do."

This perhaps struck him as going a little too far even for his
hardened readers, for he added a deprecatory "Forgive me for
describing my troubles in detail"; only to relapse into "But I
see that I'll soon be thirty (half a lifetime!) and am heartily
tired of roaming the world without results. You haven't these
unhappy thoughts and I like to think of your calm life and
pleasant occupations. Long may they last!" Unfortunately the
contrast between Roche and Aden was too much for him, and
he ended with "As for me, I'm condemned to live a long time
yet, perhaps always, in these areas where I am known and can
always find work; whilst in France I should be a stranger and
find nothing."

Before he could receive a reply the thought of his approaching
birthday turned his mind to the old bogey and he wrote again:
"Have I still to do military service after the age of 30? And
if I come back to France have I always to make up for the
service I did not do before 30?"

Madame Rimbaud, accustomed though she was to her son's
"manner of speech," could not understand why he did not bring
his savings, a sizable sum in those days, back to France where
a home awaited him. She said as much: why continue with such
uncongenial work? Only to receive the usual evasive "Thank you
for your offers. But as long as I can find work and am able to
stand it, it is better for me to continue working and scrape
some sous together."

"Scrape some sous together" was a Rimbaudism. A "small assured income" would not buy him a house of his own, would
not necessarily earn him respect, certainly would not compel

admiration. Satisfactory it might be, sensational it was not; and he who had never submitted to the ordinary, and who heard of fortunes being made on every hand, still confidently expected the dramatic stroke that would bring him back in a blaze of financial glory.

By the time this last letter was written, in July, Bardey had returned from Lyons. The firm had refused to support the Aden branch but he decided to continue the business with his brother and offered Rimbaud a definite six months' engagement in his office as coffee buyer with the prospect of a permanency if trade picked up. Rimbaud accepted, but in less than two months was continuing his tirade: trade was bad, the business was too small to prosper, the employees were poorly paid and, although he believed himself to have become acclimatized to the violent changes of weather, he had a new fear: "I feel that I shall very quickly grow old in these idiotic businesses and the company of savages or imbeciles. However, and I think you'll agree with me, from the moment I began to earn my living here—and every man is the slave of that miserable fatality in Aden as elsewhere —it was better to stay in Aden than go where I would be unknown." And he quoted, unsmiling, the Arab saying "It is written! It is life. It is not amusing."

It was true enough, as Bardey had quickly perceived, that he was the mental superior of every man in Aden, where culture was at a premium. He was far, however, from being the most successful and this disagreeable fact inspired one bitter reflection after another. Most of the money was going into the pockets of the "savages" and "imbeciles"; he, Arthur Rimbaud, remained after four years a paid clerk.

The flow of the familiar *"c'est pas injuste?"* was diverted for a moment and for the last time by Frédéric. After a legal delaying action of two years Madame Rimbaud had had to admit defeat. Frédéric was given permission by the courts to marry whom he chose. He promptly married his penniless and ancestorless girl and was as promptly disowned by his mother. Yet that was not the end of the matter; she had to witness this disgraceful creature driving his van about the district and even bringing his parcels to the very door, she knew that her first grandchild had been born to him, she heard that he was freely opening his mouth and not to her advantage: the whole world of Attigny was being told how he had been cut off without a sou, how she would not see him, refused all help. In bitter mood she wrote to the good son far away, saving every sou, braving a frightful climate, fulfilling the true Frenchman's destiny of sober living, hard work and filled money bags. She hoped that Arthur would stand with them. (Isabelle too would have nothing more to do with Frédéric and, specially, would not lend money to the déclassé.)

Her concern was needless; the model son was as shocked as she could wish. Frédéric's behavior, he said gravely, "is very vexing and could greatly prejudice us in the eyes of others. It troubles me enough, for instance, that anyone should know I have such a bird for a brother. I'm not surprised, however, not by Frédéric; we have always known that he is an absolute fool and have always marveled at the obtuseness of his brain box."

The question of money was even more serious, and the shade of the boy who had helped Verlaine to run through thirty thousand francs in a year retired behind a barrage of moral indignation. "There's no need to tell me not to write to him. As for giving him something, what I earn is too painfully accumulated for me to make presents to a bedouin of that type who I am sure is considerably less overworked than I."

There remained Frédéric's criticisms of himself—for Frédéric had been unable to see his brother as the paragon of the family —and the shade of past years receded still further as Rimbaud defended himself with some hauteur and an abundance of underlining: "My conduct is known here as elsewhere. I can send you proof of the *exceptional* satisfaction with me for *four years of service, from 1880 to 1884* which the liquidated Mazeran Company has expressed. I have a very good reputation here which allows me to earn my living decently. If I once had some unhappy moments, I have never tried to live at the expense of other people nor by bad means."

The self-righteousness of the reformed was all very well but his mother was chiefly concerned to get him to Roche even if only as a counterblast of respectability to the embarrassing Frédéric. To both her and Isabelle he was the sole man of the family and his place was at home. An even stronger emotion than peasant tradition moved Madame Rimbaud; he had long since stopped sending his savings home where she could convert them into indestructible land; he was actually walking about with thousands of francs on him. She remembered with a shudder the affair of the camera; she knew that sooner or later if left with the money he would commit a yet worse folly and lose the lot. So she made another effort to bring him back; she proposed to let out his land at Roche, she said, but would keep the house which he must consider as his own, for himself and his wife.

He approved but did not choose to take up the offer; he felt that once back at Roche and married he would not leave it, which was his mother's calculation too: "As you say, farming will never be my vocation and I have no objection to seeing the lands let; I hope that they'll be let soon and well. To keep the house is always a good thing. As for my staying there with you, this would be most agreeable to me; I should be very happy to take a rest; but I can scarcely see the chance of it taking shape. Up to the present I have found a living here; if I leave, what am I likely to come across to take its place? How can I bury myself in a country where no one knows me, where I can't find a chance of earning something? You say, I should only go there to rest myself; but to do that an income is necessary; to marry, an income is necessary; and I haven't an income. For a long time to come I am condemned to follow the trails where I can find a living until I can scrape together, by dint of hard labor, the means for resting myself temporarily."

This was not wholly frank, and he argued on, as special pleaders always do: "I have on me at present thirteen thousand francs. What do you think I could do with that in France? What kind of marriage do you think it would procure for me? Everybody can find poor and honest women! If I marry one back there, shan't I be forced to travel to make a living?"

The next month, January, 1885, Khartoum fell and Gordon was killed before the rescue force arrived. But this tragic blunder excepted, Rimbaud's pessimistic predictions, made in almost every letter, of political disaster and personal ruin, were all proved mistaken; for Bardey re-engaged him for the whole of 1885 as coffee buyer, an engagement which would, he calculated, bring his savings up to 17,000 francs by December. "Don't think of me as a capitalist," he added with imperfectly concealed pride.

He told his mother, to whom the thought of 17,000 Rimbaud francs at the mercy of her son's judgment was a sort of agony, "People who have spent some years here can't pass a winter in Europe; they would die quickly with inflammation of the lungs. If I come back, it will only be in summer, and I shall be obliged to go down, in winter at least, towards the Mediterranean."

Then, with a kind of defiance: "In any case don't reckon on my inclination to wander becoming less. On the contrary, if I had the means to travel without being forced to earn a living, I should never be seen for two months together in the same place. The world is very large and full of magnificent countries; a man would not have time to visit all of them even if he had a thousand lives. But on the other hand I don't want to roam in misery. I want to have an income of some thousand francs so that I can pass the year in two or three different countries, living modestly and doing odd spots of business to cover my expenses. But I should find it wretched to live always in the same place."

This classic challenge was followed by no less common efforts to engage sympathy. As the new year passed into spring he told her that he had gastric fever, could digest nothing, that his stomach had grown very feeble. Her remark that the weather

was exceptionally hard only drew out a "If you complain of the
cold, I complain of the heat." Forgetting his role, he castigated
the heat he was supposed to worship; it was insupportable and
a robber besides: "Every night of the year I sleep in the open
air, yet my lodgings cost 40 francs a month!" He drank nothing
stronger than water, never smoked, wore cotton always, yet "I
live horribly badly here at great cost!" His was "the most
atrocious existence in the world," no one to talk to, business
poor and himself a slave: "Every day I work from 7 to 5 and
I've never had a day off. When is this life going to end?"

And with the comprehensive jeremiad: "We are in our spring
oven; skins stream, stomachs grow sour, brains become confused, business is foul, news is bad," he left his family without
a letter until the end of September.

His lot, though dismal enough, was not so entirely joyless as
he made out. He enjoyed making plans to escape, to India,
Tonkin, Panama, Zanzibar (he spoke of them all), where money
was supposed to flow, a chance word in the office or market
being enough for him. He enjoyed his intellectual eminence. He
was proud of his reputation as a "safe" man and a wit. He was
proud of his growing savings. He was not even so lonely as he
would have his mother believe; he had a certain unwilling
liking for both the Bardeys and he had found a good listener
when he wanted to forget money, in a journalist, Franzoj, friend
of an Italian trader. Franzoj was in his spare moments a Latinist
with a passion for Horace and an admirer of French literature;
he and Rimbaud, said the trader, used to discuss this literature
"from the romantics to the decadents by the hour." Anxious to
emphasize his superiority over an employer, Rimbaud even told
Bardey that after he had made his pile he intended to re-enter
the world of letters.

He and Franzoj had become intimate enough for Rimbaud
to write to him in September when he had decided to get rid
of his girl. The note speaks for itself: "I'm sorry, but I send
this woman back without forgiveness. I shall give her some
thalers and she will go off on the ship from Rasali to Obock

where she can do what she pleases. I have watched this panto-
mime long enough. I wouldn't have been so stupid as to cart
her all the way from Choa so I shan't be so stupid as to trouble
to send her back there."

Two months later came the appeal that he had waited many
years for: "Arthur, my son, your silence is long. Why this
silence? Happy are those who have no children, happier those
who don't love them: they are indifferent to everything that
can happen to them. Perhaps I ought not to worry; at the same
time last year you neither wrote to me for six months nor replied
to any of my letters however urgent they were; but this time we
have had no news from you for eight long months. It is useless
to speak of ourselves to you since what concerns us interests
you so little. However it is impossible that you could forget us
in this way. What has happened to you? Aren't you free to move
any more? Are you so ill that you can't hold a pen? Or aren't
you at Aden any longer? Have you gone to the Chinese empire?
Truly we are going out of our minds thinking of you and I come
back to what I said: 'Happy, oh! very happy are those who have
no children or who don't love them!' Those at least have no
disappointment to dread since their heart is closed to everyone surrounding them. But what is the use of spreading myself
further? Who knows whether you will read this letter? Perhaps
it will never reach you since I don't know where you are or what
you are doing."

If this letter protested too much, Rimbaud would be the last
to see it. It would probably have tempted him home, inde-
pendence fully secured or not. But by the time it arrived he
had no choice; Madame Rimbaud's last effort to preserve his
savings had failed; he had already committed himself and them.

CHAPTER FOURTEEN

Gunrunner
1885–1887

THERE were in Abyssinia at this time two kings, Joannes of Tigre in the west and Menelik of Shoa in the south. Joannes was a smallish man. Dressed in his favorite white silk and perched aloft on a plank throne with legs folded beneath him, he looked like a white cocoon. A rather malevolent cocoon; what could be seen of his face through slits in the silk was not reassuring: two burning black eyes regarded the visitor with distrust; a thin line of mouth pursed with pleasure at thought of the punishment soon to be pronounced. For Joannes liked to punish; he told himself, the culprit and anyone else who would listen that it was God's will, but the culprit had his doubts. Joannes' view of religion was of the Calvinist variety: for instance, any of his subjects caught in the act of smoking promptly had a leg or arm lopped off. This was God's will too. All in all, Tigre was a sober place to live in.

Joannes was a crafty fellow. Menelik was slippery too. But Menelik at least looked the part of King; he was a big man and could wear a lion's skin with an air. To Europeans, it is true, his penchant for a quaker hat detracted from the general effect; this apart, he presented a majestic figure. Jovial too on occasion, for Menelik had a sense of humor. What specially pleased him was to get the better of a white man; then the big brown face would spread into a thousand creases, the large teeth gleam, the great right hand slip from its jeweled dagger hilt. Only one thing could have given him greater pleasure, to slit the throat of Joannes.

For Menelik and Joannes were not the best of friends. Both men were spoiling for a fight and were not too particular with whom, but their preference was to make mincemeat of each

245

other. Joannes irritated Menelik almost beyond endurance by styling himself the Most Christian Emperor of All the Abyssinians and, what hurt most, the Lion of Judah. That Joannes had some claim to the first of these titles even Menelik did not deny with conviction; he simply omitted to mention that he was officially a vassal of Joannes. But the Lion of Judah was another matter; Menelik proclaimed himself right and left as the One True King of Shoa, of Kaffa and of all the country of the Gallas round about, and he flew the Lion of Judah on standard, shield and royal residence. To Joannes this was in the worst of taste, and Menelik would not have lived an hour longer had he not been difficult to reach and his armies stronger than Joannes chose to admit.

Whilst Egypt was on the warpath—an expansion which culminated in the capture of Harar in 1874—both kings skulked in their fastnesses, Menelik shorn of Harar, Joannes preparing for the worst. Ten years later, with Egypt firmly tucked behind her own frontiers again, England preoccupied with the Mahdi, and France and Italy content to snatch ports on the Red Sea coast whilst no one was looking, the kingly pretensions shot back once more and there was none to say them nay. France and Italy favored Menelik; England, busily pursuing her policy of divide and rule, leaned towards Joannes, but as they could not get at either their interest remained largely academic. Apart from the appalling nature of the roadless savagery which separated them, only one difficulty kept Joannes and Menelik from each other's throats; they were too well matched for either to be sure of gaining the decision.

An obvious answer presented itself; the King who first armed his soldiers with modern weapons could safely begin the war. It is difficult to say whether this idea burst upon Joannes and Menelik spontaneously or was introduced by European gunrunners who had picked out both as excellent customers. By the time Rimbaud retired in dudgeon to Aden in 1884 one of these men, a Frenchman, Pierre Labatut, had obtained a firm grasp of Menelik's ear, had married one of Menelik's subjects and was raising a dusky family in Menelik's capital of Ankober.

Labatut was making a nice little fortune for himself by buying old rifles on the cheap, transporting them by camel from the Red Sea coast to Ankober and selling them at several times their value. He was an attractive adventurer with a convincing tongue; when he came down to Aden in the autumn of 1885 to arrange for another shipment of arms, met Rimbaud by chance and realized that the bored and impressionable young man had a useful hoard of savings, he had no difficulty in persuading him that there was big and quick money, as well as change of scene, in the business. Rimbaud, won over at once, passed on his new oracle's predictions enthusiastically to his mother: "The goods we are importing are rifles (forty years old) for which the dealers in old arms, at Liege or in France, charge 7 to 8 francs. We can sell these to Menelik II, King of Shoa, at 40 francs each . . . Barring accidents I reckon to make a profit of 20 or 30 thousand francs in less than a year."

For the idea was scarcely in his mind than without a word to Bardey he signed a contract with Labatut by which he handed over his savings and was to receive 20,000 francs, all expenses paid, when the trip was over. A few days later, having committed himself, he broke his contract with Bardey: "I have left my job after a violent quarrel with these vile misers who had hoped to stupefy me to the end of time. I have done many services for these people, and they thought that I would stay with them, for their benefit, for the rest of my life. They have done everything to try to keep me but I have told them to go to the devil with their profits and their business and their frightful house and their dirty town!" He added: "They have given me excellent references for the five years."

The addition explains all that had gone before. His rancor covered uneasiness rather than hard feeling. He had abandoned a safe job for a gamble which, as his mother would at once deduce, involved every sou he had saved in the past two years;

how better anticipate the inevitable protests than simultaneously throw doubts on his employers and flourish a testimonial from them? The Bardey brothers were not bad men (Alfred was to take the trouble to make the long journey to Madame Rimbaud after her son's death) and they had his interests in mind rather than their own when they warned him against Labatut whose reputation on the coast was none too good. This warning he rejected with loud denunciations. Bardey said afterwards that he did not try to keep Rimbaud as soon as he realized that his savings were already promised to Labatut. "In any case," he added, "one might just as well have tried to stop a shooting star." Rimbaud had not changed; at thirty-one as at sixteen when he wanted something he had to have it.

By the beginning of December he was at the village of Tadjourah in the newly formed colony of Obock (later French Somaliland) across the Red Sea from Aden. Tadjourah, an uninviting collection of mud huts, was the starting place for the caravans to Ankober. In the first days of the new year, 1886, Rimbaud, optimistic as ever when action opened out, was prophesying that by late summer he would have done his gunrunning and be at Roche enjoying his ease out of the profits.

He did not reckon with fate, at first in the form of the English who, an irate eye on this traffic of arms to the King they had not backed, made many difficulties about a permit for the rifles to be embarked. Then, the permit finally obtained and the arms assembled, Labatut became ill, grew rapidly worse and returned to France to die, leaving his affairs in confusion. Rimbaud, his money spread about in boxes of rifles and ammunition, could not face an ignominious and unprofitable retreat. He even had visions of greater profit with Labatut out of the way and tragedy turned into triumph. Unwilling to risk the long journey without an experienced companion, he arranged to travel with another caravan led by the explorer Soleillet. "I've had no luck!" he was to tell his mother, and he said no more than the truth. Misfortune continued; before the caravan was ready to leave Soleillet fell dead in the street.

By this time Rimbaud had been chafing for nine months in Tadjourah. Desperate, he set off on his own shortly before his thirty-second birthday with his two thousand rifles and sixty thousand cartridges. The journey, a long ordeal of desert crossings harassed by hostile Danakils, took him four months, twice as long as the usual fifty days of Labatut and the few others familiar with that wild country. He arrived in Ankober on February 6, 1887, tired out and anxious to get his money and be gone. But Menelik was away on a campaign to recapture Harar.

After fuming helplessly in Ankober for some weeks Rimbaud heard that Menelik had won a great victory, had taken Harar and was returning not to Ankober but to the still more remote Antotto which he had determined to make his capital. Wearily Rimbaud made his way up to Antotto and there, in May, was at last received in audience.

Rimbaud, describing the return of the victorious army, tells how the troops hastened back bearing in triumph and with a kind of wonder the genitals of the Frenchmen they had killed in Harar, the first white ones they or their families had ever seen. They were simple souls, these Abyssinian warriors of the eighties, with simple pleasures, and Rimbaud made the mistake of expecting their king to be of the same kind; he pictured Menelik's childlike delight at being permitted to buy, at five times their price, ancient rifles, many incapable of firing a shot. A few years earlier Gordon, not unlike Rimbaud in his feelings (at certain moments) of infallibility, had bearded Joannes in his lair on a diplomatic mission. He barely escaped with his life. Rimbaud was more fortunate yet not fortunate enough. Menelik had learned a thing or two from the Europeans who sold him arms and spent much of their time in his country; he was also a shrewd man. He summed up at a glance the grim-faced young Frenchman angry at his long wait, barely troubling to conceal his arrogance before a colored man, too proud to descend to tact, inexperienced in the arms traffic. He said that the arms were too dear, and offered a greatly reduced price. Rimbaud refused it contemptuously. Menelik, not at all put out,

replied that he had no particular need of them and told his
visitor to take the consignment back where he had brought it
from.

There was no arguing with this. Rimbaud had neglected
the elementary principle of his new trade; the campaign over,
Menelik was in no immediate need of his goods and could dic-
tate the terms. Furiously he agreed to sell at Menelik's price,
agreed with an openly bad grace.

Worse followed. His manner had antagonized the King, the
court and his own countrymen there. Menelik decided that he
must be taught a lesson. The consignment was in the joint names
of Rimbaud and Labatut; Labatut's creditors suddenly appeared
in shoals demanding payment, Labatut's family loudly claimed
their share. Rimbaud found himself involved in interminable
lawsuits. He could make neither head nor tail of the matter,
could not distinguish genuine creditors from fake, could not
follow the unorthodox procedure of Menelik's law court. No one
supported him. The regular European traders, offended by his
unfriendliness and air of superiority and fearful of the effect of
his meeting with Menelik on their own business, stood aloof.

He gave way and settled the debts. Then, as anxious to be
out of Shoa as he had been eager to be in it for the last few
years, and having obtained permission from the now beaming
Menelik, he joined the Italian explorer Borelli who was just
about to leave for Harar. Rimbaud took with him an order from
Menelik to Ras Makonnen, the new governor, to pay him the
much reduced sum.

In June, following the route of Menelik's march and what
was later to be the way taken by the railway to Addis Ababa,
Rimbaud was in Harar. He was paid by Ras Makonnen after
the usual delays and hurried down to Aden where he arrived at
the end of the next month, one year later than he had predicted
to his mother. From there he addressed a long and angry scream
of protest to the French consul: after twenty months "of atrocious
hardships" he had lost 60 per cent of his money. He had been
robbed! Menelik had not kept his word! He went into every

detail with meticulous care, determined that the consul should not have the excuse of inaccuracies or omissions to justify inaction, and ended with a rash "Ask anybody who was there" and a demand for redress. The consul, who had received protests from Rimbaud before, returned a smooth answer; he may have thought that for a gunrunner's profits to be cut from time to time was a minor tragedy; he knew well enough that neither Menelik nor his people would refund a sou.

Months later, whilst the affairs of Rimbaud's caravan were still being unraveled, and after the consul had been able to speak to other Europeans in Menelik's capital, there came from him what can be considered the final though tactful word: "I have verified, by the details you have given, that in effect this commercial transaction has been disastrous for you, and that you have not hesitated to sacrifice your rights to satisfy the many creditors of Monsieur Labatut"—a polite manner of praising the inescapable. "But," he continued, "I must also recognize, when I refer to the declarations of Europeans coming from Shoa whom you yourself invoked as witnesses, that your losses would perhaps have been less great if, like other traders who do business with the Abyssinian authorities, you had known or been able to adapt yourself to the particular requirements of these countries and their rulers."

CHAPTER FIFTEEN

Fame and Fortune

1887–1888

FOR the better part of a year after his return from Menelik, Rimbaud sought high and low for a way out of the future that faced him if he stayed in that area—the life of a Red Sea trader. He refused his mother's offers of help if he came home, giving always the same answers, fear of the cold, dislike of sedentary work and lack of sufficient capital. This last was the real point and never more so than then. Instead of the boasted return home with his gunrunning gains he found himself with savings diminished. Rather than endure the "I told you so" at Roche, he preferred to stay where he was.

After a few days in Aden he set off for Cairo. The Red Sea heat that year, he said, was unbearable. So were his thoughts. He was held up at Massawa which had recently been seized by Italy; his papers were not in order and the French consul there asked his colleague in Aden for references for "this individual whose bearing is somewhat suspicious."

Released, he went up to Cairo with the vague intention of getting temporary work in a more agreeable climate. He did not find work, but managed to publish an account of his travels in Abyssinia, with a comment on the politics of Menelik and Joannes, in the Cairo journal *Le Bosphore Egyptien*. He also wrote a description of his journey from Antotto to Harar, with notes on trade possibilities, which he sent to Alfred Bardey. The abuse of two years earlier when he left the Bardeys precipitately was put out of mind. He was unashamedly preparing a return to the "vile misers" if nothing better offered itself; as the end of his covering letter, a dismal "hard luck" record, shows: "I am at your service at any time when you have an undertaking in which I could be of use . . . Have the kindness to think of me." The amiable Alfred Bardey, bearing no ill will, did think of him, sending the article to the Société de Géographie as his brother had sent the account on Ogaden years before. It was printed in the Transactions of the Société in November, 1887.

But in August Rimbaud had only the one small satisfaction of the Cairo newspaper to cheer him; it was not enough to modify his view that life's scales were weighted against him. "I've had no luck!": that was the refrain of the letters he began to write to Roche after almost a year of silence. His hair had turned grey, he said, he could find nothing to do, felt exceedingly tired and was tormented by rheumatism "which drives me mad" in the back, shoulder, thigh and knee: "I suppose that my very life is in danger."

He was always sure of a hearing when he complained of aches and pains but, unconscious of the tragic irony of the intended exaggeration, he passed on to another form of suffering in which he knew his mother would share with real concern: "I'm frightened of losing the little I have. Just imagine, I carry constantly in my belt sixteen thousand and some hundreds of gold franc pieces; these weigh nearly eighteen pounds and give me dysentery."

He did not see the grotesqueness of this Hans Andersen predicament but he did eventually realize its unprofitability. One day either the dysentery or the loss of interest forced him into a bank where he put the greater part of the contents of his belt on deposit at 4 per cent. This made him easier in every way but led him straight into another impasse. Having brought himself to the point of trusting a bank he could not bear to forfeit a single sou of interest; he therefore deposited all sixteen thousand francs, leaving himself with insufficient money to pay for a passage to Zanzibar which he had half decided to take.

Unable to endure the thought of breaking into the banked money, he begged his mother the next day to lend him five hundred francs, the amount he needed to reach Zanzibar. Fearful that she would refuse, he wrote again the following day, to his "Chère Maman" this time, thus giving her the unexpected pleasure, which she had however to weigh against a reckless expenditure on stamps, of receiving three letters in three days. He begged her "not to refuse to send me the five hundred francs I have asked for" and promised to repay before the end of the year if the money had to come out of her own pocket.

He calculated correctly; if there was one consideration which would extract more money from Madame Rimbaud it was to leave capital untouched. She sent the five hundred francs which he received with a gratified "I see that I'm not forgotten."

The arrival of her letter was his only pleasure; by the time the money reached him, in October, he had drifted back to Aden, Zanzibar had lost most of its charm, and all other projects of the last three months had fallen to the ground. He was too susceptible to trade gossip and had been listening with worried attention. The Zanzibar plan of August, which he favored, he told his mother, as he had good recommendations and because "from there one can make long journeys into Africa and perhaps to China or Japan and who knows where?" became by October "I shall stay a month here before leaving for Zanzibar. I haven't decided to go in that direction with any cheerfulness, I have seen people come back from there in a deplorable state."

Yet by this time Zanzibar appeared almost a last hope. Since August one plan after another had miscarried. First in order was the old dream of receiving the financial backing of the Société de Géographie. As soon as he knew that Bardey had sent to the Société the account of his latest journey he followed with a letter asking for a definite sum of money to pay for further explorations in Abyssinia. Early in October his request was refused, no reason being given; the secretary recommended him to apply to the French government, but said he did not think that the ministry in question would pay, since "your journey would not directly cover French territory or concern French politics." Nevertheless he offered, if Rimbaud would write a monograph on Abyssina with full details, to do his best to have it published "and make it well known." This, he thought, might influence the government favorably.

Rimbaud was far too impatient, and far too reluctant to live on his savings, to wait for the leisurely reply of the Société; another chance of fame and, if not exactly fortune, excellent rewards, had sprung up—War. Massawa was, in theory, Joannes' Red Sea port; he demanded the withdrawal of the Italians; Italy replied with an assurance that her main object in settling at Massawa was to trade with Joannes and fill his coffers. But as Joannes, who was well served in the information line, knew that Italy was pouring troops into the port and had opened friendly negotiations with Menelik, he received her assurances with a certain scepticism, and expressed his doubts soon afterwards by what he hoped would be a surprise attack on one of the armed posts covering Massawa. This was in January, 1887. The attack was only moderately successful, but was followed before the month was out by the first of the many shocks which the Abyssinians were to cause Italy, the virtual wiping out of a relief force. By the time Rimbaud passed through Massawa the port had been put onto a war footing (hence the suspicion with which he was regarded there) and by the time he had been in Cairo for a few weeks everyone had begun to realize that Joannes would be difficult to defeat.

It was a real war. And who more suitable as war correspondent than Rimbaud? He offered his services to the Paris newspaper *Le Temps*. He also wrote to an old Charleville College boy, Paul Bourde, literary correspondent of *Le Temps*, asking him to put in a good word for him.

This request was more ill-timed than he could have known. Bourde had led the attack, two years earlier, on the "horrible decadents" and their "morbid and uncouth" school of modern poetry—a poetry which he exemplified by Verlaine's "Il pleure dans mon cœur"; his attacks provoked the publication of Moreas' Symbolist manifesto out of which grew the Symbolist group of poets with Rimbaud as one of their gods. Bourde, then, did not regard Rimbaud with a kindly eye. He did not recommend him for the post and took the opportunity of putting into perspective, as he chose to see perspective, the position in the Parisian world of letters: "Living so far away from us you probably don't know that to a small coterie in Paris you've become a kind of legendary figure . . . They have published in a Latin Quarter periodical your early efforts in verse and prose and have even made a small book of them. Certain young men whom I personally consider rather naïve have tried to make a system out of your "Sonnet des Voyelles." This little group hails you as master and . . . devoutly trusts that you will one day return and rescue it from obscurity. But to tell you the truth I hasten to add that, practically, this is valueless. All the same, to be frank, in the midst of a mass of weird incoherence I was struck by the surprising virtuosity of your first youthful attempts."

No help there. By this time he had heard from the Société de Géographie but was in no mood to sit down to the composition of a monograph on Abyssinia which might or might not be printed. And as Zanzibar was rapidly losing its glamour, he turned back to a pursuit of which he at least knew the rudiments. He thought of selling more arms to Menelik. Nor was this resolve so foolhardy as it appeared. He had gained confidence by his desert crossing to Shoa, and from the lamentable weeks in the King's capital had come a solitary benefit, a sort of friendship with the Swiss engineer Alfred Ilg who in the manner of those days and countries acted as go-between for Menelik and the foreigners. Ilg, a most informal kind of minister of trade, had a dry sense of humor and was not above amusing gossip. He had endured the angry Rimbaud for the sake of the "lugubrious sketches" of mellower moments and because, knowing the wiles of Menelik, he pitied the straight-dealing young Frenchman with the rigid mind. In a disarming way he had made him understand the sympathy behind his smiles. Rimbaud believed that Ilg would speak for him a second time and help him. With his mother's help, he set about obtaining a permit for the importation of arms.

But one obstacle after another was put in his way, and it seemed to him as if official obstructionism might successfully keep him dangling for years. There he was, in October, 1887, at Aden again, jobless, futureless, and infuriated by all manner of things; by talent ignored, chiefly, and by the drain on his savings, a slight drain since he lived like an anchorite but none the less hurtful to a Cuif. He had the feeling of slipping backwards; the vision of dazzling his mother with a fortune brilliantly snatched from under the noses of ordinary men, of a life of leisured ease at Roche, in Charleville, in whatever part of the world he elected to take himself to, declined into the harrowing prospect of begging for a stool in Bardey's office.

At this point, whilst negotiations for a permit dragged on, he met Armand Savouré. Savouré was the biggest "arms King" of the area, a man who did not trouble overmuch about permits. Like Labatut, he was clever, convincing, had a sense of humor and plenty of charm. Rimbaud, impatient and still hopeful, was at once captivated by lavish promises of large and quick profits. For his part, Savouré, like others before him, reckoned that he could be profitably used. In January, 1888, they came to an understanding and after some bargaining Rimbaud took Savouré's first caravan of arms to Harar in March; from Harar Menelik's governor was responsible for them. The operation was successful up to a point; the caravan evaded detection and reached Harar in good time; but commercially it disappointed. "I don't consider that your job has entirely succeeded for you haven't been firm enough and haven't had confidence in my words," Savouré wrote; by which he meant simply that, as before, after succeeding in transporting the goods Rimbaud had failed as negotiatior.

Nevertheless Rimbaud's courage, coolness and ability in handling men and animals were impressive, and Savouré put him in charge of another gunrunning expedition. At the last moment, at the secret request of the French government, he was obliged to turn the leadership over to an Arab, "because" he explained to the disappointed Rimbaud, "owing to the English attitude, Frenchmen must not appear to be mixed up in this affair." Rimbaud, finding himself for the moment without occupation again, returned to his beginnings; he agreed to open a branch in Harar for an Aden merchant. This man, César Tian, had one of the

oldest established trader's businesses in Aden. He had just decided
to set up a branch in Harar—the first trader to do so since its
capture by Menelik. Rimbaud, with his knowledge of the Hararis
and his reputation as a "safe" man, was an obvious choice as
manager. Savouré promised to use him as agent in his gunrunning
transactions, and he intended to do some business of his own on
the side. All in all, with three separate sources of income, there
appeared once more a chance of adding substantially to those
sixteen thousand francs. He did not hesitate, and by May was
back in Harar.

2　 ✐

1888–1891

He spent three years in Harar. He worked hard and with a
kind of desperation, sparing neither himself nor others; to say
that he worked himself to the bone would scarcely be an exaggeration for he ate next to nothing, went about in an old cotton
suit, rested with reluctance, was forever walking or riding out
in search of custom, and put every sou back into the business.
Rimbaud the adventurer had gone the way of Rimbaud the poet,
and Rimbaud the peasant took his place; Madame Rimbaud herself could not have worked harder nor saved more stringently.
Yet he made no fortune; his savings mounted, but little quicker
than if he had stayed in Aden with Bardey or had even taken the
despised town council job in Charleville that his mother so
earnestly wished for him. If he went into the slave traffic with
Savouré—and he certainly approached Ilg and was snubbed with
a "I have never bought slaves and I don't want to begin"—
neither this nor the gunrunning which he unquestionably did
brought in the large returns he had confidently expected. Not,
at least, to him. Savouré was altogether too sharp, too experienced
to let his junior partner take more than a junior reward. Savouré
marveled at the sheer slogging of this mistakenly dedicated man's
life, he professed fear of the temperamental Rimbaud "the

terror of underlings" and unreservedly reveled in his verbal take-
offs: "I practically never saw him smile, but he made us laugh
till we cried; he was one of the most delightful raconteurs I
have ever met." But for all his respect, pity and admiration, when
it came to the making of money he outstripped Rimbaud with
absurd ease.

In the Rimbaud house at Harar there was no more skimming
of textbooks to master all knowledge in double quick time, no
more demands for this, for that, in almost every letter to the
family, no more talk of biding his time. Rimbaud had left the
realms of the fabulous once and for all. No quick fortune for
him, he saw that after a few months; and no wandering about the
world, a monied man. But no settling down at Roche either until
he could be truly independent and respected; about that he remained adamant. He had finally lowered his sights; he would
be a trader.

To this had come the terrible "Rimbe." He would be a trader.
Yet not a very successful one. The first trader back in the town,
experienced, hard-working, infinitely superior intellectually to
all who competed with him, fortunate after a year (Joannes
having been killed in a skirmish with Mahdists) to see Menelik
proclaimed Emperor and to have won the ear of Ilg at court,
everything was in his favor: everything but himself. For money
was being made and plenty of it in that area; and if Rimbaud did
not get his fair share there were good reasons. He would not
hobnob with the other traders at the cafés and did not hear the
business tips over drinks; his resolute non-smoking, non-drinking
attitude was an unpopular as his tongue; his excessive care of his
money was a standing joke and his aloofness gave offense. Even
his honesty, though it earned him general respect, did not protect him from the less scrupulous; they, not he, made the big
profits. Time after time, carried away by love of a bargain, he
forgot that there was no point in snapping something up cheaply
if he could not sell it at any price. So Ilg is found protesting
humorously after inspecting Rimbaud's "famous bazaar" sent up
from Harar, that this included religious ornaments "which I

don't even dare to give away. The Abyssinians would easily take me for a disguised capuchin friar"; imitation pearls "which you would have done better to shoot birds with"; and cheap writing pads: "To sell these pads to people who don't know how to write and who haven't learned the way to use such things in private, this is really too much to ask."

And Rimbaud fell into the trap waiting for the Harpagons; trying to cut expenses to vanishing point, he reduced the rations of his men and animals to an extent which prevented them from serving him efficiently. When one of his caravans crawled worn out and days late into Menelik's capital, Ilg, horrified, once again reproached him: "Not a single caravan of yours has arrived here without being famished nor without all the servants being in a deplorable state, and everybody complaining bitterly of you." He pointed out, as friend to friend: "It's not worth the trouble of saving a few thalers on food only to have all the servants ill and unable to work for months."

The clever man is not always intelligent and Rimbaud had shown this in everything he touched, but most of all when he invaded commerce. For he made a stupid error, he despised both the job and the men in the job. How easy to outsmart them, hard-drinking, loose-living, ill-educated traders! Yet even when he abandoned hope of a quick fortune, he could not compete with the dull, the illiterate, the cheap with a business instinct. First he tried to be too clever, then too cautious. They had waited for the right moment to strike whilst he was trying brilliant short cuts; now he discovered that watchful application did not necessarily bring in the most profits. Savouré summed up the matter with his "Instead of believing like you that everyone is a rascal I believe too easily that all are honest." And the man who made the money was Savouré.

Rimbaud's thirty-fourth birthday passed, his thirty-fifth, his thirty-sixth. Hopeful young editors of Left Bank periodicals wrote for contributions. No answer. In Paris, Verlaine wrote the first of his great sonnets to a Rimbaud he believed to be dead. The savings crept towards forty thousand francs. Less than forty thousand francs in ten years; what was this to a man who had thought in terms of thirty thousand a year? He worked even harder and became less and less approachable, a dried up man, his soul like the parchment face, old before his time. Ilg, the only European to notice or care to notice what was happening, remonstrated in his friendly way. Not many years earlier he had been so "divinely amused" by a Rimbaud word-portrait of one of his fellow traders that he was saying enviously, "Monsieur Savouré tells me that you have written to him; I'm delighted, but I could also have done with the honor and pleasure of having my morale raised a bit by you and your good stories." But those days had passed. Even the visit of an ambassador to Harar could not stir him, and Ilg, waiting hopefully for the witty-satirical account which never came, wrote disappointedly: "You know so well how to tell a story when you feel in the mood; but it seems that big business has completely driven out the little cheerfulness left in you. Look here, my dear Monsieur Rimbaud, one only lives once; make the most of it, then, and send your heirs to the devil."

But Rimbaud was beyond the help of friendship; he had become a money-making, money-thinking automaton. Yet, half aware of this, his resentfully exaggerated complaints of loneliness, boredom, isolation continued. "What do you expect me to tell you?" he cried after his mother protested that he had not written home for months: "About the desert tribes, the stupid negroes, the lack of roads, posts, travelers? . . . That one is bored, embittered, brutalized, that one has had enough but can't stop!" And so on in this strain until Madame Rimbaud called his bluff. She knew well enough that the complaints had a purpose, and she countered again with a, Why did he not come home and marry? She began to talk in almost every letter of marriage: he was no longer young; the idea of a child of Frédéric inheriting all was bitter to her; she longed for a true heir to the Rimbaud name and property. Perhaps she had an inkling of the truth about the aches, pains and inexplicable weariness of which he complained and felt obscurely that time was short; certainly,

like everyone from whom the impossible is asked, she hastened
to give what she could. She was truly concerned about his health
and his money and said so, fulsomely for her. Where would he
go if taken ill? she wanted to know. And if he died, what of his
savings? Had he taken all precautions that the money would not
be left lying about at Harar to be stolen? If in Aden, was he sure
that it was safe? And was he certain that in any event it would
be sent to Roche?

If he were to become ill, Rimbaud replied, pleased with these
signs of interest and proud to display his sensible precautions,
he could go into the Christian mission at Harar "to which I
should entrust my will which would be sent on to the French
consulate in Aden." If he fell seriously ill he would probably
liquidate his business and go back to Aden "which is a civilized
country where one can put one's affairs in order at once." As for
his savings: "I have them with me."

He rejected his mother's renewed mention of marriage with
"When one goes into trade in this satanic country one doesn't
leave it any more . . . I have neither the time to marry nor to
think of marrying." This being something less than gracious, he
threw in another appeal to pity. One of his most admirable
traits was a refusal to make use of his charm outside the home,
in fact he laid himself out to be uncharming; when he fascinated
a Delahaye, an Izambard, Demeny, Verlaine, Bardey, Ilg, the
charm was working against the grain. His pride was in what
the charm obscured, his virility, his ability to walk further than
most men, to outlast them in everything from conversation to
physical endurance. His hair, that thick wavy chestnut hair,
symbolized this abundant energy. But it was no longer chestnut,
as he sadly and purposefully added: "I'm well but my hair gets
whiter every moment . . . I'm afraid I shall soon have a head
like a powder puff. It's desolating, this treason of the scalp, but
what can one do?"

Madame Rimbaud did not reply. She was not pleased. By this
time, April, 1890, her son had been in Harar for two years and
away from home for ten. No woman was better able to appre-

ciate the merit of a man sticking to his work and making money, but Rimbaud evidently did not like his work and was not making the pile on which he had so often declared he would quickly retire. Why, then, wear out a life in uncongenial surroundings when an aging mother was left without the support of what had virtually become an only son? She knew by long experience that he could be brought to heel by silence. She remained silent.

He became conciliatory. In August, after protesting that he had not heard from her for a long time, he asked: "Shall I come back next spring to get married at Roche?" Then, having given way, he had a vision of Madame Rimbaud ruling the household, him and his wife as well as Isabelle, and controlling the education of his longed-for son, and added with a last flicker of the rebellious poet, "But I can't agree to remain in your house or to give up my business here. Do you think I can find someone who will consent to follow me in my travels? I'd much like a reply to this question as soon as possible."

This brought the desired reply, one so satisfied that Rimbaud warned his mother again that he could not live in France, or at least not for some time. But he took the matter seriously enough to list a catalogue of the solid virtues calculated to tempt the women of Charleville or Roche, calculated too, he hoped, to impress the reader. His whole capital, he pointed out, "is at my disposal, free to be used whenever I wish." At Harar he dealt in gold, musk, ivory, coffee, et cetera, and took half profits when he worked for Tian, the whole when he did business on his own; he was at liberty to pack up and go at a moment's notice. His employer was "a very honorable trader established for 30 years in Aden." As for his own reputation: "No one at Aden can say a bad word of me. On the contrary. I have been well known by all in this country for the last ten years." Finally, if anyone wished to confirm these statements, "They have only to write to Monsieur de Gaspary, French consul at Aden, or to his successor."

And with this "Notice to lovers!" as he playfully called it, he left his mother with the understanding that he would return in the spring.

Chapter Sixteen

Homecoming

1891

O N February 20, 1891, a month or two before he planned to leave for Roche, Rimbaud wrote to his "Dear Friends." The letter did not differ materially from any other of the dissatisfied letters he had been writing for years past; it was a little more specific than usual, that was all. "I'm not well at the moment. At least, varicose veins in my right leg are causing me much pain. That's what one gets for working hard in these wretched countries! And the varicose veins are complicated by rheumatism."

He asked his mother to send him elastic stockings, and reassured her and himself with: "Varicose veins aren't dangerous but they prevent all violent exercise. This is a great bore because the varicose veins lead to sores unless one wears special stockings; yet at the same time the leg, being already irritated, will scarcely bear these stockings, above all at night. On top of this I have a rheumatic pain in that wretched right knee which tortures me, also catching me specially at night!"

For further reassurance he added: "Young Europeans of no more than 25 to 30 years old are struck down by rheumatism after living two or three years here!"

There was nothing to worry Madame Rimbaud unduly and certainly not the rheumatism which her son had been complaining of four years earlier at Cairo. However she was a woman who took bodily ills seriously, the more so because she was as strong as a horse; she went straight off to her doctor, ordered elastic stockings from Paris and sent them to Harar with a special ointment for the varicose veins and detailed instructions; for, she said, quoting the doctor, "Your ailment has reached a point which causes me a certain anxiety about the future."

But the varicose veins were not the real trouble; long before Madame Rimbaud's parcel could reach Harar the right knee had swollen to such a degree that her son could no longer walk. He had, he explained, "continued to walk and work a great deal, in fact more than ever, believing that it was a simple chill. But the pain in the knee increased. At each step I felt as if a nail had been driven into the side of it. I still went on walking, but with more and more difficulty; then I confined myself chiefly to riding a horse from which I dismounted each time practically crippled. Then the leg began to swell, the kneecap and shin to thicken. The circulation of blood grew painful and the pain aggravated the nerves from the ankle up to my back. I could only walk with a heavy limp which grew steadily worse. Yet I always had a lot of essential work to do. I began to bandage my leg from top to bottom, to massage it, bathe it, all without effect. Then I lost my appetite. An unbreakable insomnia commenced. I grew very thin and weak. About March 15 I decided to go to bed or at any rate to keep my legs up. I put a bed between my cash box, my books and papers and a window from which I could keep an eye on my scales at the bottom of the courtyard, and I paid some people to keep the business going while I lay, or at least stretched out the bad leg."

He remained in this state for nearly three weeks "unable to make a single movement, suffering atrocious pain and never sleeping." The rest did not help him: "Every day the swelling of the knee went on, until it looked like a big ball. I noticed that the inner side of the top of the shin bone was much bigger than on the other leg. Filled with the excretion which made the knee swell, the kneecap stiffened and after a few days I found with terror that it had become as hard as the bone. A week later the whole leg had grown rigid; I could only go to the privy by dragging myself along. Meanwhile the leg and top of the thigh grew thinner, thinner, the knee and shin continued to swell, petrifying or, rather, ossifying, and my bodily and moral weakness increased."

At the end of March he decided to leave. "In a few days I had liquidated everything at a loss; and, as the stiffness and pain prevented me from riding a mule or camel, I had a covered stretcher made out of a curtain." This stretcher, designed by himself, was wide, boarded on all four sides to save him from being jolted off on the rough tracks and with a sort of tent above to shield him from the sun. He hired sixteen negro porters to carry him to the port of Zeila, a trek of 200 miles across the desert.

The nightmare journey lasted twelve days. Rimbaud kept a scribbled record of it, a record of courage and parsimony. Long before it began the slightest movement roused a sickening twinge in the knee. And the journey was all movement. Even on the smoothest parts of the track the porters could not prevent the stretcher from jerking.

Trouble began soon. On the afternoon of the first day the party had to make a steep descent over rocks; very difficult for the porters, noted Rimbaud, "who stumbled over each stone, and for me who expected at every minute to be overturned. The stretcher is already half broken and the men absolutely worn out." He tried to ride a mule, his right leg tied to the animal's neck, but after a few minutes the pain became too terrible to bear.

On the morning of the second day the porters, trying to shorten the journey, began to run at a jog trot. But this caused "even more suffering than the descent" of the previous day, and had to be given up.

On the fourth day rain fell in torrents. The camels, which carried the party's food, refused to be loaded. At eleven in the morning Rimbaud decided to set off, leaving the camels to follow. After three hours' march his party halted, drenched to the skin: "All the evening and all that night we waited for the camels which did not arrive. It rained 16 hours without a break and we had neither food nor a tent. I passed this time under an Abyssinian skin."

The next day he sent back some men to find the camels; they did not return until late in the afternoon. Soaked, chilled, ravenously hungry, he had his first meal for thirty hours.

On the eighth day the tired porters handled the stretcher carelessly at their first halting place and tipped him on to the ground. "I fined them 4 thalers," he wrote, savage with pain. Each of the four stretcher-bearers lost a day's pay.

By this time everyone was at breaking point, the men pressed beyond their strength by the bitter-tongued sufferer: "My knee," he said, "swelled visibly and the pain increased continually." The record of the journey dwindled to a word or two, the last day was not recorded at all. But somehow the porters got the sick man to the port and somehow he managed to keep conscious to the end. On April 18, "exhausted, paralyzed," he was put down on the dockside at Zeila. After four hours a ship left for Aden; he was hoisted on deck on the stretcher and lay there for three days. He could eat nothing.

At Aden he had himself carried to Tian's house where he stayed a day or two trying to settled his accounts. But he became so much alarmed by the rapidity with which his knee was swelling and so stupefied by the pain that he had to abandon the effort and go into the English hospital.

This was the beginning of the last week in April. When the English doctor saw the knee he looked serious; it was a synovitic tumor, he told Rimbaud, aggravated by exercise and lack of medical care. He thought of amputating the leg immediately but decided to try a special treatment first.

After six days of this treatment Rimbaud wrote home for the first time since leaving Harar: "I am stretched out, the leg bandaged, tied up again and again and fixed so that it is impossible to move. I have become a skeleton. I am a frightful sight. My back is sore from lying on the bed; I can't get a minute's sleep. The heat here has become very great. The hospital food, for which I pay very dearly, is very bad."

As he lay there day after day, unable to move, unable to sleep, the bandaged leg suspended to prevent circulation of blood, his mind was black with worry: "I don't know what to do. For one thing I haven't yet finished my accounts with my associate Monsieur Tian. They can't be finished for another week. I ought to come out of this business with about 35 thousand francs. I should have had more but because of my wretched departure I lost some thousands of francs." He was "tempted to have myself carried to a ship and to come to France to be treated," but even this was difficult; at that season the ships were crowded by men returning on leave "and I am a poor invalid who needs to be transported very gently!"

Reading over his letter, he made an effort to soften its effect. "Don't be alarmed by all this, however. Better days will come." But he could not keep up the pose. He contrasted the planned homecoming, masculine, monied, irresistible, with the probable one. He thought of the years thrown away, talent wasted, futile labor, and cried, "All the same this is a sad reward . . . Alas! that life should be so miserable!"

"So miserable": yet his final thought was to please: "The elastic stockings you sent are no use now, but I hope to sell them."

2 ⟝

Nine days after writing this letter he left for France. The treatment had failed; his knee continued to swell, the pain grew worse. He arrived at Marseilles on May 22 and was carried immediately to hospital. There he was examined and, on hearing the medical report, telegraphed to Roche.

The next morning he wrote to "My dear mother, my dear sister. After terrible sufferings, unable to get better at Aden, I took ship for Marseilles. I got here yesterday after 13 days of pain. On arrival, being very weak and chilled to the bone, I entered the Hospital of the Conception where I pay ten francs a day, doctor's fees included.

"I am very bad, very bad. I'm reduced to a skeleton by this malady in my right leg which has become enormous and looks like a huge pumpkin. . . .

"This would have lasted a very long time if complications did not compel an amputation of the leg. In any case I shall be crippled. But I doubt whether I shall live to see it. Life has become impossible for me. How wretched I am! How wretched I have become!"

Another dread tormented him. The one tangible result of the years of struggle and sacrifice—his apology for a fortune—seemed to his tortured brain to be in danger. "I have the sum of 36,800 francs here in the branch of the Comptoir National d'Escompte de Paris. But I have nobody to go to fetch the money. I can't take a step outside my bed. And I have some money on me which I can't keep an eye on. What am I to do? What a sad life! Can't you help me at all?"

This letter was not read by Madame Rimbaud; she was on her way south before it arrived. Late the previous evening she had received her son's telegram: "You or Isabelle come to Marseilles today by express train. My leg to be amputated Monday morning. Mortal danger. Serious business to arrange."

She replied soon after dawn the next morning, "I am coming. Will arrive tomorrow evening. Courage and patience."

She arrived as promised, on the evening of Saturday, May 24. After eleven years mother and son faced each other. He had thought many times of that meeting; he would return, he had said, "with iron limbs, dark skin and furious eye," bearing proudly the proof of his claim "I will have gold." He had had another vision, expressed also in *Une Saison en Enfer:* "Women nurse these fierce invalids returned from hot countries." But the reality was not as he had pictured it; no fierce invalid, no tender nursing, but a sixty-six-year-old mother erect, indomitable, standing over a hospital bed looking down at the physical and moral wreck of the brilliant, disturbing son of little more than half her age. He could not read love into those blue eyes, he did not see admiration there; all they showed was pity and, not far behind, disappointment.

On the Monday his right leg was amputated high up the thigh. The operation over, he was calmer than ever before in his life. If his mother could not give him what he wanted, she invited peace, no thinking, rest. Above all, she was there.

But not for long. She waited until he was out of danger, then announced that she must go.

Rimbaud collapsed. A little boy again, he wept, stormed and begged her to wait until he could go with her. Later that day, June 8, Madame Rimbaud explained to Isabelle her unalterable intention. "My luggage is ready. I expect to leave tomorrow, Tuesday, in the afternoon. I shan't reach Roche before Thursday evening by way of Voncq station. No one is to put themselves out; I prefer to arrive by myself.

"I wanted to leave today but Arthur's tears moved me. However if I stayed on it would mean staying at least another month, and this is not possible. I do everything for the best: may God's will be done!"

She left as she had said. Isabelle was unwell, the farm work had to be carried on, and neither her son's tears nor her own uneasiness could move her a second time. The parting was painful. Bitterly hurt, he did not write home for nine days, and then to Isabelle who had sent him letters returned from Harar. "I was very upset when mother left me," he explained. "I could not understand it. But it is better for the moment for her to be with you to help you to get well. Beg her pardon for me and give her my greetings."

For the rest he had, he said, "a very painful neuralgia" in the stump and "I don't know how all this will end. But at least I'm resigned to everything. I've had no luck!"

Resigned he was not, as this last remark showed, and when no signs of forgiveness came from his mother, when even Isabelle did not reply within the week, he lost all control: "As for me, I weep day and night, I'm a dead man, I'm crippled for life." The doctor had told him that an artificial leg would take at least six months to get used to, and "what do I do, where can I stay all that time? If I come home the cold will chase me out in three months or less."

He ended hopelessly, "I don't know what to do at all. All these anxieties make me mad; I never get a minute's sleep. Anyway, our life is a misery, a misery without end! Why do we live?"

Before this letter reached Roche, Isabelle had written to him: police inquiries had been made about him there, she said. Her news provoked a cry of alarm. "What new horror are you telling me? What is this new story about military service? Didn't I send you from Aden when I was 26 a certificate proving that I was employed by a French business and that this exempted me?— and afterwards whenever I asked Mama, didn't she always say that everything was in order and that I had nothing to fear?" On and on he raged, with a "Prison after all I've had to suffer! Better death!" and a final appeal: "If you try to find out about this, you must never know where I am. I'm afraid that someone will discover my address at the post office. Don't betray me." Isabelle must write seldom, avoid using his Christian name, and give him immediate warning if he is sought for: "Then I can quickly take a ship from here."

That same day, June 24, he first tried to walk with crutches. To him, so proud of his strong body, his grace, his activity, the relief of leaving his bed at last was poisoned by the humiliation of taking a few ungainly paces after painful efforts. He had never been patient and he had no patience then: the crutches hurt, they were ugly, he could not balance himself properly, he had to bend forward, distort his body and twist his head, make a fool and an eyesore of himself before everyone; and with all this he moved like a snail.

"Oh well, I shall resign myself to my lot," he repeated; but he could not. Nevertheless, the fact that he could move unaided made him think of escape from the old fear of punishment by authority. Think and talk, for there was an even older fear in his mind: he was expert in reading his mother's moods, he had had no word from her since the scene in hospital, and remained uncertain of his welcome even if he dared to go home. He had his own way of finding out: "I hope to be able to go back where I was, where I have friends of ten years' standing who would be sorry for me, who would give me work so that I could live as I pleased. I shall always live there, for in France except for you I have neither friends nor acquaintances, nobody. If I can't see

you I shall return there. In any case it's essential that I go back."
And he wrote forthwith, to Harar, to Aden, and to the new
capital of Addis Ababa that Menelik was building next to Antotto.

3 ~~~~~

But at Roche, the moment his mother receded into the "unapproachable" mood noted years earlier by Vitalie and feared
by all her family, an intermediary appeared. Isabelle had received his letter ending "Why do we live?" This letter affected
her powerfully. She was then a woman of thirty-one, thoughtful,
devout, emotional under a calm exterior. She had not seen her
brother for eleven years, and previous to this, during her late
teens, he had often been away and she had been a pupil in the
convent school at Charleville. She knew that he had written
poetry, that his Charleville friends admired him, that his school
career had shown him to be exceptionally clever, and she too had
fallen under the spell of his personality. She had seen the liberties he had taken with the martinet mother, she had seen the
tightly closed purse open for him only, and she had drawn her
own conclusions. Eleven years later, single and to all appearances
likely to remain so, devoted to her mother yet unable to become
intimate with that self-sufficient woman, she remained unful-
filled. Then came Arthur's letter, and interest and duty met in
the person of this romantic, unhappy brother who wrote so re-
belliously from hospital. The fact that she scarcely knew him
was immaterial; to her he was an only brother and she knew the
one thing necessary to reinforce a strong family feeling: he was
a lost soul. She had read his letters from Aden, Harar and Marseilles with their blasphemous asides, their lack of faith.

Now the lost soul had appealed directly to her. For all her
outward softness, this unsatisfied woman had inherited the iron
of her mother. Her religion was of the jesuitical variety; any
means justified the glorious end. For this end she began to work
unsparingly and without scruple. She suddenly saw herself,

whose life had seemed purposeless, given the greatest of all tasks, to reclaim her brother for the faith.

From this moment she became his only correspondent at home, relieving her mother from a duty grown onerous. She at once busied herself about the question of military service; she had charm and perseverance and used them so effectively that by July 7 she was able to write to Marseilles to announce that the commandant at Mézières had given him a permanent acquittal and that his military situation was legal.

She did not announce the news in the manner of a good angel but like the softer version of her mother that she was. In a short letter enclosing the acquittal, a letter written on a page of cheap squared paper torn from a notebook, she says: "It is a precious document, the only proof that you are not at fault. It has needed many applications and much pleading to drag it out of the signatory, a peevish, ill-natured man of an insupportable punctiliousness in everything concerning the army." She warned him that the document was irreplaceable and advised him to send it back to her for safekeeping.

She dealt briskly with his pessimism and doubts of the doctors; if they amputated his leg, an amputation was necessary, and "If misfortunes comes unexpectedly, so does happiness."

The acquittal reached Rimbaud many years too late; he was relieved— "At least I no longer risk going to prison"—but had traveled far beyond real comfort; one anxiety lifted, another took its place. He had no sooner thanked Isabelle than, ignoring her reproof, his complaints about the crutches broke out afresh, the artificial leg was going to be expensive, difficult and perhaps too painful to use and, in short, "I begin to understand that crutches, wooden legs, mechanical legs are all a kind of lie and one drags oneself about wretchedly without being able to do anything at the end of it all. And I who had just decided to come back to France this summer to get married! Goodbye marriage, goodbye family, goodbye future! My life is over. I'm nothing more than an inert stump."

The tone was the same but the cause was changing, the affronted athlete was giving way to the frightened man. For the stump had healed, the doctor had said that he could go, yet inexplicable pains and inability to sleep worried him "and to tell the truth I don't believe I'm cured inside and I'm expecting some outbreak . . . This insomnia makes me afraid that I still have some other malady to endure. I think with terror of my other leg."

Yet it was nebulous, this feeling, and perhaps imaginary. In any case the hospital expenses were eating into his savings, the hospital routine wearied him, alarmed him too. He thought of Harar but was drawn to Roche. His mother had not replied to his apology, had not written a word. He had to see her; perhaps after all she would relent when she saw him upright and with his 36,800 francs.

On July 23 he left for Roche.

4 ～～

He felt unwell by the time he reached home, but the pain and insomnia were put down to the rigors of the long journey; all believed that after a few days he would begin to stump about on his wooden leg and that the country air would soon bring back health and strength. He quickly showed a flicker of the familiar liveliness, and his mother was obliged to confess privately that he might even yet justify his existence.

If ever she needed a son's help and comfort it was then. That spring and summer had been the worst ever known at Roche, and when she wrote to Isabelle from Marseilles, "If I stayed on it would mean staying for another month, and this is not possible," she was thinking of her stricken farm. Frost had ruined her wheat, incessant rain had flooded her fields, and it seemed, by the look of the black skies, the gales, the wildly fluctuating temperatures, that God had not yet completed his chastisement. But for what? "There are some creatures destined to endure all life's sorrows: I am one of them" she was to declare. That was her state of mind then. She was somber, irritable, martyred.

Then came Arthur from hospital, a man raised from the dead. She had a duty towards him and subdued hopes of him: another hand on the farm, a child who brought with him certain savings, savings not entirely negligible though sadly depleted by the iniquitous charges of surgeon, doctors and hospital. Perhaps providence, having taken with one hand, was about to give with the other.

This not unreasonable hope was shattered within the first week or two. The wooden leg was thrown aside after a few days; it irritated the stump too greatly. The crutch soon followed; the right armpit, like the stump, could not endure the pressure. The pain in arm and stump continued even when he did not use the crutch or wooden leg. The insomnia of the first nights showed itself as having nothing to do with his journey; it grew worse. Finally, the right arm began to stiffen.

Madame Rimbaud watched her son's rapid deterioration with a mordant eye, the eye of one who expects the worst even when hoping for the best. "Thin and gaunt," says a contemporary, "with a disdainful air, an aristocratic carriage, she presented her children with the example of a rigid piety . . . a typical specimen of the northern people who so often hide an extreme sensibility under a glacial exterior." But neither the piety nor the glacial exterior could conceal her expression. It was not lost on her son; from that moment he declared a horror of the house and spent every possible hour of daylight driving about the countryside with Isabelle in an open cart. The drives were ruined every day by rainstorms, by a close heat, by the mockery of a summer which reduced even healthy people to shivering, sweating bundles of complaint, yet he insisted on the distraction. He liked to be taken into the towns, to Attigny, to Vouziers, to watch the crowds, but this bitter pleasure could not save him from the return to Roche, to the "blue look" of his mother.

For Madame Rimbaud was not to be deceived. Her son could order a new and more expensive artificial leg, he could speak of a return to Harar where, riding a well-trained horse, he would build up his business again, he could discuss his marriage, either to an orphanage girl "wellborn and irreproachably brought up" or to "a noble Abyssinienne and good Catholic," and of the family he would raise, he could boast of "making a success in French literature" when he had retired on his Abyssinian-made fortune, he could congratulate himself on having abandoned his youthful writings "because they were bad," he could promise this and boast that. All useless, these attempts to cheat, to mollify his mother. Times had changed; he was no longer the hard worker amassing the francs, he was a useless, weeping, whining burden who took up the time of his sister and a Roche horse and cart in driving about the countryside.

Then came the night of August the ninth, a night of frightful storms, when hail beat down the remnant of the crops. It was followed the next morning by a frost which stripped the orchards. Madame Rimbaud surveyed her rotting fields and bare trees. The moment was too grave for an outburst of anger; it called for and was given a mournful but clear-sighted attention. She saw not only the ruin around her but that the ruin would have to be repaired without a man's hand. Her first reaction, in hospital, had been the right one: Arthur was finished. She was not the woman to shirk a melancholy duty. He had to be put out of her mind. She put him out of her mind.

Isabelle could not see the matter in that light. Up to then she had been not so much a shadow of her mother (so negative a term maligning a strong-minded woman) as a deliberate accessory. After the storm the women's roles diverged. Madame Rimbaud was neither a monster nor consciously unkind, she was a practical, hard-headed peasant who put first things first. To her daughter even Roche was less important than this chance to indulge for the best of reasons an egoism which had been forced to play second fiddle for thirty years. With characteristic nervous determination she redoubled her attentions to the sick man. His desperate condition, clear to her too, indicated that her time was short. From the moment of his arrival she had been his most frequent companion; now: "I supported his unsteady frame, I held his suffering, inert body in my arms, guided his goings-out, I accompanied him step by step, I took him where he wanted to go, I helped him to come back, to get up, to get down, I swept from the path of his solitary foot all obstacles, all dangers, I prepared his seat, his bed, his food. I made him take some nourishment mouthful by mouthful, I held the cup to his lips until his thirst was quenched. I watched the time carefully and at the precise moments gave him the various medicines prescribed— how many times a day! I spent my days trying to distract him from his thoughts and sufferings, I passed my nights at his bedside. I tried to bring him sleep by making music, but music always caused him to weep. When he asked me to make him some poppy soup during the night I made it, but I was afraid to be far from him and hurried back. . . ."

Yet though Isabelle was foot and arm to him, though she never left him, she was not Madame Rimbaud; to "distract him from his thoughts" was beyond her power. "Crises of nervous irritation, of despair, of tears succeeded each other without a break," she confessed.

And the pain grew daily less tolerable, the symptoms more alarming. All remedies—and she tried everything she could think of—left him worse than before; the medicines tortured his digestion, the lotions "irritated his nerves, muscles, bones horribly." His appetite disappeared. He could not sleep. The pains spread through his body. His right arm "literally died" before her eyes.

After the great storm and Madame Rimbaud's withdrawal he began to talk of Harar. He had had replies to the letters written from hospital, gratifying replies. There at least he would be welcomed. Ras Makonnen, the governor, congratulated him on his successful operation with a "I hear with pleasure that you propose to return to Harar to continue your business. Come back quickly and in good health." A fellow trader assured him that the loss of a leg need not interfere with his work and announced that preparations for a caravan to meet him were already under way. There was a typical note from Ilg; he could not find the ivory, musk or gold sent by Rimbaud in his last caravan "because his Majesty has taken everything for himself."

Rimbaud would have been even more pleased if he could have read Savouré's letter which was still in the post: "Ras Makonnen speaks of you endlessly to us, saying that you are the most honest of men and have often proved yourself his true friend." The Abyssinian said no more than the truth. Rimbaud had made a place for himself in men's minds. He was not one of them, yet he had said of the natives, "It's just a question of being human." He had been human; and although he was neither loved nor understood, respect came from all sides.

Events moved quickly; the letters from Abyssinia, the suspicion that his mother had done with him, the march of disease. Within a week of the storm he was talking hysterically of leaving at once. He would, he said, go anywhere, do anything, however painful, to keep the use of his limbs; for he was "possessed by a frightful fear of becoming and remaining paralyzed."

Isabelle tried to dissuade him, but the only word that might have kept him was not said. All she could do was to convince him that he was not well enough to make the long journey to Abyssinia. Then he would go back to Marseilles, he said, "where at least I shall have the sunshine and heat and will be cured at the Conception by the surgeon who operated on me." And "the moment I feel well enough I shall take ship for Aden."

5 ~~~~~

He left Roche on August 23, less than two weeks after the storm and a bare four since his arrival. Isabelle decided to accompany him, daring a possible explosion from her mother. Indeed he was by this time scarcely capable of dragging himself along.

The journey began disastrously. The train was due at Voncq at half past six in the morning. At three o'clock Isabelle was wakened by a feverish Arthur demanding to be dressed and off.

The servants, dazed with sleep, took an interminable period to harness the horse to the cart; and when at last horse and cart were brought to the door and Rimbaud was lifted in and arranged as comfortably as possible, only just enough time remained to cover the two miles to the station. Perhaps Rimbaud, frantic with the delay, tried too hard to urge the horse on, perhaps the horse resented its unusually early awakening; whatever the cause, it stopped in the road halfway to Voncq and refused to budge. Beside himself, Rimbaud dragged off his leather belt and beat the animal furiously. To no effect: five minutes passed before it could be induced to move; when they arrived at the station the train had left two minutes earlier.

They sat there, Rimbaud "very gloomy." The next train was due at 12.40. But any thought he may have had of waiting for it at the station was driven away by the cold clouds of the morning. He began to shiver, said he would wait at home, the cart was turned round and in a few minutes they faced a surprised and not well-pleased Madame Rimbaud.

At half past nine Rimbaud, who had gone straight back to bed, again called for the horse and cart. He was very much excited and refused to eat or drink. "Quick, quick, let us go!" he kept on crying. But on his way to the cart his mood changed; he looked round about him, at the farmhouse, the village street, the waiting servants, at his mother standing stiffly, and, with tears pouring down his cheeks, cried: "Oh my God! can't I find a stone on which to lay my head or a roof under which I can die? Ah, I would much rather not go!"

His appeal was cast in the tones and words of his mother; he had never thrown off the manner. Perhaps they were too familiar. She remained impassive, mute. He drove off.

This time they were two hours early. He and Isabelle sat on the platform under a chestnut tree. He commented caustically on the station master's idea of floral decoration, quite the Arthur of old, Isabelle thought. He drank a bromide to try to dull the pain aroused by the jerking of the cart, and watched with a sardonic eye the envious expression on the faces of the thirsty servants. This too brought out a sally in the youthful manner. But for the most part he remained silent, his face twisted.

At last the train steamed in. He was hoisted, groaning, into a compartment. The train moved off. As it gathered speed, the movement tried him severely; his back, thighs, shoulders, arms all ached violently and specially the right armpit and the stump of his leg. He began to weep. "How I suffer! How I suffer!" he cried.

Isabelle piled cushions round him, laid him full length on the seat, leaned him this way and that. No relief. He sat up sobbing and clasping the stump with both hands: "Oh what a cruel monster!" He was in despair, and Isabelle too. "I should like to hope," he told her, "but I see that it is all over. I shan't have any more pleasure, I am too ill."

At Amagne, the junction for the main Charleville-Paris line, they had to wait for the express. Sitting in the wheel chair the porters had carried him to, he began to compare his present departure with his arrival at Amagne a month earlier. The tears rolled down cheeks unnaturally flushed. Isabelle could find no comfort for him.

The express came in, he was lifted once more into a corner seat, and Isabelle wedged him into it with his valise supporting the paralyzed right arm wrapped in a rug and burnous, and the left elbow resting on the window ledge. This somewhat relieved the pressure, but the stump continued to pain him severely. "They must certainly cut off the rest of this wretched leg," he said after a time. "I suffer more than I can bear. They have left something rotten in the stump." But Isabelle was puzzled; she had examined and massaged the stump daily; it looked perfectly healthy. She hoped against hope, could his pain be nothing more serious than rheumatism or neuralgia, aftereffect of the amputation?

Worn out, he fell into a sort of torpor. For some time he was not disturbed. It was a Sunday, many people were traveling, but most went away when they saw the sick man sleeping, eyes blankly open, mouth compressed in lines of suffering, thin bloodless hands jolting flaccidly with the swaying of the train. Finally a young married couple got in, then a man and wife with two small children. The chatter of the children roused him from time to time; he looked at them with blue eyes extraordinarily brilliant but with an expression so tired and indifferent that Isabelle, watching, felt desolated.

Many times in his short life he had taken this train to Paris, always overflowing with hope and excitement; to see the Commune triumph and make a name as poet, to meet Verlaine and conquer the capital, to find a publisher for *Une Saison en Enfer*, to make a fortune in the East. This time the suburbs of the approaching city left him unmoved. He continued to doze uneasily until the bustle of the arrival at the Gare de l'Est disturbed him.

The train arrived at six-thirty in the evening. He and Isabelle had planned to sleep in Paris and continue the journey the next day. Or not to continue; for the thought came to both that perhaps he would find more skilful treatment in the capital. They decided in the fiacre that they would sleep on it.

Just then, and before they could reach the hotel, rain began to fall, the streets and pavements cleared, the bustle and brilliance of a Parisian summer evening changed suddenly to the drizzle of raindrops down the windows of closed shops and steamy cafés.

The sight of the rain roused Rimbaud from his lethargy. For a month he had seen, heard and felt rain every day. He leaned forward and told the driver to turn round and go to the Gare de Lyon. They drove silently through the glistening, empty streets. Rimbaud stared through the window. In Paris he would have been the literary sensation of the day. But he was no longer interested. His longing was fastened on the south and its sunshine; there, if anywhere, he would rediscover health, there if anywhere postpone realization of the final defeat at home.

At the Gare de Lyon, his decision made, he rose for a few moments into a gaiety which Isabelle, suspecting the future, found heartrending. The mood collapsed abruptly; at eleven o'clock he was carried to his sleeping berth prostrate, speechless.

The journey to Lyons, where Isabelle saw the sun rise, was a horror to both. He did not sleep, as his sister had hoped; instead, she had to witness "the most frightful paroxysm of despair and of bodily torture possible to imagine." In those small hours he saw where his journey was leading him.

After Lyons neither the noise of the train, nor its movement, nor the suffocating heat of the compartment as they traveled south could keep him awake. He was exhausted and slept, but his sleep was itself a kind of agony, one nightmare succeeding another. Soaked in sweat, groaning, crying, he tried again and again to move, to ease himself. In vain; he was held fast; paralysis had spread through his body.

That evening, at Marseilles, he was carried back to the Hospital of the Conception. He registered as Jean Rimbaud. Arthur Rimbaud had died on the train.

Epilogue

Isabelle to Madame Rimbaud, Marseilles, Tuesday, September 22, 1891

I HAVE received your note. You are very laconic. Are you ill? This is my greatest worry. My God, what should I do with a dying man and an invalid two hundred leagues apart? How I wish I could halve myself and be half here and half at Roche!

"I must tell you that Arthur is very ill. I told you in my last letter that I should ask the doctors privately. I have spoken to them and this is roughly what they say, 'The poor boy (Arthur) is sinking little by little; his life is a question of days, of some months perhaps. At least, he could not survive some dreadful complication which might arise at any moment. As for recovering, there is no hope, he will not get well. His illness is a diffusion by the very marrow of the bone of the cancerous infection which made the amputation of the leg a necessity.' One of the doctors, Dr. T., an old man with white hair, added, 'Since you have already been here a month and he wants you to stay on, don't leave him; in his state it would be cruel to deprive him of your presence.'

"So, dear mama, this is what the doctors have told me only, you understand; to him they say the contrary, they promise him a radical recovery, trying to make him believe that he is getting better every day. So well that, hearing them, I was so deceived that I asked to whom they lied, to him or to me, for they have as sincere an air in speaking to him of recovery as in warning me of his death. It seems to me, however, that he is not so ill as the doctors told me in private. Calm returned to him almost instantly four days ago. He eats a little more; it is true that he gives the impression of forcing himself to eat,

283

but at least he eats and the fact that he eats can't do him any harm. His complexion is no longer so red.

"On the reverse side of these small ameliorations I must mention new sufferings which I attribute to his extreme weakness. From the first his pains never stopped, nor the paralysis of his arm. He is very thin, his eyes are sunken and circled with black; he often has headaches. If he sleeps during the day he wakes with a start and tells me that he is wakened thus by a blow striking him at the heart or on the head. When he sleeps at night he has frightful dreams and when he wakes he is stiff to the point of not having the power to move (the night nurse has already found him in this state). And he sweats, he sweats, night and day, in the cold as in the heat.

"Since he has become calmer he weeps all the time. He doesn't yet believe that he will remain paralyzed if he lives; deceived by the doctors, he clings to life, to the hope of a cure. But as he always feels very ill and as at present he gives himself up to thinking about his state most of the time, he can't help sometimes doubting what the doctors say; he accuses them of making a mock of him or, in plain words, taxes them with ignorance. He wants so much to live and get well that he begs for any treatment, however painful or unpleasant, that will give him back the use of his arm. He actually wants to have his artificial leg so that he can try to get up, to walk—he who for the last month has had to be lifted up so that he can lie naked on the couch whilst his bed is being made!

"His great anxiety, his enormous worry is to know how he is to earn his living if he can't get back the full use of his right arm. And he weeps, comparing what he was a year ago to what he is today; he weeps in thinking of a future in which he won't be able to work, he weeps for the atrocious sufferings he has to endure now. He embraces me, sobbing, crying and begging me not to abandon him. I can't tell you how pitiable he is. Everyone is moved by him here where everybody is so good to us that all our wishes are anticipated. He is treated like a man condemned to death who is refused nothing; but all these kindnesses, all these small indulgences are thrown away; he never accepts them."

Isabelle to Madame Rimbaud, Marseilles, October 3, 1891

"I beg you on my knees to write to me, at least to write a word. I can't continue to live in this uncertainty; it has already made me seriously ill with fever. What have I done that you should treat me so badly? If you are so ill that you can't write, it would be better to let me know so that I can come back in spite of Arthur who entreats me not to leave him before his death. What has happened? Ah! if I could only come to you this moment! But no, without knowing definitely that you are ill I can't leave this poor unhappy creature who moans from morning to night without pause, who calls for death with loud cries, who threatens, if I leave him, to strangle himself or kill himself no matter how. And he suffers so much that I really believe he would do what he says! He has grown much weaker. They are going to try an electrical treatment; this is the last hope."

Isabelle to Madame Rimbaud, Marseilles, Monday, October 5, 1891

"A thousand thanks for your letter of 2 October. What I suffered waiting for it! But I am happy to get it. Yes, I am very unreasonable. You must forgive me; affection makes me so.

"I understand how busy you have to be. Be patient and cheerful with the servants. If they left you just now you would be even more inconvenienced. If the reapers have gone you ought to be a little less overworked, but the 'woyen' is still a bad time to get over. I hope you won't take the threshing machine now. Father Warin or someone else ought to thresh the little wheat you have if you give him fodder. How are you doing with the milk? The biggest calf ought not to drink as much as 'matron' provides. You should be able to sell milk to the milkman. I hope that you have dried up the small one; she will have her calf at the beginning of November; don't hesitate to sell her if she is in good condition. The pigs ought to be big and good enough to sell. What about Comtesse? Be careful of the other horses, especially Charmante who is so difficult I often have to give her her oats by herself. Who will 'râger' the wheat for sowing? How I suffer when I think that I can do nothing to help you!

"I can't dream of leaving Arthur just now; he goes on badly, he grows weaker every day, he begins to despair of living and I lose hope too. I ask only one thing, that he makes a good end.

"Yesterday we expected to see Ries (from Tian's office in Aden) but no one came. I don't think that Arthur could undertake any business deal at this moment, he is too ill. In any case I should try to dissuade him with all my strength . . ."

"P.S. I send you this penciled scribble which I wrote yesterday; it was my day's work. Don't give yourself much trouble to decipher it, it isn't worth reading."

Sunday, October 4, 1891. I went into Arthur's room at seven o'clock. He was sleeping with his eyes open, breathing quickly, so thin and so pale with his eyes sunken and circled with black! He didn't wake at once. I watched him sleeping and told myself that it was impossible for him to live long in that condition, he looked too ill! After five minutes he wakened and as always complained of not sleeping during the night and of having suffered greatly; he was still in pain when he awoke. As on every morning he said good morning to me and asked how I was, had I slept well, etc. I told him that I was very well. What was the use of telling him that fever, cough and above all worry had prevented me from sleeping? He has troubles enough of his own.

"He then told me of unlikely events which he imagined had taken place in the hospital during the night. This was the only remnant of his delirium which he still remembered, but it stuck so obstinately in his mind that all the morning and many times during the rest of the day he repeated the same absurdities, annoyed that I didn't believe them. I listened, then, and tried to persuade him that it was nonsense; he accused the nurses and male attendants of abominable things which could not happen. I told him that he had without doubt dreamt it but he wouldn't give way and treated me as a simpleton and imbecile.

"I began to make his bed. But for more than a week he hasn't wanted to be moved from it; he suffers too much when lifted up to rest on the couch whilst his bed is being remade. For him making the bed consists of smoothing out a hollow here, pushing down a bump there, of arranging the bolster, of putting back the blankets (without sheets)—all this, of course, with a crowd of unhealthy crochets. He can't bear a crease under him; his head is never comfortable; his stump is too high or too low; he must have the right arm completely inert on the patch of wadding, the left arm, which is becoming more and more paralyzed, wrapped in flannel, in double sleeves, etc.

"There was a knock. This was the nurse who brings Arthur's black coffee and comes to call me to Mass; it was half past seven. But I could not leave my invalid who was not yet fully made neat and comfortable; I decided to go to Mass at nine o'clock.

"I made him drink his coffee. Then came the massage. I have been given everything from the surgery that can be used externally—oil, spirits, balsam, liniment, everything that exists to soothe pain is set out for me on the washstand. When one of the other patients has to be massaged they come to me to ask the best way of doing it.

"Someone brought in the bottle of milk. He drank it at once, hoping to overcome his constipation and specially his holding back of urine. I believe that the interior organs are becoming paralyzed one by one and I'm afraid, and he too, that this general paralysis will go on little by little until it reaches the heart. Then he must die.

"The left leg is always cold and palpitating, with much pain. His left eye is half closed. Sometimes he has throbbings of the heart which stifle him. He tells me that when he wakes he feels his head and heart burning and he always has pain in the left side of the chest and back.

"A quarter past eight. Eugene brought the electric apparatus. This is the first session. The electrician set up the apparatus and applied it to the right arm for a quarter of an hour. During this Arthur's hand made several abrupt movements, opening and closing quickly, but as soon as the apparatus was taken away it relapsed into immobility; he feels no more than a sharp heat and violent pain in the hand and arm. Nevertheless the operator expressed satisfaction with this trial. By eight forty-five we were alone again. I again arranged his bed and raised him on his pillow. We tried the urinal and the basin once more.

"I put on my hat and gloves . . . I went alone to Mass . . . It was the great feast of Our Lady of the Rosary. The chapel was all lit up. The two chaplains were there. The High Mass was served perfectly by six young boys with lace surplices over sky blue. There were chanters accompanied by a harmonium and a choir of girls: all sang admirably as most people of the Midi do. The nuns were in their seats. The chapel was nearly full. It is a long time since I have taken part in such a good and beautiful service. After Mass some went, others told their beads; I hurried back, for Arthur maintains that when I am not with him he believes himself to be already in his coffin.

"He was waiting impatiently for me. Someone had brought a box containing his artificial leg; they had asked 5 francs 50 for it which he couldn't pay because I have all the money. I also found on the washstand a bowl of hot milk which the nurse, the kind nurse, had brought me as she does every day 'to help my cough to go.' I drank it straight away and went down to the office to pay the cost of the carriage of the leg; I spoke to a young man who, hearing me speak of paying for the carriage of a box imagined that the box was a coffin and compassionately asked me for details of the death of the occupant; I had some trouble in undeceiving him.

"Coming back to Arthur, I found him in tears. He was no longer able to try the leg that had been so greatly desired, so impatiently waited for! 'I shall never wear it,' he said. 'It is all over, finished, I feel that I am going to die.' I calmed him as best I could; but like him, and even more so, I thought he would have much difficulty in pulling through. That is, besides, the opinion of everyone here and they add that he would better be dead than live in his present state of suffering.

"Eleven o'clock. I made him eat semolina soup, fried potatoes and kidneys, omelette, grapes, a pear, a slice of gateau. He is always given what he wants: I chose the best for him, and that is very good, but he finds everything detestable and scarcely touches a morsel. I constantly tidied his bed, his blankets, his pillows but he was never comfortable. Perpetual groans escaped from his lips. No one but myself ever touches him, looks after him, arranges him during the day; the sight, the very thought of the nurses does him harm; and that's why during the night he leaves himself inundated with sweat, holds back all needs, rather than call on the night nurse. Yesterday he made me shave him so that no one else should come near him.

"At half past twelve the postman, so impatiently waited for, watched for with such anxiety, passed without leaving me anything. I went to lunch with death in my soul. But half an hour later, when I had only just come back to the hospital, the nurse signed to me; I hurried out at her call and she gave me two letters, one for me, the other for Arthur. Before going back into the room I read mine, for I didn't want it to be read by my brother before me. At last, after fifteen days without news from Roche, a reassuring letter! I kissed it, I bathed it in my tears. Exiled so far away with a poor invalid, it was a very long time since I had passed such a happy afternoon as that one with my dear letter. I wanted to give Arthur the one addressed to him; he refused it. . . .

"I had to tax my brains during the day to prevent him committing numerous follies. It is a good thing that I have such influence with him. His fixed idea is to leave Marseilles for a hotter climate, whether Algiers, Aden, Obock. What keeps him here is the fear that I won't accompany him further away, for he can't bring himself to leave me any more.

"Sometimes he is very good and very tender, thanking me effusively for the care I have taken of him, calling me his good genius, his only support. Above all he makes me promise not to leave him before his death and to carry out his last wishes, in particular concerning his burial. Alas! those who have only the men nurses to look after them are wretched indeed! Near us are three paralyzed men, two of whom are younger than Arthur. One of these two is getting better but has become absolutely insane and can't speak any more; the other, a French engineer, came from the island of Madagascar two weeks ago, he was delirious when he arrived. These two unfortunates are mal-treated by the men nurses; we hear their cries, their moans, and I tell myself that if I were to go Arthur would be treated in the same fashion. Instead of becoming calmer, his delirium would turn into a furious madness.

"I have written all this whilst he was plunged into a sort of lethargy—not a sleep but arising from his weakness.

"When he awakened he looked through the window at the sun, brilliant as always in a cloudless sky, and he began to weep, saying that he would never again see the sun out of doors. 'I shall be put under the earth,' he told me 'and you will be walking in the sun!' And so it goes on through the day, an inces-sant wail, an indescribable despair.

"At half past four dinner was brought in. He scarcely tasted it. He insisted that I ate the dessert. I did so to content him and to avoid his anger.

"At five o'clock, the doctor's visit. Alas! the doctors have de-ceived him so much that he scarcely believes them any more. Yet he still listens with a kind of hope to the cheerful words of the young doctor who gives him the most sympathy. As for me, no one deceives me, and between the fine words I can dis-cern very well that the success of the electrical treatment is quite uncertain.

"Then the candle had to be lit, for by half past five the room was absolutely dark. Up to nine o'clock my night attendance passes in massage, changing the linen, arranging the bed, etc. Then he delayed, minute by minute, the moment of leaving him. Then he said goodbye to me as if I should no longer find him living the next morning. And so it is every evening."

Isabelle to Madame Rimbaud, Marseilles, Wednesday, October 28, 1891

"Blessed be God a thousand times! On Sunday I experienced the greatest happiness that I could ever know in this world. It is no longer a poor condemned wretch who is dying by my side, it is an upright man, a saint, a martyr, one of the elect!

"During the course of the past week the chaplains came twice to see him; he received them, but with such weariness and despondency that they dared not speak to him of death. On Saturday evening all the nuns met together to pray that he would make a good end. On Sunday morning, after High Mass, he seemed calmer and in possession of his senses; one of the chaplains came back and suggested that he should confess to him; and he was very willing!

"When the preacher came out he said, looking at me with a strange and troubled air 'My child, your brother believes. What more can we tell you? He has the faith and I have never seen a faith of his quality.' I, crying and laughing, could have kissed the earth. O God! what joy! what joy, even in death, even by death! What does death, life, the whole world and all the happiness in the world matter to me now that his soul is saved! Savior, sweeten his agony, help him to carry his cross, have pity on him and still more pity, you who are so good! ah, yes, so good. Thanks, my Lord, thanks!

"When I went back to Arthur he was very moved but did not weep; he was serenely sad as I have never seen him before. He looked at me as I had never seen him look before. Wishing me to come very close to him he said, 'You are the same blood as I; do you believe, say, do you believe?' I replied, 'I believe. Others wiser than I have believed, believe. And now I am sure, for I have proof, this is it.' And it is true, I have had proof today! He then said to me with bitterness, 'Yes, they say that they believe, they pretend to be converted so that people will read what they write. It is a speculation!' I hesitated, then said, 'Oh no, they would gain more money by blaspheming!' He looked at me the whole time with a heavenly expression in his eyes. He held me and kissed me, then, 'We certainly should be able to have the same soul since we have the same blood. You believe, then?' And I repeated, 'Yes, I believe. One must believe.' Then he said, 'The room must be prepared, tidied; he is coming back with the sacraments. Go to see, somebody is bringing the candles and lace; we must have white linen everywhere. I am very ill!' He was anxious but not desperate as on other days and I could see very plainly that he ardently wished to have the sacraments, the communion above all.

"Since then he has never blasphemed any more; he calls on the Christ crucified, and he prays. Yes, he prays, he!

"But the chaplain has not been able to give him the communion. At first he was afraid of affecting him too much. Then, as Arthur is spitting a lot at the moment and is not able to endure anything in his mouth, there was fear of an involuntary profanation. And he, believing that he has been forgotten, has grown sad, but he doesn't complain.

"Death comes at great speed. I said in my last letter, my dear Mama, that the stump was very swollen. Now there is an enormous cancer between the hip and the belly, just above the bone. The stump, which was so sensitive, so painful, doesn't cause any more pain. Arthur has not seen this fatal tumor; he is astonished that everybody comes to see the poor stump of which he feels practically nothing; and all the doctors (ten have already come since I pointed out this terrible thing) remain silent and terrified in front of this strange cancer.

"At present his poor head and his left arm give him the greatest pain. But he is most often sunk in a lethargy which looks like sleep and during which he hears every noise with a singular clarity.

"He is given an injection of morphia each night.

"Awake, he lives in a sort of continuous dream; he says strange things very softly, in a voice which would enchant me if it did not pierce me to the heart. What he talks about are the dreams —however it is not at all the same as when he had a fever. One could say, and I believe it, that he expresses facts.

"As he murmured these things, the nurse said to me very low, 'He has lost consciousness again?' But he heard and blushed; he said nothing until the nurse had gone, then, 'They think I'm mad. Do you?' No, I don't believe it; he is almost an immaterial being and his thoughts escape him in spite of himself. Sometimes he asks the doctors if they see the extraordinary things he sees and he speaks to them softly and tells them his impressions, in terms which I can't reproduce. The doctors look in his eyes, those beautiful eyes which have never been so beautiful or more intelligent, and say to one another: 'It is strange.' In Arthur's case there is something that they can't understand.

"The doctors, however, scarcely come any more because he often weeps when speaking to them, and this upsets them.

"He recognizes everyone. He sometimes calls me Djami but I know that this is because he wants to and that this comes in his dream wish also. For the rest, he mixes everything and . . . with art. We are at Harar, we are always leaving for Aden and he tries to find camels, to organize a caravan; he walks very easily with the new artificial leg, we go for some rides on beautiful mules richly harnessed; then he must work, keep the accounts, write letters. Quickly, quickly, someone is waiting for us, we close our bags and go. Why was he allowed to sleep? Why didn't someone help him to dress? What will be said if we don't arrive on the day named? His word won't be taken any longer, no one will have any more confidence in him! And he begins to cry, regretting my awkwardness and negligence; for I am always with him and I am the one who is responsible for all the preparations.

"He eats practically nothing and that little he eats with extreme repugnance. He is as thin as a skeleton and the color of a corpse! And all his poor limbs paralyzed, mutilated, dead all round him! O God, what a shame!

"Referring to your letter and about Arthur, don't count at all on his money. After him and the costs of the coffin, journeys, etc. paid, you must realize that his possessions will revert to others; I am absolutely determined to respect his wishes, and as he would only have me as executor, his money and his concerns will be dealt with as seems good to him. What I have done for him has not been through hope of gain but because he is my brother who, abandoned by the entire universe, I did not wish to leave to die alone and without help. I will be as faithful after his death as before it, and what he has told me to do with his money and clothes I will do exactly even if I have to suffer because of it.

"May God help me and you too: we have great need of divine aid."

2 ⟶

Unfinished letter dictated by Rimbaud to Isabelle, November 9, 1891, the day before his death

"Monsieur le Directeur.

"I want to ask you if I have anything left on your account. I want to change today from this service, which I don't even know the name of, but in any case let it be the Aphinar service. Services go in all directions from there and I, helpless, wretched, powerless, can't find anything, the first dog you meet in the street will tell you that.

"Send me, then, the price of the passage from Aphinar to Suez. I am completely paralyzed, so I want to get myself on the ship in good time. Tell me at what time I must be carried on board . . ."

3

Madame Rimbaud to Isabelle, Charleville, June 9, 1899

"Yesterday was a day of great emotion for me. I shed many tears yet in spite of these tears I felt a certain happiness which I can't explain. Yesterday, then, I had gone to Mass and was already on my knees praying when someone to whom I paid no attention came close to me. From under my eyelids I saw resting against the pillar a crutch just like the one poor Arthur used. I turned my head and was paralyzed with astonishment; it was Arthur himself, the same height, same age, same figure, white-brown skin, no beard but small mustache, and one leg missing. He looked at me with an extraordinary sympathy. Despite all my efforts I could not restrain my tears, tears of unhappiness certainly but with something behind them which I could not express. I believed absolutely that it was my well-loved son who was near me.

"And that was not all. A very well-dressed lady passed close to us. She stopped and said to him, smiling: 'Come with me. You will be much better than you are here.' He replied: 'Thank you, aunt, but I'm very happy here and I beg you to leave me where I am.' The lady insisted, he preferred to stay. He was very pious and appeared perfectly at home with every part of the service.

"My God, has my poor Arthur come to fetch me? I am ready . . .'

Madame Rimbaud to Isabelle, Charleville, June 1, 1900

"I feel a sense of satisfaction impossible to express; I feel that I have done God's will.

"The vault is made and well made, though not yet quite

as I should like it. My place is ready in the midst of my dear departed; my coffin is to be put between my good father and my dear Vitalie on my right and my poor Arthur on my left. I have had built two small brick walls on which my coffin will rest and I have fixed to the wall a cross and a branch of box-wood that has been blessed. I have sent for the gravedigger and made him see exactly where I want to be. He understood me very well. All is ready. . . .

"I have done my duty. My dear Vitalie was hard working, intelligent and wise; all, in school and out of it, who knew her loved, admired and esteemed her. My good father was a thor-oughly honest man, well known to all. . . . My poor Arthur never asked anything of me. By his work, his brains and his good conduct he amassed a fortune and amassed it very honestly. He never deceived anyone; on the contrary, people made him lose much money and owed him much. And the dear child was very charitable, as is well known. You yourself, my daughter, you remember how you sent money out there to be given to his servant as he wished . . ."

Madame Rimbaud to Isabelle, Roche, June 6, 1907

"Many soldiers are passing by just as I'm getting ready to write. This makes me feel a very great emotion, reminding me of your father with whom I should have been happy if I had not had certain children who caused me so much suffering . . ."

Bibliography

The full Rimbaud bibliography is enormous and for the most part worthless. This short list is confined almost entirely to contemporary witnesses. Even so students must be warned that statements in these accounts should not be accepted without confirmation. A comprehensive bibliography of Verlaine will be found in *Verlaine: Prince of Poets*.

Public Sources

Letters, manuscripts, drawings and photographs of Rimbaud, Isabelle, Vitalie, Mme Rimbaud, Izambard, Delahaye, Nouveau, Verlaine, the Bardeys and other Red Sea traders, with additional documents relating to the life of Rimbaud, are to be found in the following publicly owned collections:

Bibliothèque Nationale, Paris.
Bibliothèque Jacques Doucet, Paris.
Archives du Département de la Seine, Paris.
Musée de l'Armée, Paris.
Maison de Poésie, Paris.
La Direction de l'Architecture, Paris.
Musée Rimbaud, Charleville.
Bibliothèque de Bordeaux.
Bibliothèque Royale, Brussels.
British Museum, London.

Books

Poesies. Edition critique, ed. Henri de Bouillane de Lacoste. Paris, 1939.

Une Saison en Enfer, ed. Henri de Bouillane de Lacoste. Paris, 1941.

Illuminations, ed. Henri de Bouillane de Lacoste. Paris, 1949.

Œuvres Complètes, ed. Rolland de Renéville and Jules Mouquet. Paris, 1954.

Berrichon, *La Vie de Jean-Arthur Rimbaud.* Paris, 1897.

———. *Lettres de J. A. Rimbaud.* Paris, 1899.

———. *Jean-Arthur Rimbaud le Poète.* Paris, 1912.

Carré, J. M. *Lettres de la vie littéraire de Rimbaud.* 1931.

Champsaur, F. *Dinah Samuel.* Paris, 1882.

Delahaye, E. *Rimbaud.* Paris, 1923.

———. *Souvenirs familiers à propos de Rimbaud.* Paris, 1925.

Etiemble. *Le mythe de Rimbaud.* Paris, 1952–4.

Godchot, Col. *Rimbaud ne varietur.* Nice, 1936–8.

Izambard, G. *Arthur Rimbaud à Douai et à Charleville.* Paris, 1927.

———. *Rimbaud tel que je l'ai connu.* Paris, 1947.

Méléra, M. Y. *Rimbaud.* Paris, 1930.

———. *Résonances autour de Rimbaud.* Paris, 1946.

Rimbaud, Isabelle. *Mon frère Arthur.* Paris, 1920.

———. With P. Berrichon. *Réliques.* Paris, 1921.

——— *Rimbaud. Ebauches et correspondance.* Paris, 1937.

Starkie, E. *Rimbaud en Abyssinie.* Paris, 1938.

Vaillant, J. P. *Rimbaud tel qu'il fut.* Paris, 1930.

Articles

Bourguignon and Houin. "Poètes Ardennais: Arthur Rimbaud," *Revue d'Ardenne et d'Argonne.* November, 1896–February, 1897. September–October, 1897, May–June, 1899, January, February, July, 1901.

Carré, J. M. "Arthur Rimbaud en Ethiopie," *La Revue de France.* June 1, 1935.

Delahaye, E. "A propos de Rimbaud (Souvenirs familiers)," *Revue d'Ardenne et d'Argonne.* March–April, 1907.

D. (R. Darzens). "Letter to the editor of the *Petit Ardennais.*" December 15, 1891.

Dullaert, M. *Nord.,* Brussels, 1930.

Emanuelli, E. *Inventario.* Rome, 1929, 1949.

Izambard, G. "Recherche sur les sources du Bateau Ivre," *Mercure de France*. August 15, 1935.

Labarrière, P. "Un témoignage tardif sur Rimbaud," *Mercure de France*. May 15, 1953.

Le Brun. "Verlaine inédit."

————. "Les Idées françaises." 1924.

Lepelletier, E. "Arthur Rimbaud," *Echo de Paris*. November 17, 1891.

Losseau, L. "La Légende de la destruction par Rimbaud de l'édition princeps d'Une Saison en Enfer." Mons, 1914.

Louys, P. "Paroles de Verlaine, Vers et prose." 1910.

Méléra, M. Y. "Nouveaux documents sur Rimbaud," *Mercure de France*. April 1, 1930.

Petitfils, P. "Rimbaud à Douai," *Bulletin du Bibliophile*. 1945.

Pierquin, L. "Arthur Rimbaud," *Courrier des Ardennes*. November 30, 1891.

Rimbaud, Isabelle. "Letter to the editor of the *Petit Ardennais*." December 19, 1891.

Vaillant, J. P. "Bulletin des Amis de Rimbaud." 1931.

Van Dam, J. J. "Arthur Rimbaud," *De Fakkel*. February 4, 1941.

Le Bosphore Egyptien. August 25–27, 1887.

Revue de L'Evolution Sociale, Scientifique et Littéraire. November, 1891.

Société de Géographie. "Comptes rendus des Séances." Paris, 1884, 1887, 1888.

Index

Abyssinia, 210, 212, 214, 215, 221, 245, 252, 254, 256, 278
Adam, Villiers de L'Isle, 107
Addis Ababa, 250, 272
Aden, 196, 213–8, 223–33, 235–9, 247, 250, 252, 254, 263, 272
Alexandria, 197, 201, 210, 230
Andrieu, Jules, 137, 151, 159, 176
Ankober, Menelik's capital, 247, 248–51
Antotto, 249, 272
Antwerp, 150, 154
Ardennes, 5–7, 92, 128, 199, 215
Arras, 6, 33, 95, 123–5, 132–3, 137
Attigny, 144, 215, 240, 275

Banville, Théodore de, 29, 45–7, 63, 66, 85, 91–2, 95, 98, 101, 109, 111, 115–8, 181
Banville, Mme. de, 115
Bardey, Alfred, 218, 219, 223, 224, 248, 253, 254
Bardey, Pierre, 212–8, 220–6, 231, 232, 234–9, 242, 247–8
Baring, Major Evelyn, Consul General in Egypt, 230–1, 235
Batavia, 195
Baudelaire, Charles, 66–9, 76, 85, 86, 87, 90, 93, 98, 99, 109, 118, 121, 127, 166
Belgian Congo, 210
Belgium, 52, 54, 128, 142–3, 150
Bergerat, Emile, 69
Billouart, Léon, 53, 54, 71
Binard, Arthur, 53
Blémont, Emile, 109–10, 129, 136, 142–3, 150
Borelli, Jules, 250
"Bouche d'Ombre, La," 32, 71
Bourde, Paul, 255

Bretagne, Charles, 32–3, 38, 40, 73, 88, 95, 99, 125, 133, 184
Brown, Oliver Madox, 137
Brussels, 54, 133–4, 137, 150, 155–7, 160, 161–4, 169, 170, 179–80, 181
Burty, Philip, 95
Buzenval, 67

Cabaner, Ernest, 108–10, 116, 119–21, 188
Cairo, 252–3, 264
Carjat, Etienne, 108, 111, 119, 123
Charleroi, 45, 53, 55
Charleville, Ardennes, home of the Rimbauds, 5–13, 19–20, 32, 33, 39, 41, 45–6, 51–2, 56–67, 70–5, 77, 82, 87–95, 99, 104, 110, 120, 123–5, 145–9, 164, 166, 170, 175, 180, 184, 187–9, 196–7, 206–10, 272
Charleville, College of, 20–5, 61, 68, 115, 137
Clair, Camille le, 178
Commune, the, 67–72, 87, 101, 137, 160, 166, 174, 281
Coppée, François, 34, 40, 69, 106, 107, 109–10, 118
Corbière, Tristan, 236
Cros, Charles, 95, 102, 104, 107–10, 115, 116, 126–7, 131, 171
Cuif, Auguste (uncle), 5, 13, 15
Cuif, Félix (uncle), 5, 13
Cuif, Marie-Catherine-*Vitalie* (mother), 5–11; *see also* under Rimbaud
Cuif, Nicolas (grandfather), 5–7, 13, 144
Cyprus, 201–3, 209–12, 235

De Brazza, 210, 230
Delahaye, Ernest, 22, 25–7, 61–4, 65–74, 75–6, 88, 96, 106, 118–9, 125, 128–30, 148–50, 169, 170, 171, 173, 178, 180, 181–4, 185, 187–91, 197, 205–7, 209, 227–8, 236, 262
Delavigne, Casimir, 81
Demeny, Paul, 34, 47–8, 50, 69–71, 74, 77, 80–1, 85, 86–8, 91–5, 106, 110, 120, 124, 182, 262
Des Essarts, M., 53–4
Deverrière, Léon, 32, 38–9, 46–52, 60–2, 65, 67, 73, 77, 80, 88–90, 96, 184
Dierx, Léon, 118
Dijon, 7, 11
Douai, 23, 27, 34, 38–9, 44, 46–53 passim, 77, 88, 123, 186
Durand, Paul, 52, 54–5
Dutch East Indies Army, 194

Egypt, 210, 216, 230–1, 233, 246

Fantin-Latour, T., 118
Forain, Louis ("Gavroche"), 108, 111, 119, 121–2, 126, 156, 170, 175, 188
Franco-Prussian War, 38, 40–1, 48, 59, 61–5, 67; Peace, 132, 209
Franzoj, 243
Fumay, 53, 54

Galla country, 216, 219, 226, 246
Garde Mobile, 61–2, 67–70
Gaspary, G. de, 263
Gautier, T., 66, 85, 98, 111, 127, 167
Gill, André, 68–9, 108
Gindre, Caroline (Izambard's aunt), 38–9, 47, 49, 52, 54–8
Givet, 7, 54–5, 68
Glatigny, Albert, 98, 111, 118
Gordon, General, 235, 242, 249

Hamburg, 197, 198
Harar, 215–23, 225–7, 232–7, 246, 249–50, 259–62, 272, 275, 277
Hicks Pasha, 231
Houssaye, Henri, 118
Hubert, Père, 65–6, 76

Hugo, Victor, 29, 30, 35, 84, 101, 111, 181

Ilg, Alfred, 256, 258–61, 262
Izambard, Georges, 28–39 passim, 42–57 passim, 57–60, 64, 71, 76–82 passim, 86, 87–90, 106, 184, 190, 196, 204, 227, 234, 262

Jacoby (photographer), 60, 63, 71
Java, 195, 196, 198, 210
Joannes of Tigré, Emperor of Abyssinia, 245–6, 252, 255, 259

Khartoum, 235, 242

Labatut, Pierre, 247, 248, 250–1, 257
Lemerre, Alphonse, 35, 43, 69, 95, 111, 207
Lepelletier, Edmond, 111, 117, 118, 139, 142, 150, 180
Lévi, Eliphas, 66
Lincolnshire, 181, 190, 191
Lisle, Leconte de, 29, 66, 69, 85, 98, 101, 107, 118, 166–7
London:
    Howland St., 137–9, 142
    8, Gt. College St., Camden Town, 150–1; Mrs. Smith, 159–60
    Stamford St., Waterloo, 174–8
    British Museum, 139, 151, 174, 176
Louis Napoleon, Emperor, 7, 31, 38, 41, 45, 48, 61, 143
Lyons, 10, 231, 237, 281–2

MacMahon, Marshal, 41, 44, 87
Mahdi, the, 231–7 passim, 246, 259
Makonnen, Ras, 250, 277–8
Mallarmé, Stéphane, 116, 120, 236
Marseilles, 187, 196, 197, 268, 273, 282; letters from, 283–94
Massawa, 252, 255
Mauté, M. de, 101–2, 115, 122, 125, 140, 151
Mauté, Mme. de, 103, 107, 135
Mauté, Mathilde (Mme. Paul Verlaine), 100–1
Mazas prison, 45, 154
Menelik of Shoa, Lion of Judah,

Menelik of Shoa (*continued*)
    245–7, 249–51, 252, 255–8,
    259–60, 272
Mendès, Catulle, 69, 98, 109, 118
Mérat, Albert, 85, 107, 110, 118,
    119, 130
Metz, 6, 41, 42, 61, 132, 204
Meuse, R., 8, 20, 41, 44, 61
Mézières, 8, 42, 52, 59–63, 273
Millot, Ernest, 62, 73, 88, 170, 206–
    7, 217
Moncomble, Elisa (P.V.'s cousin),
    98–9

Namur, 143, 150, 160
Nouveau, Germain, 171–5, 181, 188,
    227, 234

Ogaden, 234, 253

Paris, 39, 44–6, 61, 64, 68–71, 76,
    78, 88, 95–6, 97-102, 103–22,
    126–31, 132–3, 135, 150, 152,
    160, 170–3, 181–4, 281
Parnassians, 29, 35–6, 85, 94, 98, 99,
    106, 107, 120, 126, 210
Paros, 187–9
Perrin, Henri, 88, 129
Petits-Carmes prison, 162, 170
Pierquin, Louis, 62, 65, 73, 74, 88,
    111, 206–7, 210, 217
Poe, E. A., 66, 142
Ponchon, Raoul, 109, 119, 126

Red Sea, the, 195, 212, 214–5, 224,
    237, 246–8, 252, 255
Régamey, Félix, 137
Rethel, 188, 205–6
Richepin, Jean, 108, 109, 119, 126,
    170, 171, 174
Rimbaud, Captain Frédéric (father),
    7–12, 15–6
Rimbaud, Frédéric (elder brother),
    10, 14–6, 17–22, 23–7, 42, 44,
    61, 63, 106, 179, 214–5, 239,
    240–1, 261
Rimbaud, Isabelle (younger sister),
    11, 14, 74–5, 144–5, 165, 176,
    186–8, 195, 198, 215, 220, 232–
    3, 240–1, 263, 269–73, 276–82;
    letters, 283–96
Rimbaud, Jean-Nicolas-*Arthur,* early
years, 13–6; Charleville homes,
    18; advanced learning, 18–21;
    1865–70: sensational career at
    College of Charleville, 22–5;
    friendship with Delahaye, 26–7;
    1870: Izambard his class master
    first to encourage the young
    poet, 27–32; learns Demeny's
    poems, 34; secretly sends three
    poems to Banville for *Parnasse
    Contemporaine,* 35–7; gives
    Izambard MS. "Credo in
    Unam," 37; desperation at out-
    break of war, first thought of
    escape from mother's tyranny,
    37–9; *1870:* allowed use of
    Izambard's library, relieves feel-
    ings in savage poetry, one poem
    accepted by Paris daily, 40–1;
    angry and frustrated he tries
    caricature, 41; discusses books
    in letter to Izambard, 42–3;
    sudden flight to Paris, 45; ar-
    rested for debt, he appeals suc-
    cessfully to Izambard, 45–6;
    visits Demeny at Douai, 47–9;
    mother's letter causes frantic
    outburst, 50–1; returns to face
    the music with Izambard, who
    forbids him his rooms without
    mother's consent, 52–3; runs
    away to Charleroi, goes to Gin-
    dres with poems written on the
    way, 54–6; handed over to
    police for return home, 57;
    1870–1: intimate letter to Izam-
    bard, 59; friendship with De-
    verrière and Delahaye, 61–3;
    Prussian occupation, 64–5; dis-
    covery and worship of Baude-
    laire, 66–7; armistice signed,
    67; sells watch and goes to
    Paris, Gill befriends him, 68–9;
    tells Demeny of his literary dis-
    coveries, 69–70; walks 150 miles
    back home, 70–1; hopes of
    journalism, café life with
    friends, 71–5; sends test letter
    enclosing new verse to Izam-
    bard, 77–80; derided, he turns
    to Demeny, 81–8; Izambard

Rimbaud, Jean-Nicolas-*Arthur* (*cont.*)
pays another debt, 89–91;
writes fully to Demeny, 92–4;
sends five poems to Verlaine,
who summons him to Paris, 94–
6; P.V. and Cros miss him at
station, expecting fully grown
man, 103; effect on Mauté
household, 104–5; crude fervor
of first talk exhilarates P.V.,
106; meets *Vilains Bonshommes,* Zutists, all Paris avant-
garde, 106–13; bohemianism
disrupts private lives of P.V.
and Mathilde, 113–5; of Cabaner and Banville, 116; Lepelletier, 117–8; F.-Latour's *Hommage à Baudelaire,* 118; drink
leads to ugly scenes, 119–22;
1872: sent back home, 123–5;
letters to P.V. destroyed by M.,
125; returns to Paris at P.V.'s
request, 126–30; rising tension
leads to Rat Mort incident, 131;
1872–3: they go together to
Arras, 132; to Charleville and
Belgium, 133–4; disrupting influence leads to thoughts of
England, 135–7; London, 137–
40; Charleville, 140–1; back in
London, P.V. sick, 141–2; to
family farm at Roche, 143–5;
Saison en Enfer, 145–8; confiding letter to Delahaye, 148–9;
P.V.'s funds enable return to
London, 150–3; where P.V.
leaves him, 154; but writes,
155–9; return to Brussels, 160;
P.V. in danger of arrest as communard, 160; beseeches A.R. to
stay and finally fires at him,
161–3; depositions to police,
163–4; *1873–5:* returns to
Roche, 165; sense of degeneration expressed in prose poem,
166–9; mother pays for printing 500 copies of *Saison* in
Brussels, 169; Roche then Paris,
170–1; meets Nouveau, 171;
who takes him to London, 172–

5; mother and Vitalie join them,
anxious over jobless state, 176–
7; "My poor Arthur" leaves for
Scotland (?) and then teaches
at Reading, 178–9; meets P.V.
in Stuttgart after his two-year
imprisonment, 179–81; *Illuminations* has to wait eleven years
for publication in Paris, 182–4;
1875–80: desire to travel, 185;
bored with Dr. Wagner, 185–7;
the wanderer to Milan, Leghorn, Marseilles, 187; learns
Arabic and modern Greek in
Paris, 188; correspondence with
Delahaye and P.V., 189–94;
death of Vitalie, 194; *1876:* en-
lists in Dutch E.I. Army,
reaches Java, 195; deserts and
returns to Roche, 195–6; *1877:*
studies languages and goes to
Vienna, 196–7; to Scandinavia,
then ill in Italy, 198; *1878–9:*
unhappy at Roche, he leaves for
Genoa, 199–201; Alexandria,
201; Cyprus, 202–4; *1879–80:*
returns home weak from fever,
205; Delahaye's visit leads to
last reunion with school friends,
206–8; *1880:* backed by mother,
returns to Cyprus, 209–11; looks
for work in Red Sea ports, finds
it at Aden with Bardey, 212–
3; three-year contract, 212–6;
1880–1: crosses Somali desert
to Harar, 216–7; interest in
Panama Canal, 218–9; arrangements for sending money home,
220; quarrels with Bardeys and
goes to Aden, 221–3; *1882–3:*
Bardey's patience during year
in Aden, 224–6; works for
Société de Géographie, 226;
Mahdi's Holy War, 231–2;
1883–4: choice between Aden
and Harar decided by affray
with employee at former, 232;
exploration to Ogaden, his account printed in *Transactions* of
S. de G., 234–5; P.V.'s efforts

Rimbaud, Jean-Nicolas-*Arthur* (*cont.*)
to obtain recognition for A.R.,
235–6; third return to Aden;
1884–5: brother's marriage and
mother's efforts to make A.R.
return home, 237–43; finds new
friend in Franzoj, 243; *1885–7:*
dispute between Menelik and
Joannes in Abyssinia, 245–6;
meets gunrunner Labatut, 246–
51; *1887–8:* sets off for Cairo
and writes home for money,
252–4; Zanzibar, 254–6; writes
Bourde, working on *Le Temps,*
seeking job as war correspondent, 255; jobless in Aden again,
256–7; agrees to open branch
for Savouré in Harar, where he
spends three years, 257–8;
1888–9: life as a trader, does
not answer Paris editors, 259–
61; P.V. believes him dead,
260; *1891:* varicose veins develop into serious knee trouble,
264–5; carried in stretcher 200
miles to Zeila, thence to Aden,
266–7; settlement of accounts
with Tian, 267–8; telegraphs
mother to come to Marseilles,
269; leg amputated, 269;
mother insists on returning
home, 270; Isabelle his sole
correspondent, 271–2; "nothing
more than an inert stump" he
returns to Roche, 273–4; rapid
deterioration watched by un-
sympathetic mother; 275–6;
nursed by Isabelle, 277–8;
cheering letters from Harar,
277–8; back to Marseilles for
treatment, 278–80; Isabelle with
him to the end, 280–2
Cafés frequented by A.R.:
Charleville: Ardenne and Bas-
Rhin, 129; Dutherne, 73;
Promenade, 72; l'Univers, 64,
72, 129, 207
Paris: Hôtel des Etrangers, 110;
Cluny, 118; Rat Mort, 131,
153; Tabourey, 170–3;

Théâtre de Bobino, 118
Papers and Periodicals:
Bosphore Egyptienne, Le, 252
La Charge, 40, 44, 68
Le Courrier des Ardennes, 42
Le Libéral du Nord, 49–50
Parnasse Contemporain, 35–8,
98
Les Poetès Maudits, 236
Le Progrès des Ardennes, 60,
62–3, 71–2, 88
La Renaissance littéraire, 129–
30, 136
La Revue pour tous, 34
Le Temps, 255
Poems referred to, in chronological
order:
1870–1
1. "Les Etrennes des Or-
phelins," 34–5
2. "Première Soirée," 40
4. "Le Forgeron," 38
5. "Credo in Unam" ("So-
leil et Chair"), 35–8,
90
9. "Vénus Anadyomène," 40
10. "Ce qui Retient Nina"
("Les Réparties de
N."), 44, 57
11. "A la Musique," 41
12. "Les Effarés," 48, 236
13. "Roman," 55
14. "Morts de Quatre-vingt-
douze," 39, 40, 45
19. "Au Cabaret-Vert," 55
20. "La Maline," 55
22. "Le Buffet," 55
23. "Ma Bohème," 55
25. "Les Assis," 66, 76, 236
28. "Chant de Guerre Parisien," 81
29. "Mes Petites Amoure-
uses," 83
31. "Les Poètes de Sept
Ans," 50, 87
32. "Les Pauvres à l'Eglise,"
87
33. "Le Cœur Supplicié" (C.
de Pitre), 79–80, 88,
184

Rimbaud, Jean-Nicolas-*Arthur* (*cont.*)
34. "Paris se Repeuple," 73
36. "Les Sœurs de Charité," 74, 124
38. "Les Premières Communions," 73
40. "Ce qu'on dit au Poète," 91, 100
41. "Le Bateau Ivre," 96, 105, 236
42. "Voyelles," 128, 236, 256
    1872
66. "Mémoire," 44
74. "Chanson de la plus Haute Tour," 124
77. Jeune Ménage," 126–7
83. "O Saisons, ô Châteaux," 134–5, 148
    "La Chasse Spirituelle," 140
LES DÉSERTS DE L'AMOUR, 66
ILLUMINATIONS, 127, 137, 139, 142, 152–3, 182–4
    1873
UNE SAISON EN ENFER, 145–9, 153, 165–71, 177–8, 184, 187, 198, 210
Reading: 42, 65, 69, 84–5, 89–90
Rimbaud, Vitalie (mother, née Cuif), born at Roche, 5; a true Cuif, 7; meets and marries Capt. R., 7–10; life in Charleville, 12–21; tyrannical rages, 15–7; strictly religious, 18–20, 23–7, 30–2; dealings with Izambard, 48–52, 57, 64, 71; forbearance at A.'s escape to Paris, 76; maternal duty, 91–6; sees nothing practical in poetry, 125–6, 141; thrifty farmwork, 144; letter to P.V., 156–7, 165, 169; joins A. in London, 175–8; used as scapegoat by her son, 185–9; courage and patience, 198–9, 202–6, 211, 218–9, 225, 227–8, 239–40, 258, 261–2, 264, 278; letters, 283–96
Rimbaud, Vitalie (elder sister), 11,

13–4, 75, 144, 165, 175–7, 186, 188–9
Roche, Ardennes (Cuif farm), 5, 13, 16, 143, 144–5, 148–9, 153, 164–6, 175, 180, 188, 197–9, 202, 205–6, 214, 220, 225, 227, 238, 253, 257, 262

Saarbrucken, 41
Samarang, 195–6
Savouré, Armand, 257–9, **278**
Scandinavia, 197
Sedan, 41, 45, 49
Shamok, Ali, 232
Shoa, 223, 230, 246, 250, 251, 256
Silvestre, Armand, 108
Sivry, Charles, de, 100, 112, 151
Société de Géographie, La, 226, 230–1, 234–5, 253–6
Sottiro, 234
Stuttgart, 179–82, 187, 190–1, 201, 236
Symbolism, 236, 255–6

Tadjourah, 248
Thiers, 67–8, 81, 108
Tian, César, 257–8, 263, 267, **286**

Valade, Léon, 95, 107, 110–1, 118
Vanier, Léon, 111
Verlaine, Mathilde (née Mauté), 95–6, 100–3, 110–5, 117, 121–6, 130–1, 134–7, 139, 142, 158–60, 163–4, 170, 179
Verlaine, Paul, 32, 33, 43, 66, 85, 90, 94–6, 97–102; *1871:* meets A.R. in rue Nicolet after abortive visit with Cros to station, 103–5; showing off Rimbe, 106–13, 116–7; bad effect on Mathilde V., 113–5, 121–6, 130, 135–7, 150, 154, 156, 164, 170; stabbing incident, 119; office work, 126; constant bickerings, 130–1; leads to scene at Arras, 132; vagabonds, 133–7; anglophile in London, 137–42; fear of arrest, 143, 160; obtains money from mother to take A.R. to London again, 150–3; returns to Ant-

Verlaine, Paul (*continued*)
  werp, 122; thinks of suicide, letter from Mme. R., 157–8; A.R.
  comes to him in Brussels, 160–2;
  shooting affray, 162; prison and
  depositions, 162–4; two years'
  imprisonment, 170; "Loyola"
  letters, 180–2, 191–4; pleasures,
  184; Delahaye letters, 190–1,
  194, 197; dropped by A.R., 218,
  227, 234–7, 260
  Relations: Aunt at Arras, 123–5,
  132; at Jéhonville, 123, 143;
  uncle at Fampoux, 33
  Poems mentioned:
    POÈMES SATURNIENS (1866), 33,
    99
    FÊTES GALANTES (1869), 43, 94,
    99–100, 127–8
    LA BONNE CHANSON (1870), 43,
    100

Romances sans Paroles, 139, 142
Art Poétique and *Langueur*, 128
Les Poètes Maudits (1884), editor, 236
Verlaine, Stéphanie (née Dehée),
  123, 142, 151–3, 157, 161–2,
  164, 180
Vermersch, Eugène, 62, 64, 69, 137–
  8, 151
Vienna, 197
Vilains Bonshommes, 107–11, 119,
  137
Villard, Nina de, 111

Wagner, Dr., 179, 181, 185–7

Zanzibar, 212–4, 218–9, 225, 243,
  253, 256
Zeila, 215, 266, 267
Zutists, 109–10, 127